Politics and International Relations in Eurasia

Politics and International Relations in Eurasia

Stylianos A. Sotiriou

LEXINGTON BOOKS
Lanham • Boulder • New York • London

Published by Lexington Books
An imprint of The Rowman & Littlefield Publishing Group, Inc.
4501 Forbes Boulevard, Suite 200, Lanham, Maryland 20706
www.rowman.com

6 Tinworth Street, London SE11 5AL

British Library Cataloguing in Publication Information Available

Library of Congress Cataloging-in-Publication Data

Name: Sotiriou, Stylianos A., 1982–, author.
Title: Politics and international relations in Eurasia / Stylianos A. Sotiriou.
Description: Lanham, MD : Lexington Books, 2019. | Includes bibliographical references and index.
Identifiers: LCCN 2019001057 (print) | LCCN 2019004084 (ebook) | ISBN 9781498565394 (electronic) | ISBN 9781498565387 (cloth : alk. paper) | ISBN 9781498565400 (pbk : alk. paper)
Subjects: LCSH: Former Soviet republics—Politics and government. | Former Soviet republics—Foreign relations. | Asia, Central—Politics and government. | Asia, Central—Foreign relations.
Classification: LCC DK293 (ebook) | LCC DK293 .S675 2019 (print) | DDC 947.0009/051—dc23
LC record available at https://lccn.loc.gov/2019001057

Printed in the United States of America

To my mother, Metaxia

Contents

Illustrations

FIGURES

TABLES

Acronyms and Abbreviations

ACG	Azerbaijani-Chirag-Guneshli
AIOC	Azerbaijan International Operating Company
APF	Azerbaijan Popular Front
ASSR	Autonomous Soviet Socialist Republic
Bcm/y	Billion Cubic Meters per year
BRI	Belt and Road Initiative
BTC	Baku-Tbilisi-Ceyhan
BTE	Baku-Tbilisi-Erzurum
CAC	Central Asia Center
CAGP	Central Asia-China Gas Pipeline
CaspEcoControl	Caspian Environmental Service
CIS	Commonwealth of Independent States
CNOOC	China National Offshore Oil Corporation
CNPC	China National Petroleum Corporation
CPEC	China-Pakistan Economic Corridor
CPSU	Communist Party of the Soviet Union
CSCE	Conference on Security and Cooperation in Europe
CSOs	Civil Society Organizations
CSTO	Collective Security Treaty Organization
DRC	Development Research Center

EaP	Eastern Partnership
EEC	Eurasian Economic Commission
EEU	Eurasian Economic Union
EIA	Energy Information Administration
ENP	European Neighborhood Policy
ESPO	East Siberia–Pacific Ocean pipeline
EU	European Union
EUBAM	EU-Border Assistance Monitoring
FDIs	Foreign Direct Investments
GCC	Gulf Cooperation Council
GONGO	Government Organized NGO
HRW	Human Rights Watch
ICG	International Crisis Group
ICRC	International Committee of the Red Cross
IDPs	Internally Displaced People
IEA	International Energy Agency
IMF	International Monetary Fund
ISIS	Islamic State
JPKF	Joint Peacekeeping Forces
KCTS	Kazakhstan Caspian Transportation System
KMG	KazMunayGas
LNG	Liquefied Natural Gas
LoC	Line of Contact
MASSR	Moldovan Autonomous Soviet Socialist Republic
Mbbl/d	Thousand barrels per day
MDGs	Millennium Development Goals
MGB	Ministry of State Security
MMbbl	Million Barrels
MoU	Memorandum of Understanding
MVD	USSR Interior Ministry Troops
NDRC	National Development and Reform Commission
NEA	National Energy Administration

NELG	National Energy Leading Group
NGO	Non-Governmental Organization
NK	Nagorno-Karabakh
NKAO	Nagorno-Karabakh Autonomous Oblast
NKR	Nagorno-Karabakh Republic
n.m.	Nautical mile
NOCs	National Oil Companies
NPC	National People's Congress
ONELG	Office of the National Energy Leading Group
OPEC	Organization for Petroleum Exporting Countries
OSCE	Organization for Security and Cooperation in Europe
PD	Prisoner's Dilemma
POS	Political Opportunity Structure
PPP	Purchasing Power Parity
PSA	Production Sharing Agreement
RFE	Russia's Far Eastern Region
RNP	Russian Neighborhood Policy
RPGs	Rocket-propelled grenades
RSFSR	Russian Soviet Federalist Socialist Republic
SCO	Shanghai Cooperation Organization
SCP	South Caucasus Pipeline
SCPx	South Caucasus Pipeline Expansion
SELB	Strategic Energy Land Bridge
SEZs	Special Economic Zones
SGC	Southern Gas Corridor
Sinopec	China Petroleum & Chemical Corporation
SOCAR	State Oil Corporation of the Azerbaijani Republic
SPRs	Strategic Petroleum Reserves
SSR	Soviet Socialist Republic
TANAP	TransAnatolian Pipeline
TAP	TransAdriatic Pipeline
TCM	Trillions of cubic meters

TCP	TransCaspian Pipeline
TMR	Transdniestrian Moldovan Republic
UkrSSR	Ukrainian SSR
UN	United Nations
UNCLOS	United Nations Convention on the Law of the Sea
UNCTAD	United Nations Conference on Trade and Development
UNOMIG	United Nations Observer Mission in Georgia
US	United States of America
USSR	Union of Soviet Socialist Republics—Soviet Union
XUAR	Xinjiang Uyghur Autonomous Region

Introduction

Eurasia has long been a versatile region, promising but concurrently challenging. Powerful actors such as Russia, Turkey, and China have traditionally intermingled with states from the Caucasus, Central Asia, and South East Asia, forging a political and economic landscape that not only carries the imprint of past politics but is also subject to persistent geopolitical antagonisms. In this context, critical regional topics such as "frozen conflicts" and energy politics shape an intriguing amalgam in which developments at both the national and international level of analysis appear in a comparable manner as far as the underlying driving forces are concerned.

To begin with the national level and the issue of frozen conflicts, in November 2013, the European Union (EU) Eastern Partnership summit at Vilnius, aimed at both the EU and Ukraine signing political and economic agreements, reached an impasse, which served as the key pretext ahead of the formation of the most recent frozen conflict in Eurasia, in Crimea. During the summit, Ukraine's oscillatory course between the EU and Russia was exposed, with Ukraine's rapprochement negotiations with the EU standing against a pledge to participate in the Russia-supported and brewing (at the time) customs union along with Belarus and Kazakhstan (Herszenhorn, 2013).[1] In no time, both the EU and Russia were enmeshed in the fiercest standoff since the end of the Cold War, and sociopolitical upheaval broke out inside Ukraine. Soon it was transformed into an even bloodier conflict between the pro-EU and the pro-Russia parts of the country, culminating on March 18, 2014, when Crimea was annexed by Russia following a regional referendum that was conducted in a state of chaos and in the presence of Russian soldiers known as the green men, with their insignia hidden (Lally, 2014). Despite the international outcry, Crimea emerged as a frozen conflict, the latest in a series of such phenomena that have been rattling Eurasia since the onset of the post-soviet era.

During the late 1980s early 1990s, as the Soviet Union (USSR) was entering the critical juncture period of its dissolution, a tidal wave of nationalist mobilization either paved the way for the establishment of the new post-soviet states, such as the Baltic ones, or crystallized a reality, where opposing claims on power-sharing within a post-soviet state would engage in a protracted competition (Beissinger, 2002).[2] The phenomenon of "frozen conflict," according to which a clash is not terminated by a peace settlement, but, instead, goes on as a no-war-no-peace situation, rapidly gained prominence. In this context, smaller and distinct nationalities or peoples (e.g. the South Ossetians, the Abkhaz, or the residents of Transdniestria) within larger, internationally recognized (*de jure*), post-soviet states (e.g., Georgia and Moldova) have been trying to guarantee their survival and security, seeing the declaration of *de facto* statehood as a potent bulwark against the rival nationalism. The regions of the post-soviet geopolitical space that fall in the category of frozen conflicts are, next to Crimea, Transdniestria (Moldova), Abkhazia and South Ossetia (Georgia), and Nagorno-Karabakh (Azerbaijan). Each of these cases, perhaps with the exclusion of Transdniestria, had two major and highly comparable eruptions in the post-soviet era, with the first being the same for all, that during the critical juncture period of the early 1990s, and the second differing according to each case: Georgia experienced a high mobilization in both South Ossetia and Abkhazia in August 2008, as the Olympic Games were taking place in Beijing, Ukraine witnessed the emergence of its frozen conflict in Crimea in 2014, whereas Azerbaijan saw a major escalation in violence in Nagorno-Karabakh during the four day war in April 2016. All these eruptions were, to a high degree, duplicating the events of the early 1990s, raising questions regarding the persistent driving forces behind them.

But, if the collapse of the USSR generated a critical juncture period across the post-soviet space, which many states, especially those that host the frozen conflicts, would find pretty hard to regulate for the years to come, the same applies also to the international relations of the wider region, emphasis placed on the second key feature of Eurasia, the energy resources (oil and primarily natural gas) and the diplomacy surrounding them. In fact, someone could argue that the high institutional fluidity and the complete recession of norms which a critical juncture period is associated with, is a constant in international relations, much more in Eurasia.

Focusing on its underbelly, and on the Black Sea region in particular, on November 24, 2015, two Turkish F-16 fighter jets shot down a Russian Sukhoi Su-24 Fencer bomber jet, which was operating near the Syrian-Turkish border against the Islamic State (ISIS) (Khamdokhov, 2017). Bilateral accusations followed suit, with Turkey claiming airspace violation and unanswered warnings before the incident, and Russia outright rejecting any such claim (Tomkiw, 2015). In fact, the accusations advanced to the highest political level, with the incident portrayed by Russia's president, Vladimir Putin, as a "stab in the back carried out by the accomplices of terrorists," and Turkey's president, Recep Tayyip Erdogan, as "emotional" and "unfitting of politicians" (Kudenko, 2015). Immediately, the clash spilled over to the economic sphere, where both parties have been in negotiations over the construction of a natural gas network, known as the "TurkStream."[3] In particular, Russia's Economic Development Minister cancelled the project, a decision which, however, was revoked as a result of a letter of apology and a trip to St. Petersburg by President Erdogan in August 2016 (MacFarquhar, 2016).

These vicissitudes in the bilateral relationship notwithstanding, Turkey's role as an important transit state as far as oil and gas supplies earmarked for the EU market are concerned looms large. Circumventing Russia's role in the regional energy equation, special reference deserve two networks, the Baku-Tbilisi-Ceyhan (BTC), and the Baku-Tbilisi-Erzurum (BTE or South Caucasus Pipeline, SCP), the latter to be connected with the TransAnatolian Pipeline-TANAP in route to the EU market. Both networks have been commissioned since the mid-2000s and are associated with the EU efforts to enhance its energy security by primarily diversifying its suppliers (and supply routes) beyond Russia, to natural resources-rich states, such as those of the Caspian Sea region. In fact, the EU diversification plans became far more intense and systemized following Russia's fierce energy dispute with the neighboring Ukraine in January 2006, that resulted in the former cutting off gas supplies to the latter and the latter, exploiting its transit status, siphoning off supplies earmarked for the EU market and thus endangering the supply security of many Central European states (Sotiriou, 2015a). That time, the EU-Russia energy relationship entered a critical juncture, with the question "Can we trust them?" constantly raised in the institutions of the EU, particularly in the European Commission. That was also the time that the aforementioned networks (BTE and TANAP) were placed within the strategic plan of a southern gas corridor (SGC) in the wider Black Sea region, which would be primarily sourced from Azerbaijan (Baku), and possibly be connected to Central Asian states (Kazakhstan, Turkmenistan) via a trans-Caspian network, as a means of strengthening the nascent energy alliance that would counterbalance Russia's energy supremacy in Eurasia (European Commission, 2008; Sotiriou, 2015).[4]

The transcaspian prospects, however, stumbled upon the developments in the Caspian Sea, and especially upon its full and thorough delimitation. During the Soviet times, three treaties—the Treaty of Friendship (1921); the Treaty of Establishment, Commerce and Navigation (1935); and the Treaty of Commerce and Navigation (1940)—were regulating the coexistence of both the USSR and Iran in the Sea as far as navigation and fishery rights are concerned (Janusz, 2005). Nevertheless, setting a clear boundary, which would also provide for the complete exploitation of the natural resources wealth, had never been stipulated by any treaty, thus implying a condominium regime governing the "Soviet-Iranian Sea" (Mehdiyoun, 2000, p. 180). Following the collapse of the USSR, the newly independent Caspian littoral states, namely Russia, Azerbaijan, Kazakhstan and Turkmenistan, inherited the aforementioned long-going legal situation, the continuation of which was addressed by the Vienna Convention on Succession of States in respect of Treaties.[5] In particular, the legal validity was remaining intact, unless the states concerned unanimously agreed to a different legal arrangement (article 34, pars. 1–2). On these premises, all five actors adopted various, at times convergent and at times divergent, policies concerning the demarcation of the Sea and the subsequent exploitation rights of the natural resources, until they reached a unanimous agreement in August 2018.

Truth be told, the almost thirty-year procrastination towards a unanimous agreement created certain *faits accomplis* in the Caspian Sea region, if not across the whole of Eurasia's underbelly, from the Black Sea region to China. In particular, the Caspian Sea region's energy prospects were compartmentalized, with the Baku resources to have been "locked" to the Western markets, and the Central Asian resources to the Asian (Chinese) markets. Moreover, the prospects for a trans-Caspian network have remained an aloof probability. In other words, an energy "iron curtain" has been erected, juxtaposing two subsystems: the Caucasus versus Central Asia. With the Caucasus already sketched out, Central Asia is not only equally interesting but also leads up to China.

The resources-loaded Central Asian states, while "victims and victimizers" in the compartmentalization of the energy prospects of the Caspian Sea region, have sought and succeeded in bettering their prospects in terms of (economic and political) survival and security, capitalizing on China's huge financial reserves and energy needs. Specifically, Kazakhstan, Turkmenistan, and Uzbekistan have become integral parts of China's energy equation with the recent construction of two key networks: the 2,227.3km oil network from Atyrau port in northwestern Kazakhstan to Alashankou in China's northwestern Xinjiang Uyghur Autonomous Region (XUAR), known as the Kazakhstan-China oil pipeline, and the trans-Central Asian gas network from Turkmenistan, via Uzbekistan and Kazakhstan, to China's XUAR, known as the Turkmenistan-China (CAGP) gas network. With their construction having found fertile ground in Russia's protracted inelastic political and economic policies towards Central Asia and in the China-coined "loan-for-oil/gas deals," the truth is that they have made a headway to China, a single-party state with multiple challenging fronts in its periphery.[6]

Central Asia and Russia have been indispensable, albeit volatile, allies of China as far as its westernmost parts are concerned. The XUAR constitutes the largest administrative division and Islamic domain in China, spanning over 1.6 million square kilometers, and being populated mostly by Muslim Turkic Peoples (primarily Uyghurs) (BBC, 2016a). Regularly, the region experiences violent incidents between the Uyghurs and the Han Chinese, the second largest ethnic group in the region, which are subject to double inter-pretation: on one hand, China talks about exiled Uyghur separatists in collab-oration with overseas jihadist groups, whereas, on the other hand, the Uy-ghurs report their cultural and religious persecution on behalf of China (Hincks, 2017). In fact, the collapse of the USSR and the emergence of the five Central Asian states, which have been characterized by the predomi-nance of the Islamic tradition and the limited capacity of the state institutions to intercept all forms of transnational illegal activities, have heightened the Chinese fears over secessionist plans in XUAR.[7]

Therefore, in 1996 for the first time, China, Russia, Kazakhstan, Kyrgyz-stan, and Tajikistan formed, despite a historically tense background, the "Shanghai Five," seeking to facilitate regional security cooperation and nur-ture an environment of trust.[8] Later, in 2001, this group was upgraded to a regional organization, the Shanghai Cooperation Organization (SCO), grant-ing membership to Uzbekistan and signing the "Shanghai Convention on Combating Terrorism, Separatism, and Extremism" (SCO, 2001). In the years that followed, the organization expanded both in members as well as in areas of cooperation; India and Pakistan became full-fledged members on June 9, 2017, whereas the scope of cooperation reached out to areas such as culture, economics, banking, transportation, and energy (SCO, 2017).

As far as energy is concerned, the SCO Energy Club stands out as a double-purpose effort: to enhance energy security by streamlining strategies between producers (Russia, Kazakhstan, Uzbekistan, and Iran) and consu-mers, with prime emphasis placed on China, and to expand the global influ-ence of the institution as such, using energy as a very critical lever (Info-shos.ru, 2015; SCO, 2017).[9] With the territory of the SCO states to hold 20% of the global oil reserves and over 50% of the global gas reserves, the Energy Club is of major assistance to its major member-states/consumers (BP, 2017). Narrowing down to China, it is a primarily coal-and-oil-based econo-my, with natural gas constantly gaining ground in the face of frequent envi-ronmental problems, the presence of the U.S. Navy in the Indian Ocean, and the terrorism-susceptible choking point of the Malacca Straits, from where almost 80% of the country's oil imports passes. In view of these, the SCO provides a useful venue for ameliorating relations with states that China may have traditionally shared limited trust with but is critical of its policies to counterbalance such an alarming situation regarding its energy security.

Overall, two key features of Eurasia, the frozen conflicts at the national level and the energy politics at the international level, appear in a comparable manner. At the national level, the collapse of the USSR created a critical juncture period or an anarchy-resembling situation, which persisted for many years to come; at the international level, an anarchy-governed reality has been a constant in the Eurasian affairs, existent long before and certainly outliving the USSR (Kissinger, 1994).[10] In this context, actors at both levels, individuals at the national and states at the international, have been striving towards maximizing their power as the necessary, if not only, means for their survival at first, and security eventually. So the book at hand seeks to address the following question: How have actors at both levels been pursuing their interests in order to guarantee their survival and security in highly, if not totally, unregulated conditions?

Providing an outline of the book, the chapters are divided according to the two-level scheme. At the first level are chapters 2, 3, 4, and 5, while at the second level are chapters 6 and 7. Before the analysis adopts its two-level set up, chapter 1 offers the theoretical groundwork of the endeavor as a whole.

In particular, chapter 1 begins with the term "Eurasia," which at first sight constitutes a compact territorial mega-unit of many states, diachronically characterized by intense geopolitical competition. In this context, the connective strands throughout the region are examined, with a special focus on those across Eurasia's underbelly, from the Black Sea region until China. Undeniably, a political entity that stood at the heart of the region and has left deep its mark on the region is that of the USSR. Although not at the spotlight of the manuscript, it bequeathed intermingled relations between the fifteen successor states, reaching up to China, given the ups-and-owns between the USSR and China as far as political ideology is concerned. Once the USSR collapsed, a power vacuum was created, during which five post-soviet states were burdened by either frozen conflicts or the "genes" of such a phenomenon. At the same time, energy trade pushed its way up, as the second key feature in Eurasia's double identity. Once this context has been set, the analysis proceeds to the core of the political science discipline, portraying the fundamental theoretical debates, that of rational choice versus institutionalism (national level) and that of neo-realism versus neo-liberal institutionalism (international level), as a two-level game. Following that, each level is presented with a main argument, whereas, finally, all pertinent methodological issues are addressed.

Proceeding, now, to the first level of the two-level scheme, chapters 2, 3, 4, and 5 move on a west-east axis, focusing on the frozen conflicts; chapter 2 addresses the case of Transdniestria (Moldova), chapter 3 the case of Crimea (Ukraine), chapter 4 the cases of South Ossetia and Abkhazia (Georgia), and chapter 5 the case of Nagorno-Karabakh (Azerbaijan). In all these cases, the analysis adopts a domestic politics perspective, seeking, first of all, to shed light on the probable causes of the conflict, and then suggest probable solutions. Of course, this perspective does not mean the conflicts do not have an international dimension as well. It is a fact that in cases such as Transdniestria, Crimea, South Ossetia and Abkhazia, Russia played, and continuous to play, a role. Thus, in order for the primary focus of the analysis on the domestic level to be preserved, the Russia factor is mostly included as a constant one. In other words, Russia is not dealt with as a prime mover of the conflicts as such, but rather as a latecomer, so as the national politics to be held accountable for the root causes of the conflicts, much more for not coming up with a sufficient and an efficient institutional solution, which could have reversed a course that from the outset of the post-soviet era seemed as irreversible.

With the frozen conflicts and the segregated reality that they have created at the national level, chapters 6 and 7 revolve around the international energy relations across Eurasia's underbelly. Chapter 6 focuses on the developments around the Caspian Sea, and particularly the politics around its delimitation. Viewing each of the five littoral states as rational actors operating in conditions of insecurity as far the other party's intentions are concerned, it highlights how the prioritization of each actor's interests in the regional relations as well as the incumbent power asymmetry among the actors, were institutionalized in the August 2018 five-party agreement concerning the delimitation of the Sea. Moreover, it brings to light how the procrastination towards the August 2018 agreement greatly contributed to the formation of two subsystems, the Caucasus and the Central Asian one, which are *de facto* separated (west-oriented *versus* east-oriented), and if connected, this would only happen through Russia-controlled soil.

Chapter 7 picks up where chapter 6 leaves off, stressing how the compartmentalization in the Caspian Sea region dovetailed China's growing and alarming energy needs, given that not only has the country started to import more and more of its energy supplies but its coal-dominated energy mix calls for a diversification towards environmentally friendlier forms, such as natural gas, that China can retrieve from its proceed-with-cautiousness neighborhood—either Central Asia or Russia. In fact, energy cooperation, either within the SCO format or not, constitutes a potent means through which distrust and insecurity that soviet-era events have bequeathed may notably be ameliorated. Moreover, China's foreign energy policies acquire a broader analytical focus, extending to the wider region of South East Asia, since energy policy is a sector which could seriously compromise the country's international standing, much more constitute a significant lever at the hands of a third country, let alone a rival one.

NOTES

1. In 2014, the Customs Union was incorporated into the treaty establishing the much wider Eurasian Economic Union (EEC, 2016).

2. The term "critical juncture" is borrowed from the political science literature and signifies a period of profound institutional fluidity and reconfiguration within a state (Capoccia and Kelemen, 2007). It is a key concept of the manuscript at hand and is gradually placed in context.

3. In December 2013, with the Ukrainian crisis at the outset, the European Commission ruled against the construction of the Russia-favored "south stream" natural gas network (from Russia's Black Sea coast on to Bulgaria, with a 900km submerged section), citing violation of the EU law as far as competition is concerned (Euractiv, 2013). Following this ruling, Russia renamed the network TurkStream, redirecting it to Turkey instead of the EU law-bound Bulgaria.

4. See also Sankoyan, 2016. For the SGC, see https://gastechinsights.com/article/infographic-bps-visual-guide-to-the-southern-gas-corridor-1.

5. See the entry in the bibliography.

6. The Chinese loans aimed at "locking" natural resources in capital-seeking countries or regions (Central Asia, Africa, and Latin America) are termed "loan-for-oil" deals. In further detail, China, exploiting its abundance in hard currency reserves, has been offering loans in exchange for multi-year oil and gas contracts. Even more, in the case of the Central Asian states, China, aside from locking energy resources, it has also been interested in funding the necessary networks for transporting them, since the goal of energy security pursued in the region is two-fold: security of supplies and security of transport. For more on the way that the "loan-for-oil" schemes operate, see: (Jiang and Sinton, 2011, pp. 23–24).

7. Referring to the dominant Islamic tradition, some more mobilized Islamic Organizations such as the Islamic Movement of Uzbekistan and the Hizb ut-Tahrir should be included. For more, see Karagiannis, 2010a.

8. As noted by the scholar Shlapentokh, "in the 50 years after the victory of the Chinese revolution in 1949, Russians [Soviets] saw China as an ally for seven years [1949–1956], and for 30 years they looked at China as a dangerous enemy [1957–1987]" (Shlapentokh, 2007, p. 5). For a more detailed account, see Sotiriou, 2015, pp. 179–181.

9. Membership to the SCO Energy Club is open and it is not obligatory even for the SCO initial six member-states (Infoshos.ru, 2015). Indicative is the case of Turkey, which, for the year 2017, is the first non-SCO country to chair the SCO Energy Club. Adding a geopolitical nuance to this development, Turkey's president, Recep Tayyip Erdogan, highlighted the balancing options provided by the SCO, characterizing it as Turkey's "alternative to the European Union" (*Daily Sabah*, 2016).

10. It is noteworthy that at the national level, during the early 1990s, "the distinction between freebooter and founding father, privateer and president, has often been far murkier in fact than national mythmaking allows. . . . [Thus], in civil wars, as in politics, asking *cui bono* can be illuminating" (King, 2001, pp. 524 and 552).

Chapter One

Inside Eurasia

The Logic of a Two-Level Game

REGIONAL DYNAMICS AND STRATEGIC IMPLICATIONS

As earlier noted, Eurasia constitutes a versatile region, promising and, concurrently, challenging. But, why? What geopolitical significance might Eurasia hold? Providing an insight to such queries, the geographer/geo-strategist Sir Halford Mackinder and, particularly, his concept of the "Heartland," are of major assistance.

In his landmark study, Mackinder sets out by carving up the globe to twelve parts. Nine-twelfths are covered by an ocean, two-twelfths are covered by a continent (the World Island), and the remaining one-twelfth is covered by lots of smaller islands, among them North and South America.[1] In this division of the globe, the "Heartland" is the northern and inner part of Euro-Asia, that stretches from the icy Arctic coast down to the central deserts, having as its western boundary the "broad isthmus between the Baltic and Black Seas" (Mackinder, 1943, p. 597).[2] Having experienced most of the *Pax Britannica* in the nineteenth and early twentieth centuries, when naval power itself (e.g., Britain's Royal Navy) could determine realities in remote places of the world (e.g., India, Latin America), Mackinder deemed that an inaccessible land by the sea could alter the balance of power. For in his era a transition from the naval to land or air means of power was only in its formative years, every state impenetrable by the sea could become the invincible power of the world. Geographically speaking, "Heartland" assembles three prerogatives that place it at the helm of geopolitics; first, it contains the biggest valley on a global scale. Second, it is traversed by big floating rivers with inaccessible drains, either the icy Arctic sea or the land-

1

locked Caspian Sea, thus the trade of the riparian population is boosted without being susceptible to foreign invasion by naval powers. Third, extended pasture facilitates the mobilization of the locals (Mackinder, 1904, pp. 429–430).

Mackinder associated the "Heartland" with the then USSR but for one direction; setting the Yenisei River, which flows northwards from the borders with Mongolia to the Arctic Ocean, as the border line between the Soviet "heartland" and the "Lenaland" (dubbed by the Lena River), Mackinder argued that westwards from Yenisei to Romania is the Soviet "heartland," covering an expanse of 4,250,000 square miles, and hosting the overwhelming majority of population (then 170,000,000), assembled primarily in Eastern Europe.[3] Eastwards from Yenisei, the "Lenaland" expands over a natural resources rich territory of 3,750,000 square miles and is home to a minuscule population of 6,000,000 habitants, "settled along the transcontinental railroad from Irkutsk to Vladivostok"; albeit part of (Soviet) Russia, in Mackinder's analysis it was excluded from the Soviet "heartland" (Mackinder, 1943, p. 598).

Having set this context, Mackinder highlighted the antagonism and the power struggles inherent in the "Heartland," arguing that:

> Who rules East Europe commands the Heartland;
> Who rules the Heartland commands the World-Island;
> Who rules the World-Island commands the World.
> (Mackinder, 1942, p. 106)

In spite of several critics and many subsequent developments that the theory proved of limited capacity to foresee, it did succeed in underscoring the geopolitical competition throughout the region, which becomes far more evident when it comes to energy politics, given the natural resources wealth of the subsoil. Thus, a pun between the terms "heartland" and "energyland" could be permissible, emphasizing Eurasia's two key identities.[4]

FROM "HEARTLAND" TO "ENERGYLAND"

Competing Claims within the "Heartland"

Years before the official formation of the USSR and certainly after the 1917 Revolution, the civil strife-stricken Russian political system had to encounter many challenges, principal among which was that of the nationalities' policy. With the Polish and Finnish nationalisms to constitute a diachronic concern, and the Ukrainian, Belarusian and Azerbaijani ones to manifest themselves with increasing virility, the (pro-tsarist) White Army, on the one hand, and the (pro-communism) Bolsheviks, on the other, qualified separate ways on the issue; the former unswervingly upheld their so far position of a unified

Russia under Russians, whereas the latter, knowing the acrimony of non-Russians for the White Army due to prior operations in the name of the Tsarist regime (i.e., the old regime), saw the need for a compromising stance, which would differentiate them from the old regime, thus increase their probabilities of forming a (governing) alliance with the non-Russians (Zia-Ebrahimi, 2007).

Lenin, at the eighth Russian Communist Party Congress in Moscow in 1919, suggested, in contrast to the Marxist Theory, the manipulative recognition to the diverse peoples of the old regime of a distinct nationality, along with substantial concessions (Suny, 1993). In exchange for this right (codified as "Korenizatsya"), the diverse peoples would have their political rights alienated in favor of Communism (Konstitutsiya soyuza, 1924; Zia-Ebrahimi, 2007).[5]

The central administration in Moscow set up republics and a plentitude of national territories were configured to match specific ethnicities, even though in some cases, there were political considerations hidden behind the territorial adjustments.[6] "The Soviet Union became the incubator of new nations," with local languages being used across-the-board and local elites being promoted in order to establish the new, self-governed and thus voluntarily attached to the USSR, Soviet nation-states (Suny, 1993, p. 87). In reality, this effort went so deep so as writing systems to be developed for local languages that up to that point were only spoken, and official culture, official folklore, and national opera-houses to be established (Zia-Ebrahimi, 2007). In this manner, the Soviet authorities in Moscow nurtured a socio-political situation, which although it had been forged top-down, it was being presented and reproduced as a consensual, bottom-up, coexistence of fifteen Soviet nation-states (or Soviet Socialist Republics, SSRs) within the USSR; in fact, the erstwhile acrimonious and competitive relations between the non-Russians and the old regime seemed to have been succeeded by a non-competitive, peaceful, and consensual co-existence, at least during the 1920s.

The moribund attribute of such a reality soon came to the forefront. In the late 1920s and early 1930s, the strong sense of national consciousness started to pose an impediment, if not threat, to the now-emboldened Soviet central authorities and the need for expediting economic development. The directives of a centrally planned economy required a *lingua franca* in every sector of social life, in every territory of the Soviet edifice. Thus, the language of the most populous and well educated nationality—that is, the Russian, was qualified (Lieven, 2001).

Despite the strong sense of Russianness among the Russian population, which was identical to that of the old regime and against the ideology of Bolsheviks, the Soviet authorities made a political *volte-face*, betraying their thus far alliance with the non-Russians and forming a new one with the Russians; educated Russians were dispatched to less-developed republics to fill key post in their economies (i.e., public administration, education, etc.), creating a broad outmigration of Russians from the Russian Soviet Federalist Socialist Republic (RSFSR), and thus altering the ethnic composition of almost all of the USSR constituent republics (Simon, 1991).

Earlier achievements of "Korenizatsya" were totally reversed, with local political elites being thoroughly replaced, national treasures along with cultural institutions being targeted, if not outright terminated, autonomous republics being abolished, and people being deported from their lands, as a result of their rising nationalism being perceived as a hazardous threat (Suny, 1993, p. 108). It is noteworthy that by 1938 the Russian language was compulsory throughout the USSR, whereas World War II further solidified this "re-Russification" process, with Russianness to serve as a crucial mobilizational mechanism of the Soviet soldiers (Figes, 2002; Zia-Ebrahimi, 2007).

This course of action, despite some temporal and purposeful loosening brought about by Joseph Stalin's death at the mid-1950s, continued unabated, more or less, until the USSR entered its critical juncture in the late 1980s.[7] Then, nationalism emerged as a sweeping "tidal wave" across the soviet territory, avenging a past of oppression (Beissinger, 2002; Suny, 1993). The Baltic SSRs were the first wave of soviet states to declare its independence (Hiden and Salmon, 1994). A second, and final, wave of independent statehood begun with Armenia on August 23, 1990, and was completed with Kazakhstan on December 16, 1991. Nationalism, although it paved the way for the establishment of fifteen post-soviet states, it remained a powerful force, that kept being reignited at short intervals, presenting insurmountable challenges to the new-fangled states and, more often than not, being associated with the phenomenon of frozen conflict. Moldova, Ukraine, Georgia, and Azerbaijan have all experienced competing claims on power-sharing, the intractability of which has left its eponymous *de facto* imprint within their respective territories: Transdniestria, Crimea, South Ossetia, Abkhazia, and Nagorno-Karabakh.

To begin with, post-soviet Moldova is the end-result of a Soviet interwar merge between Transdniestria, a Ukrainian territory, and Bessarabia (the entire eastern half of Romania named Moldova), a Romanian territory.[8] This merge caused the diachronic influx of a sizeable Russo-phone community, mostly Slavic (Russian and Ukrainian) industrial workers, in Moldova's urban areas, increasing the percentage of Russians from 6.7% in 1941 to 13% in 1989 (Roper, 2001, p. 103). Moreover, Russians, just like elsewhere in the USSR, had been included in the higher echelons of the Moldovan socio-economic structure, while they had also been relishing disproportionate representation in key political and economic institutions (White et al., 2001, p. 292; Roper, 2001, p. 103). The Russian quickly became the language of public life, with a 40.9% studying in Russian, as of 1989, and 59.1% in the titular language (Chinn and Roper, 1995, p. 298). Even in the capital city,

Chisinau, less than half of the population was Romanian, out of which 12% designated Russian as their native language, and 75% competence in Russian (Chinn and Roper, 1995, p. 298). Vice versa, the Romanian language was spoken by only 11% of the Russians in Chisinau, being equally sidelined from the capital city's kindergartens, with only 10% of them using them as the language of conduct, and being treated as a foreign language in key educational institutions such as the Chisinau polytechnic university (Chinn and Roper, 1995, p. 298; Tkach, 1999, p. 145). Just before the collapse of the USSR, the issue of national identity was a "hard-to-define" one; 64% of the republic's 4.3 million were Moldovans, while the two main minority groups, the Russians and the Ukrainians, made up 13% and 14% respectively (Tkach, 1999, p. 137).[9] Interesting is the fact that most of the Ukrainian minority was russified, given that only 9% was fluent in Ukrainian, with 37% having no command at all (Tkach, 1999, p. 137; Chinn and Roper, 1995). Putting now this linguist polarization in geographical terms, the majority of Russians was concentrated either in the capital city, Chisinau, or in Tiraspol (41%), the administrative center of Transdniestria; as a matter of fact, the latter region would be transformed, from the early independence years, into Moldova's "frozen-conflict" legacy (Tkach, 1999, p. 137; Chinn and Roper, 1995, p. 306).

Transdniestria is a region that has served throughout the years multiple critical functions: first, it has been the economy's "pumping heart." Having in its bounds a substantial industrial complex dating back to the Soviet period, it has been capable of producing power for the entire country (Melintei, 2017, p. 52; Kennedy, 2016, p. 516).[10] To draw an analogy, while only 12% of Moldova's territory and 17% of the population, its industrial output contributes up to 40% to the national average (Istomin & Bolgova, 2016, p. 178). Thus, when the USSR started to crumble and new forces to get unleashed in Moldova, Transdniestria's first *de facto* leader, Igor Smirnov (1991–2011), claimed that a big part of Moldova's economy as well as all the energy production in the country were located on the left bank of the Dniester (Chinn and Roper, 1995, p. 307). Moreover, Transdniestria had been a militarily pivotal area from the onset of the post–World War II period, constituting the springboard for operations towards the Balkans; being part of the Odessa military district, it hosted the Soviet military forces, and in particular, the 14th Guards Army (Tkach, 1999, p. 149).[11] This Army had been stationed in Moldova since 1956 and headquartered in Tiraspol, while it had mostly been comprised, just like elsewhere in the USSR, by local residents, so as, in 1994, 60% of the officer corps and 80–90% of the soldiers were permanent residents of Moldova (Johansson, 2006, p. 509; Lamont, 1993, p. 599; Sanchez, 2009, p. 157; Tkach, 1999, p. 149).[12]

The innate centrifugal forces within the republic started to come to the surface at the dusk of the USSR, when issues of political power dressed the "language" cloth. While language is associated with identity and constitutes the channel through which social interaction is achieved and culture is constructed, it is also linked to power and political control (Prina, 2015, p. 54). Linguistic human rights fall within the fundamental human rights, and if denied, the "parity of esteem" between people evaporates, signifying the "hallmark of the repression of minorities"; therefore, minorities, moving across the national identity types' spectrum (figure 1.1), stake their survival under the ethnic type of nationalism as the only means of security in an otherwise atomized and institutionally fluid environment, rife with resentment, hatred, and lack of trust (Hansen and Hesli, 2009, pp. 4–7; Prina, 2015, p. 54, 63–64; Cash, 2013; Van Parijs, 2011). [13]

In the post-soviet era, the sparring aura between Moldova and Transdniestria became evident from the very beginning and from the very fundamentals, with both declaring their independence back-to-back as a sign of their competing claims over the Moldovan territory; Moldova declared its independence on August 27, 1991, and Transdniestria on September 2, 1991, with the erstwhile self-declared Pridnestrovian (Transdniestrian) Moldovan Soviet Socialist Republic of 1990 to be renamed into Transdniestrian Moldovan Republic (TMR) (Roper, 2001, p. 107). [14] In the first half of 1992, a brief war took place, which resulted in 425 being killed, tilting the balance of power towards the 14th Army-supported Transdniestria, and further consolidating its *de facto* statehood orbit (Batt, 1997, p. 42; Lamont, 1993; Tkach, 1999, pp. 146–147). In view of these, Moscow offered to broker an agreement to de-escalate the tension, with the presidents of Moldova and Russia, Mircea Snegur and Boris Yeltsin respectively, to agree on July 21, 1992 to a cease-fire (Chinn and Roper, 1995, p. 309; Lamont, 1993, p. 592; Roper, 2001, p. 109; Sanchez, 2009, p. 163). Nevertheless, after a period that conflict and intractable animosity had dovetailed the permeating polarization resurfaced by the language law, there was no trust left between the two rival

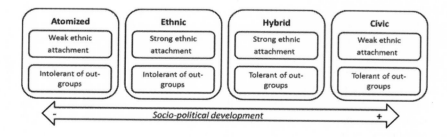

Figure 1.1. Types of national identity and their correlation to socio-political development.

parties, let alone desire towards a workable solution ever after (Johansson, 2006, pp. 510, 515; Korosteleva, 2010, p. 1277; Lamont, 1993, p. 603; Tkach, 1999, p. 147). This situation would remain stagnant even in the framework of the Organization for Security and Cooperation in Europe (OSCE), given that since February 4, 1993, the Moldovan government has internationalized the issue (Tkach, 1999, p. 153).[15]

Overall, the course followed within the republic would not be much of a deviation; in fact, it would accentuate the "atomized" type of national identity which has diachronically been instilled in Moldova. The short-lived war fought in 1992 as well as the theoretically critical juncture-terminating Moldovan Constitution were possible due to the "unformed (or atomized) nature of Moldovan national identity which allowed room for flexibility" (Batt, 1997, p. 46).[16] As previously became apparent, the conflict has essentially been "political in character," since presenting it as "a showdown between ethnic Moldovans and the Russian-speaking part of the Moldovan population . . . [would be] a gross simplification" (Kolstø et al., 1993, p. 975). The political elites led the way in instrumentalizing the language issue, which served as a critical lever in creating to an otherwise diverse public of "atomized" rational actors a correlation between language (alliance) and survival, transferring them across the national identity types' spectrum from the "atomized" to the "ethnic" one, but only temporary and only for reasons of survival. When the "cycle of mobilization" and the "tide of nationalism" would come full circle, the residents of Moldova would return to the ever-present reality of the "atomized" rational actor, this time, however, burdened by the frozen conflict stagnant aura.[17]

Sharing borders with Moldova and moving eastwards in the Black Sea region, Ukraine has embarked on a tumultuous course throughout the post-soviet era; first and foremost, it has encountered the fundamental issue of polarization between its main, or better constituent, nationalities (or ethnic groups), the Ukrainians in the west and the Russians and the Russian-speaking in the east. Studying political party development in divided societies such as Ukraine, it has been shown that "each individual's regional place of residence, language use and national identification" constitute sufficient knowledge in predicting voting behavior (Hesli, Reisinger, and Miller, 1998, p. 235). By asking questions such as "Ukrainian language only for public business," "Ukraine should join federation with Russia," and "Ukrainians and Russians have basically the same culture," not only the incumbent polarization within the society emerges (west versus east), but also the way that west perceives east and vice versa (Hesli, Reisinger, and Miller, 1998, p. 241). In fact, the "Russian question" has been proven to exert the most "salient independent effect on vote choice," adding a geopolitical perspective to the polarization and setting the bar high for the state's policies as far as the issue of nationalities is concerned (Hesli, Reisinger, and Miller, 1998, p. 235; Mak-horkina, 2005).

Going deeper, beyond polarization and ethnic lines, the country's ethnic groups, and in particular, the Ukrainians, the Russians, the Hungarians and the Roma, have all presented the "atomized" as dominant national identity type, with the "ethnic" coming right after, whereas the Crimean Tatars has been the only ethnic group in which the "ethnic" type has been dominant one (Hansen and Hesli, 2009, pp. 4–7). Focusing on the majority of the sample and given that the "atomized" type stands for intolerance of out-groups and weak ethnic attachment, it plausibly emerges that aside from the apparent divisions along ethnic lines, there is a more profound aspect, that of ineffi-cient state institutions evaporating any social trust (Makhorkina, 2005, p. 254; Sotiriou, 2016, p. 7; Wilson and Birch, 1999, p. 1050). Consequently, citizens return to a situation very close to that of the state of nature, whereas rational egoists seek to either maximize their capacity individually or form alliances in pursuit of their survival and security, making their country even more vulnerable in an occasion of a bitter standoff with a powerful neighbor such as Russia.

With these facts on the ground, Ukraine has been at the heart of a geopo-litical tug-of-war which involves the EU and Russia. Entering the triangle, Ukraine, at first, has been following a balanced, if not indeterminate, stance in its foreign policy, reflecting its constituent parts; the east has been gravi-tating towards Russia in political, economic, cultural, linguistic, and histori-cal terms, whereas the west and the center have been prioritizing their rap-prochement, if not membership, with western institutions, and particularly with the EU and the NATO (Proedrou, 2010, p. 453). A carefully forged balance had been struck, at least up to Crimea's annexation in March 2014, with the secession card, held by Crimea and other eastern regions from the early post-soviet period, to have been serving as a leverage guaranteeing the oscillatory course between western institutions and Russia (Proedrou, 2010, p. 454).

No doubt, this balance has had its ebb and flow; the "Orange Revolution," that signaled the transfer of power from Kuchma to the pro-western Yush-chenko after two months (November 2004 to January 2005) of peaceful protests in Kiev's Independence square, was a focal point in Ukraine's post-soviet history (Kuzio and D'Anieri, 2018, pp. 73–76). Albeit the inbred east/west divide in the election results, the Kremlin did not impose any economic sanctions or encouraged any act of separatism in Ukraine. In contrast, Russia welcomed the rerun of the Presidential election as well as the desire for joining the EU (Tsygankov, 2015, p. 12). Thus, it "planned to co-opt Yush-chenko by mobilizing its soft power and the two nation's economic, cultural, and institutional interdependence" (Tsygankov, 2015, p. 12).[18] Given these, it plausibly emerges that, for many Ukrainians, the issue at stake has been connected more with democracy, fighting corruption, and economic improvement, rather than with regionalism and foreign policy, corroborating, in this manner, the widespread "atomized" perception across the Ukrainian society (Kubicek, 2005, p. 286; see above).

Entering the crisis period (2013–), dubbed the "Dignity Revolution," the "atomized" character of the Ukrainian society had remained intact. The civil society's perpetual demand against flagrant corruption and abuse of power was once more resurfaced, whereas the civil society as such figured as a vital institution within the checks and balances structure, able to maintain "pressure on government for reform" as a means of intercepting another critical juncture in Ukraine's course as a state (Cleary, 2016, p. 7, 20).[19] The crisis soon (re)turned to the long-lasting, if not fundamental, issue of different constituent parts within a weak and polarization-driven state, where the political system had been governed by the logic "the winner takes it all," and social groups (e.g., the Russian diaspora) as well as independence-era demands were being relegated to the margins (Loshkariov and Sushentsov, 2016). During the conflict, a national identity "affiliated more with region rather than ethnicity" emerged, in which the "loyalty" attribute was feeble, making it easily "affected by the pressure of circumstances" (Matveeva, 2016, p. 26). Ideas, political-social norms and emotions ranked higher than cost-benefit calculations for the formation of pro-Kiev battalions, with paramilitary groups (both pro-government and rebel), proxy agents and auxiliary forces all together to pave the way for Russia's intervention in Crimea (Blank, 2008; German, 2016, p. 165; Karagiannis, 2016, 2014; Malyarenko and Galbreath, 2016; Rauta, 2016).

Alike Ukraine, Georgia has been gravely rattled since independence, not least due to its "frozen conflicts" or *de facto* statehoods. To begin with, January 1992 saw the end of Zviad Gamsakhurdia's administration, the first ever after the collapse of the USSR, which was marked by a feverish nationalist mobilization and an intractably confrontational style (Suny, 1999/2000, p. 163). Eduard Shevardnadze, the former Communist Party boss, rose to power, without, however, succeeding in alienating the leaders of the two dominant paramilitary groups: Tengiz Kitovani, Gamsakhurdia's defense minister and head of the "National Group," and Jaba Ioseliani, a bank robber-turned-theater critic and head of the "Mkhedrioni" (Horsemen) (Wheatley, 2009, p. 123). In August 1992, the former played a critical role in gravely exacerbating secessionism in Abkhazia, a region which would henceforth become one of the two "frozen conflicts" within Georgia.[20]

By the end of 1994 and mid-1995, the state power would gradually be enhanced. Georgia's police force ranked atop Shevardnadze's priorities, who, at times, sought the cooperation of the paramilitary groups; yet, this alliance would be deprived of any permanence. In the power struggles that ensued, Kitovani would be arrested in January 1995, as a result of an unsuccessful attempt to retake Abkhazia and promote his relative gains by firmly, if not dominantly, establishing its standing within the political elite. Ioseliani, too, would be arrested in August 1995 on account of an assassination attempt against Shevardnadze (Wheatley, 2009). In this manner both principal paramilitary groups were liquidated in favor of state authority (Suny, 1999/2000, p. 163).

The latter, nevertheless, would found severe difficulties in conducting its core functions, falling short of reigning over the logic of individual power maximization and alliance formation, dominant in anarchy resembling conditions.[21] Built amidst intense domestic armed conflicts (Abkhazia, South Ossetia), economic collapse, and pervasive official corruption, a situation of private profiting at the cost of providing public goods emerged (Wheatley, 2009). In fact, the "public goods" had been replaced by the "network goods," offered through a "personalized network that linked (particular citizens) to an individual in a position of state power" (Wheatley, 2009, p. 124). Such a "networking" was excluding large areas, particularly rural and those inhabited by national minorities (e.g., Abkhazia, South Ossetia). Moreover, it forced the people to sense a situation pretty close to that of the state of nature, whereas rational egoists should seek their survival and security by their own individual means, given their exclusion from the possibility to form an alliance (i.e., get networked) with the ruling political elite.

In this regard, the legitimacy, if not territorial integrity, of the Georgian polity was gravely endangered. The extensive disrespect for the rule of law, along with clientelism and unconstrained corruption served as indicators of the "ethnic" and much more of the "atomized" type of identity within the Georgian society. No doubt, things would become even more difficult in the occasion of a bitter standoff with a powerful neighbor such as Russia, when the "atomized" rational actors, aside from their individual efforts towards survival and security, would also have to take sides seeking inescapably a trustworthy alliance.[22]

To cut a long story short, Abkhazia and South Ossetia, two emerged as Georgia's "frozen conflicts." They have exhibited two major explosive points throughout the country's post-soviet history: first, in the early 1990s, when the status of the frozen conflict as well as the course towards *de facto* statehood, were becoming solidified. Second, in the mid-2008, when Russia's military presence was widely felt across Georgia, and both breakaway regions were recognized as independent states by Russia and its Latin American allies (BBC, 2017; 2016b; Fabry, 2012; Nielsen, 2009). Between 2008 and 2015, there was a series of bilateral agreements between Russia and both South Ossetia and Abkhazia. In effect, 78 agreements were signed, which could be classified into three categories: (a) the 2008 "friendship" ones that sketched out the bilateral relationship, (b) the more refined ones that fleshed out this relationship, and (c) the "alliance" and "integration" ones that set, *mutatis mutandis*, the sturdiest possible ties (Ambrosio and Lange, 2016, p. 1). Although Russia recognized the statehood of both break-away regions, the South Ossetian leadership, in contrast to the preference of many citizens, continued to rely on Russia as the only means of survival and security (German, 2016, p. 164). Thus, in 2015, it signed an integration Treaty with Moscow, which holds Russia accountable for the provision of the basic attributes of statehood (German, 2016, p. 164).

Advancing to Azerbaijan, its post-soviet course has been intertwined with the "frozen conflict" in the region of Nagorno-Karabakh (NK). On February 20, 1988, after persisting dissatisfaction with the Azerbaijani rule and efforts towards sovereignty or union with Armenia, the Armenian-populated en-clave within Azerbaijan dubbed Nagorno-Karabakh Autonomous Oblast (NKAO) voted in the soviet (parliament) of Stepanakert, the capital city, for its transfer to Armenia (Huttenbach, 1990; Mihalka, 1996, p. 17). Bilateral tension among rational actors that had allied themselves along ethnic lines in pursuit of their survival and security reached an explosive point, leading to multiple grave and lethal incidents, such as the Sumgait massacre and the "Black January," in the early 1990s (BBC, 2001; De Waal, 2013; Toal and O'Loughlin, 2013b, p. 165; Tokluoglu, 2012, p. 323).

In this context of hard-to-control mobilization, Ayaz Mutalibov came to power, who, however, did little to reverse emerging *de facto* realities; the NK Armenians declared the Nagorno-Karabakh Republic (NKR) on September 2, 1991, three days after Azerbaijan had done the same, in an effort to block Azerbaijan becoming the internationally recognized successor of the Soviet Azerbaijan (emphasis on the borders), benefiting from the international law principle *uti possidetis* (Toal and O'Loughlin, 2013b, p. 166).[23] The ongoing unfortunate, for the Azerbaijani side, developments in the NK front claimed the presidency not only of Mutalibov, but also of his successor, Ebulfez Elcibey, the leader of the Azerbaijan Popular Front (APF) (Tokluoglu, 2012, p. 323). A stabilization aura started to spread throughout the country, when Heydar Aliyev rose to power, in June 1993 (Tokluoglu, 2012, p. 323).

A Russia-brokered ceasefire in the NK conflict was reached in May 1994, with the NKR forces, nevertheless, to have outdone the Azerbaijani military forces, and be in control of swaths of territory never claimed before by the NKR (Toal and O'Loughlin, 2013b, p. 168). Particularly those in the south and in the east served as buffer zones shielding the Karabakh proper against any potential Azerbaijani military action, and were considered a potent lever-age in any final settlement (Toal and O'Loughlin, 2013a, p. 168).

With the NK conflict to have come to a standstill, Aliyev turned his focus on strengthening his political standing. Azerbaijan is a highly diverse coun-try; although Azerbaijanis constitute the titular nationality (78% of the popu-lation), there are also 115 ethnic and sub-ethnic groups, all craving for differ-ent levels of autonomy, thus making national unity a hard-to-attain task

(Kechichian and Karasik, 1995, p. 59; Tokluoglu, 2012, p. 334).[24] In this context, "family, clan and regional ties have dominated the political landscape in Baku" (Kechichian and Karasik, 1995, p. 59). Just like Mutalibov was linked to the Azerbaijani intellectual community in Baku, and Elcibey to sub-clans from Ordubad in Nakhichevan, Aliyev was linked to another regional network in Nakhichevan (Kechichian and Karasik, 1995, p. 59). Thus, when he assumed the presidency, national posts were filled by Aliyev clansmen from Nakhichevan, with all those who did not belong to the "President's political clique" to be "left out in the cold" (Kechichian and Karasik, 1995, p. 61).

Indisputably, Aliyev adopted a personalized style of leadership that dovetailed with the control mentality that the Azerbaijani people were accustomed to, during the Soviet era, and even before, during the Khans era (Altstadt, 1997, p. 133). Aliyev stood as a strong leader, who being aware of the long-forged control, or better said, dependence mentality of a diverse amalgam of "atomized" rational actors in a state of insecurity, assumed the responsibility of guiding, as a father figure, the new-born republic through the "troubled waters" of the early independence period.[25] The Aliyev administration soon became a firmly established regime, with survival-guaranteeing alliances in the society. Nevertheless, the whole structure has been "fluid and gathered around common interests and powerful individuals" (Tokluoglu, 2012, p. 335).

To guard against potential dangers, since 1993, Political Opportunity Structures (POS), which refer "to political and structural aspects of the domestic context, such as the relatively open or closed nature of a political system" have been seriously cracked down (Gahramanova, 2009, p. 779). Non-governmental organizations (NGOs), operating within a context where NGOs have been perceived as anti-governmental and the terms "non-state" and "non-governmental" are barely distinguishable, have faced insurmountable difficulties; in fact, the suspicion that many of the NGOs may be associated with rival political clans of the power struggles of the 1990s, plus the soviet legacy that the state is the one and only authority defining and providing for the public good, has led the NGO sector to atrophy (Gahramanova, 2009, p. 787). In parallel to the NGOs, local self-governance, which, theoretically, brings citizens closer to the central authorities and serves a double function: (a) to transfer everyday demands to the central political arena, and (b) to "check-and-balance" elected politicians by holding them accountable, thus guaranteeing the democratization of the political system, has encountered certain difficulties in Azerbaijan (Chrysogonos, 2003). In particular, the 1999-founded and externally suggested institution of "municipality" has encountered various problems, among which, its undetermined legal status, the blurred allocation of responsibilities between it and the Executive Committees (who are appointed and controlled by the President), and its meager economic and fiscal provisions. Generally, the institution of "municipality" has widely been perceived by the ruling elite as incubator of political dissent, favoring a rival clan (Gahramanova, 2009, p. 790). As a result, a vicious circle has been at work, with confined POS to lead "to a resource-poor civil society, which in turn leads to a level of social capital that is too low to challenge the reduced POS"; an almost absent "set of informal values and norms shared by group members for supporting cooperation between them . . . [and] . . . networks of voluntary associations that permit people to coordinate and cooperate for mutual benefit," has bred social apathy and lack of horizontal trust (Fukuyama, 1999; Gahramanova, 2009, p. 789). In this "atomized" socio-political situation, the institution of "family" has remained dominant, with almost any individual to exhibit strong in-family ties and be identified with its family's interests, distrusting any other civic construction beyond the family circle (Gahramanova, 2009, p. 789).

Aside from the tight control on any POS, the Aliyev regime has been seriously reinforced by the natural resources wealth of the country (Radnitz, 2012). Azerbaijan, being one of the world's oldest petroleum producing countries, has profoundly counted on foreign investment to develop its volu-minous oil and natural gas fields off the Caspian coast (Gulbrandsen and Moe, 2007, p. 816). While a non-oil industrial sector including chemicals, petrochemicals, manufacturing and other export sectors has traditionally been existent, since 1991, petroleum revenue has become critical, wrapping up diachronic deficits of the national budget at the expense of a diversified economy (Gulbrandsen and Moe, 2007, p. 817; Corden and Neary, 1982).[26] To further systematize the effort, in 1992, the State Oil Corporation of the Azerbaijani Republic (SOCAR) was created, which brings foreign actors into the industry in the form of Production Sharing Agreements (PSAs). Even more, the regime's economic potential was skyrocketed with the flamboyant 1994 "deal of the century," a multi-decade offshore contract between the BP-led Azerbaijan International Operating Company (AIOC) and the govern-ment (Gulbrandsen and Moe, 2007, p. 817; Lee, 2004). More often than not, the regime spends the petrodollars, *inter alia*, on ego-promotion mega pro-jects, dubbed "white elephants," which albeit economic senseless, serve pop-ulist purposes, such as allocating lucrative construction contracts to critical individuals-allies for the subsistence of the regime, keeping the largest part of the population employed, and creating the impression that development in the country is as dazzling as the "white elephants."[27] In this manner, a neopa-trimonial structure of personal relations has been created, where the political elite, acting as a patron who strategically redistributes the wealth, seeks to both stave off challengers of the president's inner circle and establish firmer the regime in the society. In fact, the prefix "neo" stands to signify that the networks of power are built not only around family, kinship, or regional lines, but they have also elements of rational choice, including cooperation with influential oligarchs and business networks (Franke et al., 2009, p. 112; Herb, 2005; Kendall-Taylor, 2012).

Patronage, corruption, bribery and nepotism have become endemic. Within this context of "atomized" rational actors, Azerbaijan has never become disentangled from the intractable "frozen conflict" in NK; since the 1994 cease-fire agreement, the conflict has been gravitating in a no war no peace course, with the terms "frozen conflict" or "de facto" state to barely make up for a situation of enduring rivalry, and a second major eruption, following that of the early independence period, to have taken place during the four-day war in April 2016 (Broers, 2015; De Waal, 2010). The liquidation of any trust left and the highest possible prioritization of security on behalf of the NKR have kept the two sides of the conflict at the oppose sides of a hard-to-bridge gap (Freizer, 2014, p. 3; Toal and O'Loughlin, 2013b, p. 169; Voronkova, 2013, p. 115). Azerbaijan counts on the "wall of money" as well as on the international interest that its resources may attract, especially on behalf of the EU, the US, and Turkey in order to tilt the balance of power towards its side, and reverse the status quo to its favor, outside the context of any peaceful resolution (German, 2012, pp. 218, 224–225; Cornell, 1998; De Waal, 2010 p. 160).[28] Moreover, Azerbaijan has been very careful from the very beginning as far as Russian involvement is concerned; being aware of the indirect support that the latter has been granting, especially during the early years of the conflict, to the Armenian side in terms of arms, fuel and support, it has opposed any peacekeeping scheme within the OSCE Minsk Group could grant Russia the general command, as it had happened in the early 1990s in the neighboring Abkhazia and South Ossetia (Ambrosio, 2011, p. 100; Brzezinski, 1997; De Waal, 2010, pp. 166–167; Freizer, 2014, p. 4; Mihalka, 1996, p. 28; Panossian, 2001, p. 28; Torosyan and Vardanyan, 2015, p. 568). [29]

Competing Claims within the "Energyland"

While the Black Sea region and the South Caucasus, in particular, have been rattled by "frozen conflicts," creating the impression that war and desolation are among the key features representing the region, the truth is that aside from the disadvantage of "frozen conflicts," there is also the advantage of its strategic location; being at a crossroads between Europe and Asia and bordering the Black and the Caspian Seas, the South Caucasus relishes the significant status of a transport corridor, especially in energy terms. As early as in the nineteenth century, Azerbaijan (then borderland of the Russian Empire) developed into the world's first commercial oil industry, with the Rothschilds fostering the region's export potential by funding the Transcaucasian railway, that carried oil from Baku to Georgia's Black Sea port of Batumi (German, 2009, p. 346; O'Hara, 2004, pp. 139–140). That rail link, completed in 1883, opened up the landlocked Caspian Sea region, converting the South Caucasus into an indispensable avenue to and from the hydrocarbon-rich Caspian Sea area (EIA, 2013; German, 2009, p. 346).

The dawn of the post-soviet era has been marked by intense geopolitical struggle among regional actors such as Russia, Turkey and Iran, and international ones such as the EU and the US. With the potential of a "new Silk Road" that would include "pipelines, railways, fiber-optic cables and power transmission grids linking Western China with Europe," the EU, the US, and Turkey have allied themselves in an area that Moscow considers its own "strategic background" (German, 2009, p. 345). Although Russia remains the dominant actor in terms of economic and military power in the wider region, the US has identified the area as a foreign policy priority, seeking to increase its political influence; moreover, it has supported the EU, Georgian, and Turkish efforts to anchor the Azerbaijani, and if possible the Turkmen, natural gas output, so as to strengthen the European (EU) energy security (Karagiannis, 2002; O'Hara, 2004).

The issue of the European energy security is a vital one, since 35% of the EU imported supplies originates from Russia and is transported *via* Russian networks; thus, a diversification of both the source of supplies as well as of the transport networks could seriously and pragmatically address the issue (Bilgin, 2009, p. 4487; Eurostat, 2014, p. 69; Sotiriou, 2015, pp. 123–177; Umbach, 2010, p. 1239; Zimnitskaya and von Geldern, 2011, p. 13). To this direction, the Baku-Supsa (Georgia's Black Sea coast) oil pipeline came on stream as early as in the end 1990s, being the first network to carry Caspian Sea hydrocarbons to the western markets independently from Moscow. In the mid-2000s, two other networks, the BTC oil pipeline, and the BTE (or SCP) natural gas network came on stream, multiplying the Caspian resources in the EU; the first network spans over 1768km, starting from Baku, crossing Georgia (Tbilisi), and ending up to the Turkish deepwater port of Ceyhan on the Mediterranean Sea. The second one is 692km long, follows the same line, except for the end, which is in the Northeast Turkey, where it connects with the Turkish domestic supply network, with the supplies to be enough for export as well (16 billion cubic meters of gas per year, bcm/y) (German, 2009, p. 350; Zimnitskaya and von Geldern, 2011, p. 13; Sotiriou, 2010, pp. 69–72). Moreover, since 2006, the EU has further systemized its attempts towards "integrating" the Caspian producer countries (primarily Azerbaijan, and prospectively Turkmenistan) into its market. The BTE has been expanded and upgraded into the South Caucasus Pipeline Expansion (SCPx), which, along with the TANAP and the TransAdriatic Pipeline (TAP), are to form the EU "Southern Gas Corridor" (European Commission, 2008, p. 4).[30] This will carry, initially, the Azeri resources, through the South Caucasus and Turkey, to the EU market, having as entry point Greece, and then proceeding onward to Italy, under the Adriatic Sea (Euractiv, 2013; BP, 2018a).

Certainly, Russia, in view of the European advances in the region, has not exhibited the slightest apathy; on the contrary, it has tried to remain the dominant actor in the region, projecting its power and counterbalancing these efforts (Umbach, 2010, pp. 1237–1239). Since the end of the 1990s, the Baku-Novorossiisk (Russia's Black Sea coast) network has been transferring oil from the Caspian to the Black Sea, and then onward, to the international markets (the European included).[31] Moreover, seeking to disengage Turkey from the pro-western "energy chariot," the "Blue Stream" network came on stream in February 2003; this 1213km-long pipeline connects the Izobil'noe area (Russia) to Ankara (Turkey) *via* a 396km-long sub-merged section at the bottom of the Black Sea, directly supplying Russian natural gas to Turkey and onward to Southeastern Europe (at the designed capacity, the network is able to deliver up to 16bcm/y) (Gazprom, 2018a; Sotiriou, 2015a, p. 107). In parallel, on October 10, 2016, the governments of Russia and Turkey signed an agreement on the construction of "TurkStream," a natural gas network in the place of the erstwhile "South Stream," intended to run parallel to the "Blue Stream" and supply the same markets (Gazprom 2018b). The construction of "TurkStream" has commenced on May 7, 2017, off the Russian coast, and when completed, it will consist of two strings, each able to supply up to 15.75 bcm/y (Gazprom 2018b).

In this EU-Russia geopolitical tug-of-war, Russia has had "an ace in the hole": the legal regime of the Caspian Sea (Mammedov, 2000, 2001; Mehdiyoun, 2000; Sotiriou, 2015b).

It has been assessed that for the EU plan towards a SGC to flourish and become sustainable, (trans-Caspian) cooperation between Azerbaijan and Turkmenistan in the form of an underwater pipeline is indispensable; in fact, "without Turkmen gas," any project such as the SGC "would not make any sense" (Bilgin, 2009, p. 4491; Bilgin, 2007, p. 6387; Comfort and Bierman, 2010). On these grounds, Russia has kept an eye out for any possible transit routes could lead to an unchecked regional diversification, undermining its pipeline dominance (Bilgin, 2009, p. 4487; Kazantsev, 2008, p. 1084). For almost thirty years until the August 2018 five-party agreement, the absence of an institutional arrangement over the Caspian Sea's legal regime created a power vacuum, which the littoral states, serving as rational actors, tried to take advantage of and establish hard-to-reverse *faits accomplis*, primarily through the tactic of bilateralism (O'Lear, 2004, p. 182; Raczka, 2000, p. 218; Rywkin, 2010, p. 9; Stulberg, 2007). Russia, principally, greatly benefited from the compartmentalization of the region's energy potential, with the Sea to be transformed into an "iron curtain" separating the South Caucasus from Central Asia, and all the EU-earmarked Central Asia resources to be transited via Russia-controlled networks (Kazantsev, 2008, p. 1085). Of course, in the mid-term, the rise of the energy resources-seeking China in Central Asia made the issue of the Caspian Sea delimitation a secondary one, giving to the oil and gas producing states of the region a lucrative outlet, and thus limiting their losses from not being able to get directly connected to the western markets, the EU included (Kubicek, 2013, p. 180; Sotiriou, 2015, pp. 179–200). New, east-oriented networks from Central Asia to China were laid down, whereas the Beijing-funded implementation of the Belt and Road Initiative (BRI) (or Beijing's Marshall Plan for Asia), as a means of Eurasian connectivity, has magnified the "China" factor in the region (Contessi, 2016, p. 5; Freeman, 2017, p. 15). In fact, this infiltration, while endangering a Russian reaction given that Central Asia is deemed part of the former's traditional sphere of influence, is considered a necessity by the Chinese leadership, much more in view of the US naval dominance in the Straits of Malacca, the chokepoint through which almost 80% of China's oil supplies is being imported (Dadwal, 2007, p. 895; Sotiriou and Karagiannis, 2013, p. 312; Kusznir and Smith Stegen, 2015, p. 102).

In essence, energy security has been atop the policy agenda of Beijing. The conversion of the country into a net oil importer since 1993 and the dominance of two resources in its energy mix, the environment-damaging carbon and the oil, have rendered China constantly vigilant; the sustainability as well as the diversification of the energy mix in terms of resources and suppliers are vitally correlated with two fundamental policies of the state, the industrialization and the urbanization (Sotiriou and Karagiannis, 2013, p. 301). Thus, consistent efforts have been made at all aspects of the state, both internal (e.g., the verticalization of power as far as the energy policy is concerned) and external (e.g., formation of energy alliances with Asian producers) (Cheng, 2008; Downs, 2004, 2009, 2010; Kreft, 2006, p. 118; Meidan et al., 2009; Seaman, 2010; Sotiriou, 2015a, pp. 179–207; Zhao, 2008, p. 225; Xu, 2007; Xu and Reisinger, 2018).

THEORIZING THE TWO-LEVEL GAME

These two levels are rational actors within institutions (national level) and rational actors unconstrained by institutions (international level).

Rational Actors within Institutions (National Level)

Delving into the two levels of analysis, that is, rational actors within institutions and rational actors unconstrained by institutions, it would be rather helpful to briefly draw back to the very fundamentals, and try to visualize, in very broad terms, how are polities being constructed and how do politics play out. Starting from scratch, someone could observe successive stages through which the individuals, or the rational actors, have regulated their everyday life at the national level.[32]

At first, the individual, being exposed to the absolute insecurity that a totally unregulated (i.e., anarchy) everyday life entails, tries to ensure his survival, and then security. In doing so, he engages in two fundamental actions: individual power maximization, and alliance formation (against a more powerful actor that, potentially, could constitute a threat). These two actions notwithstanding, the conditions of insecurity and lack of trust that anarchy goes hand in hand with are not terminated, and constant vigilance remains a constant. Therefore, all individuals, whether acting alone or within alliance, never forget to seek their relative gains, that is, "who will gain more if we cooperate," since any imbalances in this cooperation may benefit tomorrow's rival, and pose an insurmountable impediment to the lagging actor's survival.[33]

Putting this situation within a more regulated context, the individuals have gradually become subjects of the law (i.e., an enforceable institution); in the eighteenth century, the personal rights (*status negativus*), first and foremost, have been institutionalized, protecting the individuality of the person against the power-holders (i.e., the state) and the other persons. Subsequently, in the nineteenth century, the civil rights (*status activus*) followed suit, "clothing" the individual with the right to participate in the state's preferences. Finally, in the twentieth century, the social rights (*status positivus*) have institutionalized the obligation of the state to intervene in a constructive manner in the protected sphere of the individuals (Chrysogonos and Vlachopoulos, 2017, p. 68, 73). As a result, the individuals have been converted from subjects constantly exposed to the insecurity of the unregulated reality into subjects of the law, with their existence to be guaranteed by the institutional framework of the state.

As illustrated in figure 1.2, at the beginning, there is only the society, permeated by human nature-attributed informal institutions such as family ties, language, and ethnicity. This group of people is exposed to the invariable insecurity of the unregulated reality. Once rights become institutionalized for each individual, and the path for survival, security and subsequent progress is established, elections are carried out, with the political parties to serve as the transfer belts of the civil society's demands; in parallel, the trilateral division of powers among the executive, the legislative, and the judiciary, serves as the "engine," which sets any newfangled state in action (Chrysogonos, 2003; Heywood, 2002, pp. 345–493).

More specifically, figure 1.3 describes the functioning of the state. After the elections have been conducted, the newly formed assembly (legislative) draws up, in its first convention, the Constitution (the fundamental law), that stipulates the way that the state should be governed. Then, the trilateral division of powers continues in its ordinary function, with the legislative and the executive to negotiate and adopt new legislation, and the judiciary to adjudicate the disputes that emerge across the whole structure (citizens *vs*

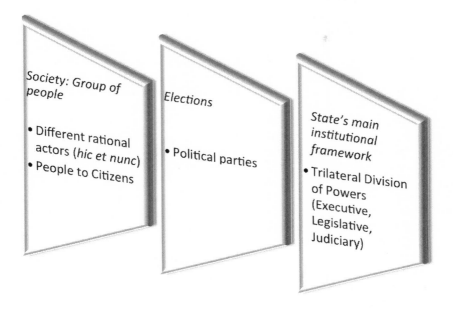

Figure 1.2.   Security at the national level: The formation of the state.

citizens, citizens *vs* state, state *vs* state); in this manner, it is guaranteed that those in power will abide by the Constitution and call elections in the stipulated time. Moreover, the civil society, as a *hic et nunc* (constantly changing) total, is being respected, given that, at one time, it may be represented in power by Party A, and, another time, by Party B (Chrysogonos, 2003, pp. 293–307).

In this way, the once unregulated reality of constant insecurity is transformed into a governable one subject to enforceable rules (i.e., institutionalized). As a result, rational actors are embedded in institutions.

Theorizing politics at the national level, since the 1990s, institutions (re)gained primary emphasis, a fact codified under the rubric "New Institutionalism." Juxtaposed with the "Old" one, "New Institutionalism" goes beyond the "descriptive, a-theoretical, parochial and non-comparative" focus on formal-legal structures, bringing society-centered approaches, and in particular, the role of groups, classes or simply civil society to the fore; thus, it does not only supplement the incumbent analytical scope, but also expands it towards "which institutions matter . . . and how they matter" on political outcomes (Hall and Taylor, 1996, p. 937; Lecours, 2000, p. 510).

Chapter 1

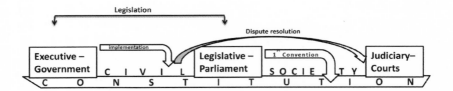

Figure 1.3. The functioning of the state.

The "New Institutionalism," nevertheless, could be considered as an "umbrella-theory," being constituted by three variants; "Historical Institutionalism," "Rational Choice Institutionalism," and "Sociological Institutionalism," each one offering its own account on two fundamental issues: (a) the relationship between institutions and behavior, and (b) the process whereby institutions originate and change (Hall and Taylor, 1996, p. 937).

If presented within a spectrum, "Rational Choice Institutionalism" would stand on the one side, adopting a "calculus approach" as far as explaining the relationship between institutions and individual action is concerned; presenting the individual as a rational actor in pursuit of utility maximization (or interest promotion), the institutions are constructions of his strategic calculations, whereas their change is contingent upon their capacity to satisfy the rational actor's utility maximization goals (Hall and Taylor, 1996, p. 945). Departing from the "Rational Choice Institutionalism" and the self-interested rational actor, "Sociological Institutionalism" would stand on the other side, adopting a "cultural approach," according to which shared attitudes and values are not only reflected on, but also influenced by, the institutions; in, fact, there is a "mutually constitutive" relationship between institutions and behavior, with the origin and change of institutions contingent on the approval by the "broader cultural environment" (social legitimacy) (Hall and Taylor, 1996, pp. 946–950).

Standing in the middle and benefiting from both, "Historical Institutionalism" draws to both the "calculus" and "cultural" approaches, stipulating that institutions and behavior are subject to an interactive procedure; institutions, on the one hand, shape the rational actors' strategies, preferences, goals, interests, ideas, and even identities, while, on the other hand, they are subject to a reconfiguration by the latter, spearheaded by the rational actors or the primacy of the agency (Huntington, 1968; Lecours, 2000; Peters, Pierre, and King, 2005, p. 1296; Tilly, 1992). Consequently, "instances of change-of-policy paths" come under scrutiny and stand better chances of having their causality thoroughly addressed (Peters, Pierre, and King, 2005, p. 1296).

In this line of reasoning, history is a "contingent product of the interactions of a diversity of actors and institutions" (Lecours, 2000, p. 514). Moreover, it is possible to isolate slices of history, juxtapose them, and through comparison to "explain the causes . . . and similarities of particular phenomena," especially those related to power (James, 2016, p. 88; Lecours, 2000, p. 515). Power relationships are at the core of social and political outcomes, a fact that becomes apparent even from the rudimentary stage of human society, when anarchy prevails, and power-seeking actions, either in the form of individual power maximization or alliance formation (against a common threat), are the necessary means for survival and security on behalf of rational actors. It is noteworthy, though, that even when human society takes steps towards regulation, the rational actors do not become oblivious of their prior actions towards survival, but, on the contrary, these actions are filtered through institutions, with the latter critically mediating and configuring their societal impact (Lecours, 2000, p. 514). This is illustrated in figure 1.4.

Setting, now, "Historical Institutionalism" in motion, long periods of path-dependent institutional stability (institutional equilibrium) are succeeded by abrupt and short episodes of institutional fluidity (critical junctures), where chances for change are high (Capoccia and Kelemen, 2007, p. 341). Of particular importance is the concept of "path-dependence," since it depicts the way that causal factors, primarily of institutional nature, propel "historical development along a set of 'paths'" (Hall and Taylor, 1996, p. 941).

Distinguishing between "path-dependencies," there are two types, the self-enforcing and the reactive sequences (James 2016, p. 89). In the first case, "initial steps in a particular direction induce further movement in the same direction such that over time it becomes difficult or impossible to reverse direction" (Mahoney, 2000, p. 512). In the second case, there are

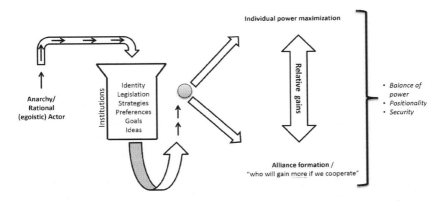

Figure 1.4.   Rational actors within institutions (national level): The filtering of power.

"temporarily ordered and causally connected events . . . where each event . . . is both a reaction to antecedent events and a cause of subsequent events" (Mahoney, 2000, p. 526). Given these, a multitude of causal factors is in play within an unpredictable historical continuum, impacting on behaviors and policies and, ultimately, triggering changes in existing policy paths. Nevertheless, the "catch," at this point, "is to explain what precipitates . . . critical junctures, and, although historical institutionalists generally stress the impact of economic crisis and military conflict," further refinement is needed (Hall and Taylor, 1996, p. 942).

Rational Actors Unconstrained by Institutions (International Level)

At the international level, there is a relapse to the rudimentary stage of human society, where no regulation exists and anarchy prevails. Although, at the national level, even at this stage, there are ties pertinent to the human nature, such as familial ties, language, and ethnicity, at the international level, there are very few, if any, connective strands among states, so the latter stand as unitary rational actors.

Diachronically, the international level lacks the organization structure of states (figure 1.3), so there is no prototype of governance, which could enforce the law (maintain order) and guarantee security. In this condition of high uncertainty, territorially organized groups (tribes, city states, or modern states) interact as unitary rational actors in pursuit of maximizing their utility. "Take care of yourself" looms as the biggest imperative, with the principle of self-help to highlight the absence of trust and render states in constant vigilance (Waltz, 1986, p. 103).[34] Yesterday's ally can be tomorrow's enemy, and the only means by which a state can ensure its position in the international field is power; "whether as an end or as a necessary means to a variety of other ends," the magnitude of power has been aptly encapsulated by Thucydides' saying: "the strong do what they can and the weak suffer what they must," indicating, in this manner, that survival and security are always at stake (Keohane, 1986, p. 165; Kauppi, 1995; Morgenthau, 1973, p. 208; Platias, 2002, p. 27; Strassler, 1996, p. 352).

Engaging the dynamics of the international system, the interaction of states creates a structure, which has a life of its own, given the ability to constrain states "from taking certain actions while propelling them towards others" (Waltz, 1990, p. 74; Keohane, 1986). With the concept "dynamics" to borrow from physics and be briefly defined both as an "energy in motion" and as "the action of forces on bodies in motion," states and structures are in a mutually constitutive relationship; nevertheless, behaviors and outcomes cannot be determined, since "the shaping and shoving of structures may be successfully resisted" (Waltz, 1986, p. 343). Determinant of these processes is the distribution of capabilities (power) across states. "States are differently

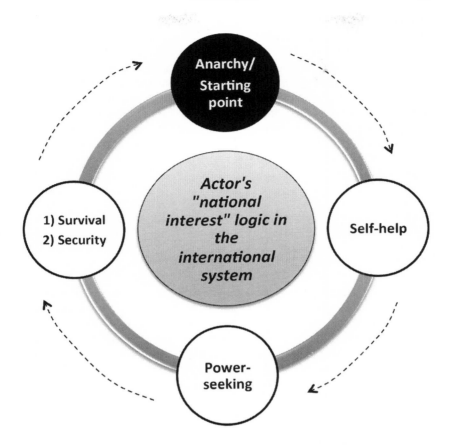

Figure 1.5. The states' "national interest" logic in the international system.

placed by their power, and differences in placement help to explain both their behavior and their fates" (Waltz, 1990, p. 31). Power, however, is perceived more as an instrument and not as an end, because the ultimate goal of states is to maintain their position in the system and be secure, i.e., positionality and security (Waltz, 1986, p. 127; 1979, p. 126).

Since the era of the Peloponnesian War, the content of the term of "power" has been treated in its totality, with Thucydides to have elaborated on every single one of its aspects, namely, the economic, diplomatic, and the military one (Sotiriou, 2015, p. 33). The economic, as control over resources and accumulation of wealth, is met as early as fifth century BC, when the Spartan King Archidamus argued that "the war is conducted less with arms and more with money" (Platias, 2002, p. 48). There is no doubt that as per the ancient Greek historian, money and power are highly correlated, whereas the accumulation of wealth is behind the pursuit of power and prosperity (Gilpin, 1984; Sotiriou, 2015, p. 33).[35] In a like manner, foreign trade favors relationships "of dependence and influence between nations," with the weak and dependent states (B, C, D, etc.) to try diversify their supplies away from the powerful state-supplier (A) as a means of disempowering it, and A to try to averse such actions as a means of increasing its national wealth, relative gains, and influence (Hirschman, 1969, p. 16). The difficulty, however, for states B, C, D, etc., in diversifying (balancing) the trade conducted with A, thus guarding their independence and autonomy, is contingent upon three main factors:

- The total net gain to B, C, D of their trade with A
- The length and the painfulness of the adjustment process which A may impose upon B, C, D by interrupting trade
- The strength of the vested interests which A has created by its trade within the economies of B, C, D (Hirschman, 1969, p. 18)

Reading between the lines of interstate cooperation, the primacy of positionality and security concerns forces states to adopt a *zero sum* perspective (one's gains are the other's losses), and focus on the relative rather than the absolute gains, i.e., "who will gain more if we cooperate" (Grieco, 1993, p. 319; Lamy, 2001, p. 187). This is due to the fact that, in anarchy, "one state may use its disproportionate gain to implement a policy to damage or destroy the other" (Grieco, 1993, p. 319). So, although absolute gains contribute to the maximization of power, the gap in the gains of both rational actors is what matters the most, and may prove, more often than not, crucial stumbling block to any prospect of cooperation. Further to this direction, "States prefer to join the weaker of two coalitions . . . [since] the goal the system encourages them to seek is security" (Waltz, 1986, p. 127).

All of that having been said, when in anarchy, states engage in two strategies: (a) internal efforts, such as increases in the economic and military capabilities, or/and (b) external efforts, such as the formation of alliances in order to strengthen their own status and wane the rival one. In this manner, balances of power are created, ensuring the states' position and overall security (Waltz, 1986, p. 117; Kissinger, 1994), as shown in figure 1.6.

While, at the national level, interests are moderated by institutions, at the international level, the relationship between anarchy and institutions is a constantly challenged one, allowing, many times, for the primacy of national interests *vis-à-vis* international institutions.

International institutions invest in the positive and trust-building prospects innate to human nature and "rationality" and see international cooperation as a means of strengthening ties among nations and multiplying benefits

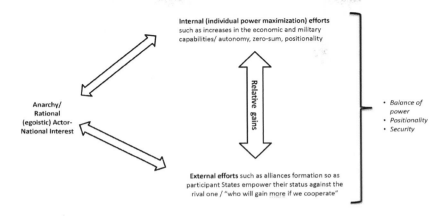

Figure 1.6. Rational actors unconstrained by institutions (international level): Unfiltered power.

for each side (Kegley, 1995). According to this positive perspective on international relations, states focus on the absolute rather than the relative gains from a cooperative scheme, playing down any possible asymmetries in the gains and avoiding any correlation with positionality concerns (Lamy, 2001). The erstwhile *zero sum* considerations give way to a win-win logic. Further to this direction, interdependence could place security within an evolutionary linear course, a far cry from the circular and anarchy-bound functioning of the international system (figure 1.5).

Nevertheless, despite the benevolence encapsulated in the "rationality" of the actor, states do not stop thinking as rational egoists seeking to maximize their own, absolute gains, much more, when in a condition of anarchy. Thus, any cooperative scheme is hard, if not impossible, to escape the problem of cheating, which, in turn, leads away from Pareto's optimal outcome, that is, a situation of perfectly balanced gains among involved actors, where it is impossible to make one actor better off without necessarily making another worse off (Georgakopoulos et al., 2002; Lipson, 1984; Powell, 1991; Snidal, 1991; Sotiriou, 2015, pp. 40–41; Stein, 1982).[36]

Fixing this problem, the role of (international) institutions is critical; conceived as communicative practices and rules that define the "appropriate behavior for specific groups of actors in specific situations of international life," (international) institutions, first and foremost, display an obligatory or coercive attribute, able to implement practices and propel behaviors *via* rule-building (Risse, 2002, p. 604). In addition, these rules (institutions) regulate any cooperative scheme, constraining "the sequence of interaction among the actors, the choices available [and] . . . the payoffs" (Risse, 2002; Weingast,

Figure 1.7.   The evolutionary linear course towards security under (international) institutions.

2002, p. 661). Consequently, the prioritization of the ego by the rational actors in pursuit of their absolute gains, including cheating, is contained, allowing for Pareto's optimal outcome to be fulfilled. Finally, the (international) institutions' capacity to clarify the meaning in a relevant issue area makes it "easier to establish a reputation for practicing reciprocity consistently," striking a balance among the gains (interests) of all actors involved (Axelord and Keohane, 1985, p. 250). On the whole, legally binding rules, allocation of choices and payoffs, as well as reciprocity, are the means through which international institutions harmonize a state's behavior with the long-term, evenly benefiting, Pareto's optimal outcome.

Summarizing, there are two schools of thought, with each holding a different viewpoint as far as the functioning of the international system and the attainment of the ultimate goal of security are concerned; according to the first one, which goes by the name "Neorealism," there is an endless power-seeking, with the security to be achieved through the creation of balances of power. The more symmetric these balances are, the more sustainable the security is. On the contrary, the second school of thought, which goes by the name "Neoliberal Institutionalism," upholds that although the endless power-seeking is a reality, as portrayed by states cheating in a cooperative scheme among otherwise good willed rational actors, security is better achieved through the creation of institutions. The more symmetric, in terms of all the actors' interests being taken into account (Pareto's optimal outcome), the more sustainable the security is. All of that having been said, the Neorealism vs Neoliberal Institutionalism debate (the so-called "Neo-Neo" debate) is formed, shown in table 1.1.

With the debate to represent the extremes, contemporary world affairs seem to stand somewhere in between; neither as anarchic and unbending as Neorealism holds, nor as politicized and fully-recalibrated via international institutions as Neoliberal Institutionalism maintains. An "anarchic society" takes shape, where, despite the absence of a formal supra-national government above states, economic interdependence, international institutions and widespread cooperation mushrooms (Bull, 1977). There is no doubt that "the world has become interdependent in economics, in communications, in human aspirations. . . . No one nation, no one part of the world, can prosper or

Table 1.1. The Neo-Neo Debate

Assumption	Neorealism	Neoliberal Institutionalism
1. States: rational unitary actors (rational egoists)	Yes	Yes
2. Anarchy: governing principle in the international system	Yes	Yes
3. Means of survival	Power-seeking (relative gains)	Power-seeking (absolute gains)
4. Prospects for cooperation	Negative	Positive
5. International institutions facilitate cooperation	No	Yes
6. Security achieved through	Balances of power	Institutions

be secure in isolation" (Kissinger, 1975, p. 197). Interdependence is a *fait accompli*, with economics and international institutions to be critical parts of this reality, if not the central ones. But, what does this mean for the "Neo-Neo" debate? Has Neoliberal Institutionalism come out on top of Neorealism? Or even worse, have states, acting as rational (egoistic) actors, become oblivious of their power-seeking as the necessary means of survival in conditions of anarchy? Is there any role reserved for "power" in this interdependent reality?

To begin with, where "there are reciprocal (although not necessarily symmetrical) costly effects of transactions, there is interdependence" (Keohane and Nye, 2011, p. 8). This can, actually, be understood in two ways: (a) the joint gains and losses, and (b) the relative gains and the distribution of capabilities (Keohane and Nye, 2011). The first is thoroughly addressed by the economists, who, given each state's comparative advantage, qualify free trade as the means serving the interests of all participant states, thus underlining the precedence of the neoliberal win-win logic (De Lima and Guizzo, 2015, p. 595; Georgakopoulos, 2002). The second, however, is more profound, seeking to address the question "who gets what out of a cooperative scheme?"

"It is important to guard against the assumption that measures that increase joint gain from a relationship will somehow be free of distributional conflict" (Keohane and Nye, 2011, p. 9). Interdependence does not replace the *zero-sum* logic, dominant in conditions of anarchy, by the win-win one. Therefore, while international relations are founded upon a mutually complement basis, the preservation of the "balance of power" is the vital factor that guarantees their sustainability (Keohane and Nye, 2011, p. 9).

Addressing such situations, "institutional balancing" figures as the befitting, "middle-ground," approach, that, initially, informs the "neo-neo" debate, so as to be able to cope with contemporary "anarchic society," and then, turns this update in Neorealism's favor. Beginning from the neorealist assumption that institutions are "epiphenomenal" in international politics, it sets out to tackle the question: "if institutions do not really matter, why do states devote resources and energy to them?" (He, 2008, p. 490).

Elaborating on this, it is specified "that (1) high economic interdependence makes states choose a new realist balancing strategy—institutional balancing—other than traditional military alliances to cope with threats or pressures from the system, (2) the distribution of capabilities in the regional system indicates how states conduct institutional balancing" (He, 2008, p. 492). Following these, point (1) underscores the fact that traditional power politics of hard balancing and military buildups have been overshadowed by the soft balancing of economics and interdependence, without this meaning, however, that when competition and insecurity run high, there is not the possibility of backtracking from soft to hard balancing again (He, 2008; Sotiriou, 2015, p. 44). The more economic interdependence grows, as is the case with energy, the more states are propelled to exhaust their "rationality" as actors by filtering their actions through a strict cost/benefit analysis, thus rendering the military balancing a far secondary option. In this case, institutions appear to matter, but in reality, they are perceived as "empty shells," serving to the interests of states, which seek to maximize their power, a fact which, in turn, will allow them to have the military advantage once the circumstances call for such a transformation. At this point and with the issue of "power" being at the center, point (2) comes to the forefront; the "institutional balancing" by states depends on the distribution of capabilities in the regional subsystem. Reading between the lines and recalling long-established scholars such as Thucydides, "the strong do what they can and the weak suffer what they must." In other words, the more powerful a state is, the more it will jump in and out of institutions' regulations, or better said, it will seek to adjust these regulations to suit and fulfill its interests.

Bringing the National and International Levels Together: Expected Outcomes in Eurasia's Two-Level Game

Starting at both levels from the point of anarchy, rational actors, either individuals or states, are after two strategies: (a) individual power maximization efforts (internal efforts at the international level), and (b) alliance formation (external efforts at the international level). Both lead to the balance of power among actors within a system, the assurance of position, and, ultimately, security. Although actors may get involved in cooperative schemes in pursuit of the aforementioned goals, relative gains never lose their prominence. In fact, actors are highly sensitive to what could become of the gaps emerging out of cooperative schemes, since this asymmetry may be turned against them, thus putting the fundamental objectives of survival and security at grave risk.

Doing justice to the argument by distinguishing between national and international level, at the national one, even when fully unregulated, there are some human nature-bound connective strands among actors, i.e., familial ties, language, and ethnicity, that, at times, are used to form alliances under their banner (e.g., language). Further to this, the more the socio-political development progresses and deepens, the more social capital is generated, and the less sharp the relative gains concerns become.[37] But this, in turn, does not mean that the existence-connected relative gains concerns are eradicated. On the contrary, they are alleviated, ready to regain their pure and intense form, once the level of socio-political development slips back to anarchy-bordering and "atomized" conditions.

By comparison, at the international level, there are very few, if any, connective strands; so states stand as clear-cut unitary rational actors, pursuing the strategies of power-seeking and relative gains in their absolute form. Co-existence within the compounds of international institutions is not an easy task to accomplish, given the diverging interests and the preoccupation of actors with relative gains concerns. Even in cases where cooperation within international institutions is highly advisable, if not inescapable, states uphold their interests and strategize around legally binding provisions, knowing how power and gaps in the distribution of capabilities may function. In situations like these, "institutional balancing" offers an inclusive account, underscoring the capacity of powerful states to "jump in and jump out" of institutions at will, opting for binding provisions that safeguard and promote their interests, even at times where high (economic) interdependence seemingly leaves a narrow window of opportunity.

Blending this two-level theoretical scheme into the content of the book, at first, at the national level, all five "frozen conflicts" of the post-soviet space—Transdniestria (Moldova), Crimea (Ukraine), Abkhazia and South Ossetia (Georgia), and Nagorno-Karabakh (Azerbaijan)—are addressed. The collapse of the USSR constituted a critical juncture throughout the post-soviet space, with the old, Moscow-centered, institutional equilibrium to give its place to fifteen new ones. This transition (critical juncture) period, however, until the new constitutions were enacted, and thus a new institutional equilibrium was established, was not a-free-of-socio-political challenges situation. On the contrary, the formerly and primarily Soviet citizens found themselves in "atomized" conditions bordering anarchy, and acting as rational egoistic actors sought to ensure their survival and security by maximizing their power either individually or through alliance formation. Conflicts broke out, pitting otherwise "atomized" rational actors under language or ethnicity banners in an effort to claim for their group a substantial part in the unraveling power-sharing, as a means of survival and security. Most of these conflicts outlived the critical juncture period of the early post-soviet period, having exhibited second major eruptions, or in the case of Crimea, the seeds for becoming a "frozen conflict" in March 2014 had been sowed since the early independence period, and remained slowly brewing ever since.

Following these and being in search of the conflicts' causal mechanism, Historical Institutionalism along with the logic of self-enforcing sequences, according to which "initial steps in a particular direction induce further movement in the same direction such that over time it becomes difficult or impossible to reverse direction," are employed to support the following hypothesis: "Lasting regional political throughout the conflict zones, embedded in an ethnicized national identity on behalf of the titular nationality (i.e., Moldovans, Ukrainians, Georgians, Azerbaijanis), have been serving as the main destabilizing factors."

Of course, in each case, there have been secondary and rather critical causes, such as the comparatively weak economic growth (GDP per capita, Purchasing Power Parity-PPP) and unemployment by the hosting states (Ukraine, Georgia), and certainly, the role of Russia (Transdniestria, Crimea, Abkhazia and South Ossetia), which is included as a contextual factor, given the focus on the state-level analysis (i.e., domestic politics).

Summarizing, at the national level, the lasting regional political preferences is the independent variable, whereas the type of national identity of the hosting states along with the interstate comparison in terms of GDP per capita, PPP and unemployment are the intervening variables. Russia is included as a contextual variable.

Advancing to the international level, with states, now, being rational actors in pursuit of their survival and security through power-maximization efforts, the energy developments across Eurasia's underbelly come under the spotlight. The Caspian Sea region, and particularly the protracted negotiations around the demarcation of the Sea until the five-party agreement of August 2018, reflect the heightened competition; this is because it could not only assist the EU in counterbalancing its energy overreliance on Russia, but it could also provide the states of Caucasus and Central Asia with a direct access to a lucrative export market such as the EU, thus further undermining Russia's stature. In light of these, a series of hypotheses emerge:

- Beginning from the most powerful actor, it is expected that Russia it will have been opting for provisions befitting its interests, whereas the other Caucasian and Central Asian states will have been succumbing to Russia's choices as an indication of the incumbent power asymmetry.
- Likewise, the foreign policies of states in Caucasus and Central Asia will also have been informed, in the direction of counterbalancing Russia's

powerful energy status. In particular, it is expected that these states will have engaged in (a) internal efforts, that will have opened their energy market to foreign investors so as to amplify their own, self-standing, energy profile by boosting production, thus healing their sensitivity to Russia's unilateral actions, and in (b) external efforts, creating new energy alliances (i.e., construction of export networks) with powerful and lucrative markets such as the EU and China, so as to make up for potential (economic) losses, thus minimizing also any vulnerability and becoming solid energy powers themselves.[38]

• Reaching, now, to the other end of Eurasia and to the seaborne supplies-dependent China, it is hypothesized that it will have adopted the same *modus operandi*: in particular, (a) in terms of internal efforts, it will have attempted at building up a more self-reliant energy status able to substitute for its imports, thus mending its sensitivity, whereas (b) in terms of external efforts, it will have established new energy alliances with rich-in-resources actors such as Russia and the Central Asia states, able to offset any external disruption, thus lessening also its vulnerability to potential losses (cut offs).

METHODOLOGY

The book is structured around a "case-study" approach, where case-studies at both national and international level are examined, primarily, for the period following the collapse of the USSR. In this manner, elements of both a synchronic (or cross-sectional) and a diachronic (or longitudinal) dimension are allowed into the analysis, facilitating the establishment of valid comparisons across space and time (Gerring, 2001, p. 222). Further to this, the wider the geographic extent and the time span, the better the chances for shedding light on the intrinsic causality. In essence, "by watching the progress of a single unit (a country, a city, a person) over time and by paying attention to variation within that case . . . often observe, or at least intuit, a complex causal relationship at work" (Gerring, 2001, p. 215).

Taken the national and the international level together and being assessed as far as their sufficiency is concerned, all case-studies are checked against the criteria of plentitude, boundedness, comparability, independence, representativeness, variation, analytic utility, mechanism, replicability and causal comparison (Gerring, 2001, p. 202). It is true that in social sciences there is not, yet, the possibility of reproducing social, political, and economic contexts so as to "test, in an experimental fashion, individual groups and responses," thus most of the foregoing criteria encounter certain limitations (Gerring, 2001, p. 202). Yet, in the present analysis, these limitations are mitigated.

To begin with, at the national level, the phenomenon of "frozen conflict" is well taken care of, since all incidents in the post-soviet space are brought under the spotlight, addressing the criteria of plentitude, boundedness, independence, representativeness, and variation. Furthermore, the fact that their examination starts from the critical juncture period of the early post-soviet years with brief flashbacks, when the USSR was a reality and most of the "frozen conflicts" trace their roots back to, facilitates the illumination of the mechanism at work. Moreover, the full consideration of all cases separately as well as the across-case comparisons, satisfy the criteria of comparability and causal comparison. Finally, the thorough within-case and across-case investigation, with the employment of both political and economic variables, adds to analytic utility of the case-studies, enhancing also their prospects for being replicated to other areas in the world that experience a similar situation.

The same, more or less, could be argued for the developments at the international level as well. The nature of the topic (energy-natural gas diplomacy), the extent (Eurasia's underbelly), and the actors involved (Russia, Azerbaijan, Iran, Kazakhstan, Turkmenistan, Uzbekistan, and China), cover the whole analytic spectrum, meeting the criteria of plentitude, boundedness, independence, representativeness, and variation. Even further, the analysis of the case-studies, that starts from the critical juncture period of the early post-soviet years and thoroughly presents each actor's options (strategies) when operating in anarchy, unravels the mechanism at work. Finally, the across-case comparisons corroborate the criteria of comparability and causal comparison, whereas the within-case and across-case study produces a well-substantiated guide, replicable not only to other areas, but also to other issues of the world scene, adding to its analytic utility. On top of all, both levels of analysis refer to situations bordering the condition of anarchy. Thus, coherence runs throughout the analysis.

At this point, the question that calls for further elaboration revolves around the measurability of the argument, i.e., how is the argument(s) measured. Addressing this, there is a wide array of primary and secondary sources that comes in handy.

To start, again, from the national level, "regional political preferences," first and foremost, are measured by resorting to primary data from institutions of the *de facto* entities (e.g., central election commissions, governments, etc.). Certainly, a credibility issue arises, given the nature (*de facto* not *de jure*) of these institutions. To overcome such a situation, these data are being cross-checked, either by data from various other institutions (e.g., Razumkov Center, GfK Ukraine), or by placing them within a historical continuum, so as to produce valid associations through comparison. Proceeding to the "national identity types," this is a more complex issue, which is dealt with, jointly, by both employing indicators and resorting to direct opinion polls. Discussing indicators first, the artificially "ethnic" type of nationalism which, in essence, is "atomized" is proved by the excessive levels of corruption. This indicator is employed to designate rational (egoistic) actors who, in conditions of institutional fluidity and high insecurity, project the "egoistic" feature of their rationality, putting the selfish behavior atop. Corruption is measured by resorting to primary data from organizations such as the Transparency International (Corruption Perceptions Index), and the World Bank (CPIA transparency, accountability, and corruption in the public sector rating, 1 = Low to 6 = High). Of course, as earlier said, there is also the availability of data from opinion polls that seek to ascertain in a more direct manner the types of national identity; special reference is made to Ukraine and Crimea, in particular. Coming, now, to the "interstate comparisons in terms of GDP per capita, PPP and unemployment," which serve as core-indicators for the quality of life, the primary data from the World Bank and the International Monetary Fund (IMF) are critical.[39] Next to all the above, the argumentation is further supplemented by indispensable secondary sources (scholarly work, internet, and policy-analyses), providing it with inclusivity and thoroughness.

At the international level, there is, too, a mix of primary and secondary sources. Setting out from the former, emphasis is, first and foremost, given to government and UN documents regarding each Caspian littoral state's position on the demarcation of the Sea. Next to these, another primary source is the archive of major energy companies (e.g., the Russian "Gazprom," "LU-Koil," "Transneft," and "Rosneft," the British "BP," the American "Exxon-Mobil," the Kazakh "KazMunayGas, KMG," and the Chinese "China National Offshore Oil Corporation, CNOOC," "China National Petroleum Corporation, CNPC," and "Sinopec"), since, along with their respective governments, they have played an equally critical role in the implementation of all energy policies (mainly upstream and midstream) in the region.[40] In this archive, there are also interviews from key actors, assisting to the full illumination of the cases in point.[41] In the same line of reasoning, data and reports from key organizations, such as the International Energy Agency (IEA), for example the World Energy Outlook, and the Energy Information Administration (EIA), offer critical input, with, other, well-informed reports (e.g., BP Statistical Review of World Energy) to complete the whole picture. Finally, secondary sources (scholarly work, internet, policy-analyses) are also employed, so as to further buttress and enrich the argument.

CONCLUSION

The book in hand presents the national and international level in comparable terms, since the existence of case-studies that are materializing in conditions, either bordering anarchy (national level), or absolute anarchy (international level), allows for the linearity between the two levels to come to light.

At the national level, the "frozen conflicts" across Eurasia are traced back to the early post-soviet period, when the erstwhile institutional equilibrium of the USSR entered the critical juncture period of the early 1990s; then, institutional fluidity swept the Soviet socio-political construction, creating a situation similar to that of the state of nature, where anarchy prevails. In this context, former soviet citizens have been acting as rational (egoistic) actors seeking a favorable power-sharing in the emerging republics, either through individual power maximization efforts or through alliance formation, so as to ensure their survival and security. Facilitators to these efforts have been features intrinsic to the human nature, such as family ties, language, and ethnicity, that "clothe" the rational actors, creating what is, at present, termed rational actors within institutions.

At the international level, developments follow a plainer path; with anarchy to pose in absolute terms, relieved from attributes such as the birthbound ties at the national level, states, which replace citizens as rational (egoistic) actors, project and pursue their national interest unconstrained by institutions. Power-seeking, either through internal efforts (domestic policies) or external (alliance formation), aims to ensure survival, at first, and then, security. Relative gains remain always sharp, since any gaps in any kind of a cooperative scheme could put states' security at stake. Presenting the aforementioned in the form of a testable model, the national interest is the independent (explanatory) variable, whereas the internal efforts and/or the external efforts are the dependent variables. International institutions more reflect the interests of the actors rather than shape and shove the behavior of the latter, at least in the cases in point.

Eventually, in terms of methodology, both levels of analysis are structured around the case-study approach, which, albeit small sized, the within-case as well as the across-case variation endow it with the potential for well-grounded arguments, projectable on a much wider scale and serving as theoretical models.

NOTES

1. The World Island consists of Africa, Europe and Asia, whereas the Islands are North and South America, Great Britain, Japan, Australia and Malaysia. It follows that the World Island is the largest, most densely populated and resource rich compared to any other possible land combination.
2. For a map illustrating the "Heartland," see https://birminghamwarstudies .wordpress.com/tag/mackinder/ (date of retrieval 17-07-2017).
3. The population showed an upward tendency of three million per year (Mackinder, 1943, p. 599).
4. As far as the developments that Mackinder's theory did not foresee, reference is made to: (a) the rapid rise of China to a great power status despite predictions for a "Sino-Japanese

empire," (b) the speedy pace of technological progress and its consequences that have rendered the US, albeit an insular power, at the helm of today's international affairs, and (c) the role of asymmetric warfare, an indicative case being the Vietnam War (Mackinder, 2006). It did, however, manage to capture the geopolitical fears of the two world-level sea powers, Great Britain and the US, *vis-à-vis* the prospect of a Russo-German alliance leading, at first, to the domination of the "world-island" and, subsequently, of the world (Mackinder, 2006). For more, see Sotiriou, 2015, pp. 1–3.

5. On this line of argumentation is also mentioned that the Russian word "коренизация" stems from the word "корен" which means "root."

6. As stated in chapter 1, Article 1b of the Constitution of the USSR, the central authorities in Moscow maintained the jurisdiction to address questions that pertain to the change or readjustment of borders between the Union's republics as well as of the external borders of the Union *per se* (Konstitutsiia soiuza, 1924). It is essential to mention, though, that power politics considerations never left the scene. The tactic of reallocating populations and territories (or ethnic engineering) had been made apparent more than a few times throughout the years of the USSR. Indicatively speaking, below are mentioned the cases of Nagorno-Karabakh, Abkhazia and South Ossetia, Transdniestria, and Crimea.

The formation of Nagorno-Karabakh: A nowadays *de facto* breakaway state but *de jure* within the territory of Azerbaijan, Nagorno-Karabakh has been a mostly Armenian-populated region (the mountainous part), that after a series of brief wars between Armenian and Azerbaijani forces in the period 1918–1920, it was belatedly awarded on November 26, 1924, the status of "Autonomous Region" by the Azerbaijani authorities (Saparov, 2012, p. 319). Taken seriatim, the Bolshevik institution for the establishing the communist rule in the Caucasus, Kavburo (Kavkazskoe Biuro), had initially (first half of 1921) promised Nagorno-Karabakh to Armenia, in a "chain reaction" logic according to which the fulfillment of the principles of "Korenizatsia" would attract public support, establishing, ultimately, their authority in the Zangezur region, which, by the time, had been unyieldingly defended by the nationalist forces of Nzhdeh and Dashnak party (Saparov, 2012, p. 307). However, the complete liquidation of the Armenian opposition in Zangezur by the Bolsheviks (Red Army) by mid-July 1921 strengthened the diplomatic position of the latter by evaporating the very reason for awarding Karabakh to Armenia (Sarapov, 2012, pp. 309, 320). Thus, the Kavburo decided to preserve the long-lived status quo, solidifying the two ethnically mixed, if not engineered, *gubernii*—Erevan (Armenians) and Elizavetpol (Muslim)—which the erstwhile Tsarist regime had forged in the early nineteenth century (Saparov, 2012, p. 286). In this manner, the Bolsheviks attested to the precedence of national interest over the nationality issue, with the latter coming at the service of the former whenever required.

The formation of Abkhazia and South Ossetia: Remaining in the wider neighborhood and, in particular, in Georgia, the cases of Abkhazia and South Ossetia, nowadays *de facto* states but *de jure* within the territory of Georgia, constitute another two cases of the kind; in 1921, the Red Army liquidated Georgia's brief independence (1918–1921), making Abkhazia an independent and sovereign SSR, associated with the Georgian SSR upon a *par inter pares* union agreement (CCPA, 1925, Art. 3). Moreover, it was stipulated that the state language would be Russian, without this, however, impeding the other nationalities within Abkhazia to develop their own language and culture in every aspect of their socio-political life, according to the "Korenizatsia" principles of the time (CCPA, 1925, Art. 6). Later, however, when the Stalin administration would freeze, if not totally reserve, the policy of "Korenizatsia," and in 1931, would downgrade the status of Abkhazia to that of an autonomous republic within the Georgian SSR, the former would have already been adequately "Russianized" to serve as a means of control of the Georgian SSR on behalf of the central authorities in Moscow (BBC, 2015a). In similar footsteps is the case of South Ossetia. Ossetians are considered to descend from the Alans, a Sarmatian Iranian tribe (Lang, 1966). Settled in the mountainous areas of the broader Caucasus region, they differed from the other peoples of the region not resisting the Russian empire as it was expanding into the area in the eighteenth and nineteenth centuries (BBC, 2016b). When the Bolshevik forces occupied Georgia, Ossetians sided with them, whereas in the carve-up that followed, the South Ossetian Autonomous Region was created within the Georgian SSR, and North Ossetia within the Russian Soviet Federative Socialist Republic

(RSFSR) (BBC, 2016b). Such a development had been perceived by the Georgian SSR as a byproduct of the manipulation of ethnic groups in the form of "divide and rule" on behalf of the central authorities in Moscow, and in particular by the RSFSR (Birch, 1995, p. 44).

The formation of Transdniestria: Chronologically placed, the Molotov-Ribbentrop pact (or officially "Treaty of Non-aggression between Germany and the USSR") contributed much to the aforementioned tactic of ethnic engineering. On August 23, 1939, the Foreign Ministers of Germany and the USSR, *inter alia*, agreed to a secret protocol that stipulated the division of North, Central East and Southeast Europe into spheres of influence; Finland, the Baltic states, Poland, and Romania (the entire eastern half of Moldova or Bessarabia) constituted the Soviet sphere of influence (The Molotov-Ribbentrop Pact, 1939). Without delay, in September 1939, the Red Army completed its advance to Polish regions and their subsequent annexation to the Ukrainian and Belarusian SSRs respectively, which became double their size, with the process of Sovietization to proceed apace throughout the new parts (Roberts, 1995, pp. 674, 690–696). A couple of months later, in June 1940, an ultimatum was issued to Romania, which in a matter of days, conceded the demanded regions of Bessarabia and Northern Bukovina to the USSR (Athanasiadis, 1988, p. 131). On August 2, 1940, the Moldovan SSR was formed by joining Bessarabia with a strip of land east from the Dniester River, called Transdniestria, which up to that time had been part of the Moldovan Autonomous Soviet Socialist Republic (MASSR), a region purposefully constructed within the Ukrainian SSR between 1924 and 1940 by the Soviet authorities in Moscow (Batt, 1997, p. 29; Cash, 2013, p. 60). The reason behind that lied in the desire to indirectly claim the neighboring Bessarabia (then Romanian land), and once the power asymmetry tilted towards the Soviet side, to directly annex it, as actually happened (King, 1998, pp. 60–61; Cojocaru, 2006, p. 263; Iglesias, 2015, p. 235). As incisively put forth in a Soviet publication of the time, "once the economic and cultural growth of Moldavia (MASSR) has begun, aristocracy-led Romania will not be able to maintain its hold on Bessarabia," allowing for the corroboration of the Thucydidean dictum: "the strong do what they can and the weak suffer what they must" (King, 1998, p. 61; Roper, 2001, p. 103; Strassler 1996, p. 352). For an exact map of the geopolitical rearrangements of the Molotov-Ribbentrop pact, see http://www.allrussias.com/soviet_russia/war_3.asp.

The formation of Crimea: In addition to the aforementioned cases of ethnic engineering on behalf of the Soviet Authorities, there were also other cases of reallocating populations and territories. One such case is that of Crimea. Briefly said, Crimea had been part of Russia from 1783, when the Tsarist Empire belatedly annexed it after defeating the Ottoman Empire, until 1954, when the Soviet government approved the transfer of the region from the RFSR to the Ukrainian SSR (UkrSSR) (Kramer, 2014). In particular, at the meeting of the Presidium of the Supreme Soviet of the USSR on February 19, 1954, the joint submission of the Presidiums of the Supreme Soviets of the RSFSR and the UkrSSR on transferring the Crimean Oblast from the RSFR to the UkrSSR was accepted on the grounds of "Crimean Oblast's territorial inclination towards the UkrSSR, the commonality of the economy, and close economic and cultural ties between the two" (Postanovlenie Soveta Ministrov RSFSR, 1954; Prezidium Berkhovnovo Soveta SSSR, 1954). In further detail, the ineradicable friendship between the Ukrainian and the Russian peoples as well as the desire of all the peoples to follow the impersonated by the Soviet government Communist ideal were highlighted as the main, if not the sole, causes behind this decision, leaving no room for alternative interpretations (Prezidium Berkhovnovo Soveta SSSR, 1954). The consideration of the recent past, however, would help provide a differently weighted reading of the aforementioned reasoning. Back in May 1944, the Stalin administration had aggregately and irreversibly deported to Central Asia a large population of Tatars that had been inhabiting Crimea for centuries, along with a smaller population of Armenians, Bulgarians and Greeks. As a result, it forged an ethnic population of 75% ethnic Russians and 25% Ukrainian in the 1950s, which was plausible to had closer cultural ties with the RSFSR than the UkrSSR (Kramer, 2014). What is more to these, Crimea has been a point of strategic significance from the Tsarist era onwards, symbolizing the Imperial Russia military might *vis-à-vis* that of the Ottoman Turks (Kramer, 2014). In the same line of reasoning, critical is also the role played by Nikita Khrushchev, the USSR's leader during Crimea's transfer, who from the late 1930s until 1949 had served as the head of the Communist Party of Ukraine; being responsible for the side of the Soviet government in the civil war that had broken out in the post-Molotov-Ribbentrop pact annexed western regions of Ukraine, especially Volynia and Galicia, Khrushchev exerted all means of power in an effort to establish a firm and profound hold (Kramer, 2014). All things considered and returning to the previously mentioned reasons of the transfer, a differently weighted reading, indeed, emerges; that which prioritizes the control of the UkrSSR by the central authorities in Moscow, with an extra 860,000 ethnic Russians to fortify the already sizeable Russian minority in Ukraine (Kramer, 2014).

7. Following Stalin's death, the contenders' need for support by the non-Russian periphery, and the critical, if not irreversible, tensions among peoples that the harsh "re-Russification" policies had engendered, called for a change of action. It is true that, although many of the peoples of the Eurasian "heartland" were "latecomers" in the "nation-state" reality, the use of a national language as well as the extensive literacy and education of the 1920s facilitated the establishment of a firm, if not intractable, national consciousness (Zia-Ebrahimi, 2007). Thus, Nikita Khrushchev, once in power, initially transferred some economic-administrative competencies to the republics, with numerous non-Russians being promoted to positions in the central and local administrations, in an effort to decompress the Soviet politics (Simon, 1991, pp. 234–258). This relapse, however, would be of very limited impact and time, since many of these transfers were repealed in the short term, and the language, the key element of identity, remained the Russian. Thus, an indirect form of control had been horizontally established as a guarantee even in cases, where local leaders may be operating with increased autonomy (Caucasus and Central Asia), the latter being an inexorable concession on behalf of the central authorities in order to keep the unity of the USSR (Zia-Ebrahimi, 2007).

8. For a detailed account, see endnote 6 and chapter 2.

9. As far as a full picture of the minorities is concerned, the other minorities were Gagauz (3.5%), Bulgarians (2%), and Jews (1.5%) (Tkach, 1999, p. 137).

10. Four big and internationally competitive enterprises stand out: the Moldova Steel Works (Молдавский металлургический завод) (1985), the large textile manufacturer Tirotex (Тиротекс) (1973), the Moldovan State District Power Plant (Молдавская государственная районная электростанция) (1964), and the Rybnitsa (Rîbniţa) Cement Plant (Рыбницкий цементный комбинат) (1961), with about 100 smaller industrial enterprises surrounding the "big four" (Istomin and Bolgova, 2016, p. 178; CISR, 2010, p. 2; Melintei, 2017, pp. 50–52).

11. In the post-soviet-period large share in the world market as far as small arms and ammunition are concerned comes from Transdniestria (King, 2000, p. 206). It is highly likely that a large part from Transdniestria's arms exports may have reached regions such as the north Caucasus (Chechnya) and Kosovo, which at the second half of the 1990s had been challenged by intense fighting (King, 2000, p. 206). Of course, it is plausible to conjecture that other conflicts in the wider area of Caucasus (Abkhazia, South Ossetia, and Nagorno-Karabakh), which resemble in nature that in Transdniestria, may have had part of their weaponry coming from the latter.

12. Many military formations in the republics of the former USSR were comprised by local residents (Tkach, 1999, p. 149).

13. At this point, of particular significance is the "weak state syndrome"; in this case, citizens as (atomized) rational actors in a condition pretty similar to the state of nature, showcase increased levels of insecurity, which, in turn, results in a "crisis in statehood" and in the attachment "of statehood to ethnolinguistic attributes," as necessary means towards survival and security (Prina, 2015, p. 64). In further clarification, the ethnic type draws extensively on the German romanticists' concept of "primordialism," which qualifies language, culture and religion as the key determinants of nationality, and develops the notion of unquenched and unchallengeable rights over specific territories among the members of such a nation (Wheatley, 2009, p. 121). In this manner, it opens the door to *zero-sum* geopolitical competition. Figure 1.1. draws on Hansen and Hesli, 2009, p. 4.

14. This competition in the declaration of independence is far from symbolic and is related to the international law principle of *Uti possidetis* ("as you possess"); according to this, the possessor of a specific territory or property at the end of a conflict (i.e., critical juncture period where institutional fluidity, if not gap, prevails) becomes the rightful owner, unless there is a treaty providing for otherwise. Simply put, the *de facto* (i.e., the acquired by force during the

war), becomes *de jure* (i.e., legally recognized). For more on the issue, see Shaw, 1997, pp. 491–492.

15. Up to December 1994, the Organization for Security and Cooperation in Europe (OSCE) was named Conference on Security and Cooperation in Europe (CSCE).

16. The phrase "or atomized" has been added by the author as a synonym of the word "unformed," so as to better fit into the text in terms of context and intended meaning.

17. For the terms "cycle of mobilization" and "tide of nationalism," see Beissinger, 2002, p. 69.

18. Discussing the wider geopolitical influence on Ukraine, the EU has, since 2003, initiated the European Neighborhood Partnership (ENP), and later, in 2008, the Eastern Partnership (EaP) as a specialized part of the former, with Russia having also its own, unofficial, neighborhood policy (RNP) (Wilson and Popescu, 2009). In fact, comparing the two, the RNP has proved more efficient in guarding its interests in the near abroad than the ENP, employing both hard power (oil and gas embargoes, raising energy prices, infrastructure takeovers) and soft power (cheap energy, economic growth, open labor market, citizenship and pensions) means (Kubicek, 2005; Sotiriou, 2015; Wilson and Popescu, 2009, p. 328).

19. The check and balances structure, if properly established, serves as the fundamental democratic institutional framework of modern states, guaranteeing the *hic et nunc* of the sovereign people. Most, if not all, times, it is extensively described in the Constitution-Fundamental Law of the State (Chrysogonos, 2003, pp. 294–307).

20. Discussing the weakness of state institutions to establish control across the Georgian territory in the early 1990s, indicative, *inter alia*, are the cases of Adjara, Samegrelo, Javakheti, and Kvemo Kartli. To begin with, Adjara was unyieldingly ruled by Aslan Abashidze, a Gamsakhurdia appointee, from 1991 until 2004. The western region of Samegrelo was in Gamsakhurdia devotees' power. The mainly Armenian-populated region of Javakheti was controlled by the local ethnic Armenian self-help organization "Javakh," whereas Kvemo Kartli, a region largely inhabited by Azerbaijanis, was dominated by numerous Georgian and Azerbaijani criminal crews, heavily benefiting from smuggling activities along the principal arteries driving to Armenia and Azerbaijan (Wheatley, 2009, p. 123).

21. Given that Georgia had been experiencing its first years of independence in the early 1990s, the core functions of the state should resemble those of a "night-watchman state" which provides its citizens with the army, the police, and the courts, as shields against aggression, theft, breach of contract, and fraud. Concurrently, it implements property laws (Heywood, 2002, pp. 95–98).

22. In fact, since 2004, both the Abkhaz and the South Ossetian governments had been eagerly facilitating Russia's passportisation program, which completed in 2008, as a means of survival and security. As argued by Valery Arshba, then Vice-President of Abkhazia, "The President of the Russian Federation is the guarantor of protection of the citizens of the Russian Federation, no matter where they live. . . . Political protection implies military protection" (Chivers, 2004). Therefore, "an attack on the *de facto* states now amounted to an attack on Russia itself" (Artman, 2013, p. 690). In this manner an alliance had been formed to balance the power of the dominant, titular nationality of Georgians within a political situation rife with "ethnic" and much more "atomized" types of identity.

23. For this principle, see endnote 15.

24. A member of the Musavat Party and former minister during the Elcibey administration stated as far as national unity in Azerbaijan is concerned: "we are divided on the basis of groups, tribes, villages, and cities . . . there were *khanates* in Azerbaijan and each *khanate* considered itself a state. Since these units were not able to unite under the roof of a state, there was never national unity" (Tokluoglu, 2012, p. 334).

25. Discussing further the personalized style of leadership in Azerbaijan, in the 1995 parliamentary elections, political party ideology had totally surrendered to the individual standing of each candidate (Akin, 2000, p. 109). See also Rasizade, 2004, p. 158.

26. In this line of reasoning, see also *IMF News*, 2016.

27. Further on this, see Franke et al., 2009, p. 130.

28. Of special interest is the Azerbaijani-Turkish relationship, with President Heydar Aliyev describing the two countries as "two states, one nation" (German, 2012, p. 222). Following in

his footsteps, his son, Ilham Aliyev, clinched in 2010 two agreements with Turkey, one stipulating for a strategic partnership and mutual assistance, and the other for the establishment of an Azerbaijani-Turkish high-level Strategic Cooperation Council (German, 2012, p. 222).

29. The group's permanent members are Belarus, Germany, Italy, Finland, Turkey, along with Armenia and Azerbaijan (OSCE, 2017a). Also, on the role of Russia in the region, see *Strategic Comments*, 2010.

30. For the routing of the TANAP and the TAP networks, see http://new.abb.com/oil-and-gas/case-studies/midstream-transportation/tanap.

31. Truth be told, this network has proved to be less favorable, given that it is longer and more expensive than its parallel network from Baku to Supsa. Furthermore, it dilutes the AIOC crude with other crudes during transit, thus negatively affecting its value. On top of all, it does little in reducing the South Caucasus states' reliance on Moscow (German, 2009, p. 350).

32. "Rationality" is a fundamental political science concept, and it could be briefly defined as the innate ability of the actor to assess his/her interest upon a cost/benefit analysis.

33. For a detailed bibliography on these, see Theorizing the Two-Level Game: Rational Actors Unconstrained by Institutions (International Level).

34. Thomas Hobbes, perceiving the human nature as sinful and wicked and encapsulating the high insecurity that anarchy entails, qualified constant war and conflict as the inevitable terminal point in world politics (Hobbes, 1651; Kegley, 1995). As put in chapters 13 and 14 of *Leviathan*, there is "a war of every one against every one" (bellum omnium contra omnes) (Hobbes, 1651, pp. 77–80).

35. Indicatively, Thucydides draws on the Greek experiences under the dominion of Minos to illuminate the role of economics in structuring power relations. For more, see Sotiriou, 2015, p. 33.

36. For the problem of cheating, as well as for Pareto's Optimal Outcome in any cooperative scheme, see the two-actor Prisoner's Dilemma (PD). For more on the issue, see Sotiriou, 2015, pp. 40–41.

37. When discussing socio-political development, reference is made to both formal (official) and informal (e.g., strategies, preferences, goals, interests, ideas, and even identities) institutions, that propel society towards achieving the wider good, i.e., Pareto's optimal outcome. Putting it in a more testable manner, it is about institutions that help the rational egoistic actors to endow their automatically ignited egoistic patterns of behavior with the rationality-illustrating mental maturity; in this way, actors distinguish between good and evil, benefit and cost, and factually contribute to a society where all interests are balanced and open to falsification. In these conditions, a wider socio-political institutional equilibrium is forged.

38. Defining the terms "sensitivity" and "vulnerability," "sensitivity means liability to costly effects imposed from outside before policies are altered to try to change the situation," whereas "vulnerability can be defined as an actor's liability to suffer costs imposed by external events even after policies have been altered" (Keohane and Nye, 2011, p. 11).

39. As far as the variable "GDP per capita PPP" and its employment in interstate comparisons are concerned, the assessment of nation's domestic market becomes very accurate. In detail, this variable accounts for the relative cost of local goods, services, and inflation rates, taking into account the distortive effects that the international market exchange rates may have on the real differences in the per capita income.

40. In brief, in the energy business, three sectors are identified. The first is the upstream, which refers to the exploration and development of oil and gas fields. The second is the midstream, which focuses on the construction of networks (pipelines) that transport the resources either to oil refineries and gas processing plants for further processing/purification, or, if purified, to storages. Of course, aside from networks, tankers also serve as a means of transport, carrying either oil or liquefied natural gas, LNG. Lastly, the third is the downstream that distributes the resources to the final consumers. For more on the issue, see Sotiriou, 2015, p. 71, and http://naturalgas.org/.

41. As far as the issue of interviews is concerned, the present analysis has sought to collect statements and interviews by key figures through the official archives of major energy companies, either state-owned or private, and through official newspapers, attempting, in this manner, to overcome not only trust problems which otherwise could have emanated, thus impeding the

present argumentation, but also the fundamental obstacle of accessibility, since in social sciences "we have considerably less access to elites" (Gerring, 2001, p. 204).

Level I

Domestic: "Frozen Conflicts"
in Eurasia

Chapter Two

The Case of Transdniestria (Moldova)

THE FORMATION OF TODAY'S MOLDOVA AND REGIONAL POLITICAL PREFERENCES

Studying regional political preferences, today's Moldova has followed a tumultuous course throughout the centuries, having been dismantled and subject to different social-political influences multiple times. Having existed as a distinct political entity, i.e., the Principality of Moldova, only in the mid-fourteenth century, it has, ever since, resembled a pendulum, whose oscillation has been determined by the geopolitical competition between the West and the East, which have, diachronically, laid claim to its lands.

The Ottoman Empire was the first to place the Principality under its suzerainty in the mid-fifteenth century, with this infiltration to become more profound in 1538, when Moldova's southeastern region between the Dniester and the Danube was directly annexed by the former. These developments have left their imprint deep, with the region, albeit Ukrainian territory as of today, to retain its Turkish name, Budjak (Batt, 1997, p. 28). When the Ottoman Empire was disempowered, the Principality was once more up for grabs, with the Habsburg Empire to be the first to come on the scene; in fact, it annexed the Principality's north-western tip in 1775, converting it to the Austrian Province of Bukovina (Batt, 1997, p. 28). Russia was the second actor to enter the picture, annexing the eastern half of the Principality, between the rivers Prut and Dniester. Moreover, it reunited it with the also conquered Budjak, forming, in total, the Russian province of Bessarabia, which, to a very large extent, coincides with today's Moldova (Batt, 1997, p. 28).[1] Throughout the nineteenth century, large numbers of Russians and Jews immigrated into the newfangled province, in an effort by the Tsarist

43

administration to fade the Romanian character of the people (Batt, 1997, p. 28; Chinn and Roper, 1995, p. 293).

The Principality of Moldova, in view of the power struggles at play, tried to ensure its survival and security by forging an alliance with its Romanian sister, the Principality of Wallachia (Batt, 1997, p. 28). In particular, with the region west of the Prut to be the only one to have been left as a self-standing political entity, the Principality of Moldova sided with the Principality of Wallachia (Batt, 1997, p. 28). Even more, the two principalities proceeded to their unification, with the election of a common Prince, Alexandru Ion Cuza, to serve as the "bonding" event and signal the birth of the modern Romanian nation-state (Batt, 1997, p. 28). Vitally strengthened by these developments, the new-found state bounced back to the regional balance of power, reclaiming the alien-ruled "Romanian lands," emphasis placed on Bessarabia, Bukovina and Transylvania (Batt, 1997, p. 28). At the end of the First World War, the collapse of both the Russian and the Austro-Hungarian Empires allowed for these claims to be materialized (Batt, 1997, p. 28).

But this was only for a while; the successor of Tsarist Russia, the USSR, would not relinquish its ambitions in the region, much less accept Bessarabia within Romanian borders. Therefore, it devised a strategy, the endgame of which would be the return of Bessarabia under Russian/Soviet influence. Taken seriatim, the Moldovan Autonomous Soviet Socialist Republic (MASSR) was, first, established within the Ukrainian SSR, on a strip of land on the left (east) bank of the Dniester. There, the Moldovans constituted a small proportion (30.1% of the population) compared with the Ukrainians and the Russians who had also been residing within the MASSR (Batt, 1997, p. 28). Acting in this manner, the Soviet authorities had been fundamentally aiming at cooking up the historical-political grounds of the Principality of Moldova, presenting the MASSR as its legal heir, thus carefully fomenting an irredentist context *vis-a-vis* Bessarabia, exploitable when the general situation would prove fertile.

When Bessarabia united again with Romania in 1918, the Moldovan leaders had been under the false anticipation of a federal regime that would institutionally guarantee their distinctive identity, and would stipulate for free elections, civil (political) rights and minorities' rights (Batt, 1997, p. 36). Resentment, as a result, mounted up, in a political regime which was self-centered, "ruled by . . . a cabal of politicians who represented no-one," and in which Moldova figured as Romania's economically and politically most forsaken province (Eyal, 1990, p. 125; Rothschild, 1974, p. 286). The Soviet authorities vigilantly waited for the moment that they could dovetail the painstakingly fomented irredentist context with the widespread disillusionment of the sidelined citizens of Bessarabia, living within Romania. Indeed, it was not long before this moment came, with the Molotov-Ribbentrop pact between Germany and the USSR in 1939, and particularly its secret protocol that stipulated for geopolitical rearrangements, to pave the way for power politics to come to the forefront and signal the endpoint in the Moldovan issue (Eyal and Smith, 1996, pp. 235–236). Following the pact, the USSR recaptured Bessarabia and northern Bukovina in June 1940, only to lose them again in 1941 (Athanasiadis, 1988, p. 131). Even more, in 1942, an essentially reinforced Romania with its alliance with the forces of the Axis, answered back the Soviet constructed pro-Moldova irredentism, invading Ukraine east of the Dniester, and advancing past the MASSR, to a far larger stretch, which it called "Transdniestria."

Notwithstanding these advances, at the end of the war, the USSR imposed its pre-war (August 1940) arrangements on the region; the Northern Bukovina and most of Budjak were transferred to the Ukrainian SSR, whereas the new-found Moldovan SSR was formed by the remainder of Bessarabia, plus Transdniestria (Batt, 1997, p. 29; Chinn and Roper, 1995, p. 293).

The prevalence, finally, of the Molotov-Ribbentrop logic brought different peoples from different regions together, keeping the issue of regional political preferences as central as it used to be throughout the pendulum-like historical course of the once Principality of Moldova. With these facts on the ground, the Russian population of the Moldovan SSR experienced an upward trend, growing from 6% of the total in 1940 to 13% in 1989, with the 1989 census to reveal that 48% of Moldova's Russians and 33% of Moldova's Ukrainians had not been born in Moldova (Chinn and Roper, 1995, p. 294; Minority Rights Group International, 2018). Given these, the issue of regional political preferences, aside from central, had been also subject to machinations and manipulations of top-down control and power.

Indeed, the Soviet administration made no secret of its intentions, employing language as its cardinal tool towards "russifying" and "Sovietizing" the Moldovan identity; in fact, this would homogenize the inbred divergence among the peoples of the SSR, whittling away any pro-Romanian attachments, namely historical, cultural, and potentially political (Batt, 1997, p. 31; Eyal and Smith, 1996, p. 231). In more detail, the Cyrillic script was inserted in the written language, so as to familiarize the non-Russian peoples with the Russian language, and eradicate any intimacy with the Romanian. Furthermore, the Romanian literature had been either controlled or "transliterated" into the Cyrillic script, with history to had been also tampered with, so as to ensure that critical junctures, such as the interwar unification of Bessarabia with Romania, to be portrayed as "unfortunate interlude(s) of foreign occupation" (Batt, 1997, p. 32; Eyal and Smith, 1996, pp. 226–230). Finally, taking "russification' and "sovietization" to a more interpersonal level, any communication between Moldovans and Romanians had been intercepted, and border passages had been "secured" (Batt, 1997, p. 31).

The broader socio-political reality had also been affected by these policies. The Russians and the Russian speakers were much better placed. The

artificial increase of their number, accompanied by the fled of many intellectuals from Bessarabia to Romania at the end of the Second World War, or
their removal as a result of the Stalinist purges of 1940–1941 and the period
right after, opened up vital space for the Russians and the Russian-speakers;
in fact, they did not only move to the cities, but also took on the most critical
and well-paying jobs, emphasis placed on the more technical jobs of the
everyday life and on the positions at educational institutions (Chinn and
Roper, 1995, p. 293). The Moldovans, conversely, had been either marginalized, if residing in the cities, or relegated to less prestigious and well-paying
jobs, such as agriculture, mostly in the outskirts. In this manner, the "Russian
culture dominated urban, technical and educational life" (Chinn and Roper,
1995, p. 294). Moreover, this dominance was also reflected on the state
institutions, since most posts were filled with non-Bessarabian cadres de-
scending either from the MASSR and, particularly, from Transdniestria, or
from other Soviet republics (Batt, 1997, p. 33). Bessarabians, on the
contrary, were viewed as Romania-leaning, in a context where Romania, and
the Romanian Communist Party Members, in particular, were not accepted to
one of the most, if not the most, critical, institution of the USSR, that of the
Communist Party of the Soviet Union (CPSU) (Batt, 1997, p. 33).

Despite the harshness and the discriminations that these top-down policies had created within the Moldovan SSR, they did not succeed in stifling
regional political preferences. On the contrary, they did cloak them, enmeshing the russified population of Ukrainians plus the Russians, on the one hand,
and the Romania-influenced population, on the other hand, in an implicit,
across-the-board, *zero-sum*, power struggle, ready to explode when the
USSR would enter its critical juncture period at the end 1980s.

THE CRITICAL JUNCTURE PERIOD AND REGIONAL POLITICAL PREFERENCES

The national revival of Moldova in the late 1980s was a far cry from a
homogenous movement (Batt, 1997, p. 31); in fact, it was the (opportunistic)
alliance of "atomized" rational actors with divergent political agendas and
interests under the umbrella of the "Moldovan idea," so as to counterbalance
the Russian influence in the republic.

Formed in 1989, the Popular Front of Moldova was the synthesis of two
groups of Moldovan intellectuals: the "Democratic Movement in Support of
Restructuring," aligned with the Gorbachev administration's directives for
fundamental political and economic reforms, and the "Alexei Mateevici Lit-
erary-Musical Circle," absorbed by the language issue, and particularly by
the reinstatement of the Moldovan at the education system as well as at the
public sphere of the nascent republic (Batt, 1997, p. 31). It is a hard-to-deny

fact that, comparing the two groups, the second was the one with the wider impact on society, thus serving as the necessary filter through which the reforms proclaimed by the former should pass if they were to resonate with the masses (Batt, 1997, p. 31). Moreover, the award of official status to the Moldovan language dovetailed the reform agenda of the Soviet authorities at the time, which saw this pro-democratization development as a re-invigoration of the cumbersome relationship between the Soviet state and the people (Batt, 1997, p. 31).

The restoration of the Latin alphabet, however, would bring to light a language same as the Romanian, uncovering, in this way, the Soviet machinations behind the artificial nature of the Moldovan SSR together with the historical ties with Romania (Batt, 1997, p. 32; Kosienkowski, 2017, p. 118). Certainly, such a reality caused fissures within the Popular Front, given the rift between intellectuals who were fond of the rapprochement with the Romanian literature and thought and considered Romania as a superior and European principles-leaning country, and others who, drawing on the ominous unification experience during the interwar period, highlighted the prospects of becoming second-class citizens again, relegated to the margins, with no influence and political say in the affairs of a unified republic (Batt, 1997, p. 33).

Uniting these divergent tendencies within the Popular Front and spearheading its opposition potential, the defection of numerous cadres from the Moldovan Communist party and *nomenklatura* to its side played a critical role; the Popular Front provided the Moldovan political staff (i.e., the Bessarabian cadres) with an opening to remove the Transdniestria-descending Russian and Russian-speaking communist elite in favor of establishing their position in the power structures after almost fifty years (Batt, 1997, p. 34). Taking advantage of the widespread institutional fluidity, it switched allegiances, dropping the weakened (communist) side and embracing the rising and strengthened one, presenting itself as the political leadership of the up-and-coming Moldovan republic (Batt, 1997, p. 34). Truth be told, the Popular Front's emphasis on the language issue, which mobilized the masses and connoted the restoration of the erstwhile *status quo,* chimed in with the interests of the turned-nationalist political elite, forging an alliance that prioritized nationalism, despite viewed from different perspectives.

This "togetherness" took a more concrete form on August 31, 1989, when the republic's Supreme Soviet, under the influence of the Popular Front, adopted the Language Law (Crowther, 1998, p. 148; Kosienkowski, 2017, p. 118). The Law defined the Moldovan, in Latin script, as the state language, whereas the other nationalities were awarded the right to use their own language at the regions of residence (Eyal and Smith, 1996, p. 233; Roper, 2001, p. 104). As far as the Russian language is concerned, it was awarded the status of the "language of inter-ethnic communication," without this mean-

ing, however, that the Russian were relishing a "'shared' official status" next
to the Moldovan (Batt, 1997, p. 34; Prina, 2015, p. 62). In fact, this interpre-
tation, or possibility, was rejected, and if taken into consideration that the
staff of the administration and local authorities would have to acquire facility
in Moldovan within five years and use it constantly when in their official
capacity, it is easy to ascertain the political implications at work; the Russians and the russified populations of the republic were to replace the Moldovans as the secondary citizens of the republic for the first time since 1940, the
very same moment that the latter were seeing in the government's Language
Law the "rebirth" of the republic on Moldovan terms. By distinguishing
between the dominant nationality and all the other ethnic groups which were
not "nations" but rather ethnic minorities, it was a historical chance to set the
score straight; although their rights should be respected and provided for,
they could not, in any occasion, be deemed equal to those of the majority,
much more take primacy over them and allow for their members to dominate
the positions of political power and govern the affairs of the republic (Eyal
and Smith, 1996, p. 233). The relationship between language and political
power was already on the ground.

Further to this direction, the March 1990 elections for the Supreme Soviet
of the republic added to the Popular Front's power at the expense of the
Communist Party. The latter, even though the main political force, authorized independent candidates to stand in 373 of 380 electoral districts (King,
2000, p. 146). As a result, the Front, not only gained 27% of all seats in the
Supreme Soviet, but also managed to win the majority of seats, insofar as
moderate Communist Party deputies, primarily from the rural districts, sided
with its reformist agenda (King, 2000, p. 146). The pro-establishment camp
of chiefly Russian-speaking deputies from urban centers, Transdniestria, and
the southern regions, that once was in control of most, if not all, of the
political system, had, now, been dethroned and constrained to a small opposition (King, 2000, p. 146). In fact, it would be further marginalized, when
deputies from Transdniestria and Gagauzia would leave the Supreme Soviet
objecting the new elite in office.

Although the fault lines within the Popular Front remained multiple, the
truth is that the pro-Romania fracture was not espoused by the wider public;
only 3.9% of the Moldovans and even fewer from the minorities endorsed the
unification, with the path of independence and internal reforms to an autonomous Moldovan republic to gather the approval of 54.8% of the Moldovans
(King, 2000, p. 147). Certainly, the Russians and the Ukrainians did not
consent to this path either, given their tit-for-tat marginalization from the
emerging Moldovan political preferences. While the Romanian orientation
could have served as an extra alliance-formation tool next to the language,
based also on another fundamental element of the human nature, that of
ethnicity, its past-informed prospects of overshadowing, if not eradicating,

the independence of the Moldovans boosted and instituted the independence orientation. Mircea Snegur, who in September 1990 was elected by the Supreme Soviet to the post of the President of the Republic, headed the pro-independence alliance within the Front (King, 2000, p. 148).[2]

These incidents that gradually established the Moldovan political preferences at the expense of those of the Russian-speaking population certainly impacted on the regions of Transdniestria and Gagauzia. A new era of polarization arose, where zero-sum considerations governed the affairs within the society of Moldova, as it would be expected in conditions pretty much close to those of anarchy, where survival and security become imperatives. The more the Popular Front was gaining socio-political ground the more insecure the populations of Transdniestria and Gagauzia were becoming. In fact, it was a security dilemma similar to those that states encounter in international relations, where, under conditions of anarchy, all the actions taken by a state to strengthen its security, such as increases in the military power, commitment to the use of weapons or formation of alliances, lead the other states to follow them up in a spiral, given that intentions are unknown and there is not supranational authority able to enforce the principle *pacta sunt servanda* (Jervis, 1978). Much more in the case in point, where a laden past increased the probabilities of retaliation rather than just of a political power reallocation and of a new balance of power formation, where the Russian-speaking would have chance to counterbalance (even asymmetrically) the dominant Moldovans.

> In the Transdniestrian and Gagauz leadership, the republican government had taken up a position against the national minorities, counter to the "internationalist" message preached by Moscow and the Communist Party. The minorities thus found themselves at odds with government itself, rather than just with individual nationalist political groups that had hitherto been the main supporters of cultural and political change. (King, 2000, p. 147)

Transdniestrians and Gagauz instantly came to the realization that self-help posed as the only way out of imbroglio. Experiencing the institutional fluidity of the critical juncture period at the time, the tool of language, just like in the case of Moldova, played a central role in mobilizing and allying otherwise "atomized" rational actors. In fact, if the existential threat hidden behind the Moldovan Language Law is taken into consideration, then it is plausible to conjecture that the mobilization in Transdniestria and Gagauzia under the (Russian) language banner was far more radical and the alliance formed far more solid. To this direction also contributed another fundamental element of the human existence, that of ethnicity, which, in contrast to the case of Moldovans that remained an undetermined and divisive issue, in Transdniestria and Gagauzia it further solidified the ongoing mobilization and alliance-formation.[3] The epitome of these developments was the formulation of the

Transdniestrian and Gagauz political preferences in the form of creating their own governmental structures and declaring the "Republic of Gagauzia" with its center in Comrat in August 1990, and the "Pridnestrovian (Transdniestrian) Moldovan Soviet Socialist Republic" with its capital in Tiraspol in September 1990 (King, 2000, p. 147). In this context, they also proposed a tripartite federation (Moldova, Transdniestria, and Gagauzia), which, however, was dismissed by the Moldovan parliament (King, 2000, p. 191).

A new round of tension began around the August 1991 coup in the USSR, with the newly established Moldovan government led by Snegur to take the side of the Gorbachev administration and the hard-line members of the CPSU, and Transdniestria and Gagauzia that of the putschists. The escalation culminated in Gagauzia declaring its full independence on August 19, 1991, Moldova on August 27, 1991, and Transdniestria on September 2, 1991, with the erstwhile self-declared entity of 1990 to be renamed Transdniestrian Moldovan Republic (TMR) (Roper, 2001, p. 107).[4]

Deciphering now the pro-conflict tendencies in each of these regions, interesting is that Gagauzia differed qualitatively from the other two cases. In particular, the Gagauz is the fourth largest ethnic group in the republic, which, in contrast to the other examined regions, cannot resort to a "protector" state abroad, i.e., Romania, Russia, or Ukraine (King, 2000, p. 209). It is geographically concentrated to the southern Moldova, in Budjak. In 1989, close to 78% were living in Moldova and particularly to Basarabeasca, Comrat, Ceadîr-Lunga, Taraclia, and Vulcăneşti, whereas the remaining 22% to the Ukrainian city of Odessa, once part of the historical Bessarabia (King, 2000, p. 209). Thus, the Republic of Moldova is "as much as their homeland as the Romanian (Moldovan)-speakers" (King, 2000, p. 209). The conflict that erupted between them and the Moldovan administration had nothing in common with the Transdniestrian cause. The demands put forward focused on cultural issues and their preservation, with the Gagauz leadership to cease the opportunity of the fluid and rapidly reconfiguring environment of the late 1980s and early 1990s to attempt a reversal of a long history of marginalization and disregard of the southern districts (King, 2000, p. 210). In essence, it demanded greater (minority) rights, which a devolution of power to the local level would be enough to satisfy, terminating the standoff (King, 2000, pp. 209–210). The "fixable" prospect of the souring bilateral relations became evident also on August 27, 1991, when during the vote on independence by the Moldovan parliament, Gagauzia's twelve deputies got divided between "approval" (six votes) and "abstention" (six votes). The same, however, cannot be argued for Moldova and Transdniestria, which had engaged in an intractable, *zero sum*, struggle of political preferences. Moldova, on the one hand, in its declaration of independence referred to the "liquidation of the political and legal consequences" of the Molotov-Ribbentrop pact, implying, in this manner, the prospect of reunification with Romania (King, 2000, p.

151). Transdniestria, on the other hand, experiencing such a nebulous situation that increased its security concerns, had no alternative than strive towards guaranteeing its position. An all-out war was *ante portas*.

THE WAR IN TRANSDNIESTRIA AND REGIONAL POLITICAL PREFERENCES

Putting the general mobilization in territorial terms, the Moldovan government had established its control at the western side of the Dniester, whereas the Transdniestrian at the east bank of the river, along with some parts of the western bank that were Romanian prior to 1940, the most important of which being the strategic, largely Russian-populated, city of Bender (Chinn and Roper, 1995, p. 309).[5] By the summer 1991, the leader of the Transdniestrian administration, Igor Smirnov, had cut off any communication between the Moldovan government and the USSR, taking advantage of the fact that main rail and road links to Ukraine and beyond crossed the east bank cities of Rîbnița, Dubăsari , and Tiraspol.[6]

A critical role in the war would also be played by the Soviet 14th Army, which had been headquartered in Tiraspol since 1956. The Moldovan authorities had been complaining, since March 1991, to Gorbachev and the Soviet Defense Ministry that there was military support of the Transdniestrian cause (King, 2000, p. 191). Protest notes had been making reference also to the deployment of the Soviet OMON special forces into the region, calling for the 14th Army Officers to exhibit military discipline and abstain from taking sides (King, 2000, p. 191).[7] It is a hard-to-deny fact that there was increased osmosis between the Soviet 14th Army and Transdniestria's newly formed army, the "Dniester Guards." Much of the latter's weaponry had been acquired by the disorganized and inadequately guarded stores of the 14th Army, whereas, administratively, the officer corps of the Soviet troops was having also the central command of Transdniestria's forces (Beissinger, 2002, pp. 320–384; King, 2000, p. 192; Tkach, 1999, p. 146).[8] With 60% of the Soviet Army's officer corps and 80–90% of the soldiers to be permanent residents of Transdniestria, the latter as well as the Russian language figured as the means around which a broader survival-and-security-providing alliance would be forged against the rising Moldovan nationalism. When Yeltsin would place the 14th Army under the Russian command on April 1, 1992, the "transfusion" of men and provisions to the Transdniestrian side would have already been quite large (Chinn and Roper, 1995, p. 308; Roper, 2001, p. 108; Tkach, 1999, p. 146). Even more, this would ensure the de facto engagement of the Russian Army by the side of Transdniestria in critical instances of the 1992 war.

The Moldovan government, on the other hand, would also increase its military power, embarking on an attempt to build a 15,000-man professional army, relishing the support of a 10,000-man force of Carabinieri, or troops by the Ministry of Internal affairs (King, 2000, p. 192). Moreover, placing these efforts within a wider context, Moldovans admitted that Romania had provided them with weaponry, a fact corroborated also by Russian military and political sources, who identified the presence of Romanian military advisors and pilots in Moldova (King, 2000, p. 192).

On December 31, 1991, serious hostilities broke out, when Moldovan police officers encountered Transdniestrian irregulars around Dubăsari, and attempted to remove their weaponry (King, 2000, p. 92). This incident was the opening scene for the much more intensive fighting along the river throughout the first semester of 1992, during which local police officers would take center stage in multiple occasions, posing as the (main) guardians of the infant and organization-lacking Moldovan Republic (King, 2000, p. 192). The hastily assembled Moldovan forces—the police, armed civilians, troops by the Ministry of Internal affairs, and Moldovans soldiers previously loyal to the Soviet system—were more or less acting on their own, each carrying the burden of "guarding Thermopylae." Such a situation could aptly be reflected also on the words of Georgia's President, Zviad Gamsakhurdia, who, encountering in early 1990s conflicts (South Ossetia, Abkhazia) similar to that in Transdniestria, called on "all Georgians who can carry gun" to do so, in order to succumb regional political preferences to the command of the nationalized center.[9]

The first semester of 1992 witnessed the escalation of the conflict, especially over the spring and the summer. During that period, the *zero-sum* geopolitical competition became apparent around west-bank cities, such as Criuleni and Bender, with ceasefires to be agreed only to be violated again, and the regional powers, Romania, Ukraine, and Russia to issue joint statements along with Moldova in the context of the OSCE and beyond, seeking a end to the conflict (Lamont, 1993).

President Snegur, despite mass demonstrations calling for a general mobilization, declared a unilateral ceasefire, effective at 07.00 on March 18, which was supplemented by Ukraine's President, Leonid Kravchuk, special regime in a 50km zone along the common border, aimed at intercepting the flow of arms and armed troops (Lamont, 1993, p. 582). Moreover, on March 24, following Moldova's protests at the OSCE's Helsinki Foreign Ministers' Conference against the escalation of violence by Transdniestria, a joint statement was issued by the foreign ministers of Romania, Moldova, Russia, and Ukraine, seeking once more the termination of hostilities (Lamont, 1993, p. 583).

However, the conflict had taken its own upward spiral; Smirnov, on the one hand, ordered partial mobilization of men not exceeding the age of forty-five, as a response to Moldova's overall militarization, testified by the misappropriation of weaponry and military gear from the Commonwealth of Independent States (CIS) military units placed at Moldovan soil, the call to arms of all the men under legal obligation, and broader terrorist actions. [10] Snegur, on the other hand, declared, on March 29, a state of emergency all over the Moldovan Republic, summoning, concurrently, Transdniestria to abstain from any act of separatism and concede to the Moldovan government's authority (Lamont, 1993, p. 583).

Despite a meeting in Chisinau among Moldova, Romania, Russia and Ukraine on March 31, where all parties consented to the principles of the Helsinki agreements on the stability of borders and on finding a resolution respecting Moldova's integrity, violence had become an inescapable reality (Lamont, 1993, p. 583); multiple ceasefires were agreed and then violated, either due to Transdniestrian incursions to seize police stations and local government offices, or to the Moldovan government's efforts to reinstate its authority (King, 2000, p. 193). In this context, Transdniestria resorted to Russia for security reasons, whereas Moldova relished the covert Romanian military support, despite the fact that the latter's Defense Ministry declined, on April 1, any military involvement in the ongoing conflict. Moreover, on April 1, the same day that Russia's President, Boris Yeltsin, placed the 14th Army (also known ever since as Ground Forces of the Russian National Army) under Russian jurisdiction, special units by Moldova's ministry of internal affairs assaulted Bendery, causing the death of at least ten people (Tkach, 1999, p. 146; Lamont, 1993, p. 585).

While the 14th Army, in many occasions, got involved in the unraveling conflict, the position held by the official institutions, either military or political, was that the Army was ostensibly serving a pacifying role in the conflict, serving as a buffer force in the region, and to the extent that it had joined the "Dniester Russian Forces," this had occurred on its own initiative and not on the Russian President's (Yeltsin's) orders (King, 2000, p. 193; Lamont, 1993, p. 588). [11] Supplementary to the former and perhaps more elucidating is the speech by Russia's vice-president, Aleksandr Rutskoy, in the opening session of the Russian Congress of People's Deputies, on April 6. Although he argued that the Congress "had to defend Russians throughout the former Soviet Union," he reiterated and supported Transdniestria's demand to see its regional political preferences institutionalized in the form of a new federative structure within a single Moldova, a perspective a far cry from that of secession (Lamont, 1993, p. 586). [12]

The fighting, however, kept raging, and in early May, ceasefire-violating attacks by the "Dniester rebels" at the Moldovan police-controlled bridgeheads over the Dniester river resulted in six Moldovan policemen and two Russians getting killed (Lamont, 1993, p. 587). These incidents were immediately brought to the attention of the international community by Snegur, who tried to form an as much as possible broad alliance by reaching out to the world through the UN Security Council (Lamont, 1993, p. 587). Moreover, he identified the "Russian aggression in his country" as the impediment to Moldova's drawing up of a political solution (Lamont, 1993, p. 587).[13]

With trust to have been completely evaporated, if ever present, and the need for security to figure as urgent as never before, on May 27, Russia's Defense Minister, General Pavel Grachev, underscored that the 14th Army "may be withdrawn following a special bilateral agreement" (Lamont, 1993, p. 588). In this manner, he highlighted the survival-assisting and security-guaranteeing role of the 14th Army in a totally unregulated socio-political environment, where *zero-sum* considerations on both sides made the line between aggressor and defender very relative, and a negotiated political settlement posed as the sole way out of the dead-end.

Nevertheless, the drawing up of a political settlement was far from possible, given that both the Moldovan and the Russian administration stood at the exactly opposite sides; the former perceived the latter as instigators, whereas the latter diagnosed the improbability of a political settlement between the Moldovan and the Transdniestrian side away from the presence of the 14th Army.

Deepening and polarizing as the conflict could possible get, in early June, Transdniestria resurfaced its steady demand to convert Moldova into a federation of three republics—the "Moldovan," the "Dniester," and the "Gagauz" one (Lamont, 1993, p. 592). Path-dependently, President Snegur declined the suggestion, arguing that "it lacks any ethnic, historic, or legal basis"; instead, he stated Chisinau's willingness to negotiate some kind of territorial autonomy, probably as a means of defusing the widespread survival and security concerns, but, certainly, nothing that reached up to federalization (Lamont, 1993, p. 592). This proposal would, indeed, resonate with the Gagauz, who, as shown earlier, were more preoccupied with reversing a long-lasting situation of cultural disrespect and marginalization, but as far as the Transdniestrian side is concerned, this would be far more difficult, if ever achievable; with most of the cadres who had been holding almost the monopoly of political power since the inception of the Moldovan SSR in the 1940 to originate from there, and Transdniestria itself being the whole republic's power house for fifty years, the odds of capitulating with a regime of territorial autonomy were close to none. Much less when its cause was militarily and politically supported by irregulars and defectors from the 14th Army.

In fact, this support became very obvious and critical on June 19, 1992, when the fighting reached a turning point. That time, the Transdniestrian forces, armed by the Russian army depots, assailed the final police station in Bender still loyal to the central government in Chisinau (King, 2000, p. 194). Red alert signaled throughout the region controlled by the Moldovan forces, which quickly regrouped in an effort to claim back the city. The venture was as critical as an indispensable one. With all of the eastern bank of the river to be controlled by Transdniestria, and the bridges at Dubăsari, which had been connecting Chisinau to the rest of the former Soviet republics, to have been destroyed earlier in the conflict, Bender was the only city on the only major road and rail artery left leading up to the ex-Soviet space (King, 2000, p. 194). Moldova's main trading partners were laying eastwards, thus its economic sensitivity and vulnerability were alarmingly increased should it loose this strategic chunk of territory. To add fuel to the fire, Bender, next to its economic weight, it had also a security one, being home to a major weapons warehouse, which, depending on which side would control it, would critical affect the balance of power in the whole republic; if the Moldovan government managed to control it, it would have made serious steps towards guaranteeing the survival and security of the newfangled state. If not, it would have been gravely, if not irreversibly, exposed to a strengthened Transdniestrian side, paving the way for the preservation of a "frozen conflict" or the establishment of a de facto state should a political settlement became, finally, unachievable.

With these facts on the ground, Moldovan troops unleashed an air-supported mortar attack on the city. Heavy fighting ensued, with the 14th Army to intervene on the night of June 21–22 on the side of the Transdniestrian forces, intercepting the advances of the Moldovan troops (King, 2000, p. 194). This intervention was reasoned by the Russian political establishment as an act of protection against "a bloody slaughter" on behalf of the Moldovans, which was putting at stake not only the security, but the very survival of the Russians that resided at Bender (King, 2000, p. 194).[14] At the end of the day, the Bender fight was a victory for Transdniestria, producing a chain of events that led to the transition of the conflict to its, current, "frozen" status, and to the *de facto* institutionalization of Transdniestria's regional political preferences.

On June 23, Ukraine, witnessing the impasse to which the conflict had been brought to and despite its earlier support to the Snegur administration, admitted that the status of an autonomous republic should be granted to Transdniestria, and Moldova as republic should adopt a federal set up (Lamont, 1993, p. 590). Furthermore, on July 3, the Presidents Snegur and Yeltsin met in the Kremlin, where they agreed in principle on the necessary steps towards defusing the standoff; in particular, they qualified:

- the implementation of a ceasefire,
- the separation of forces through a demarcation corridor,
- the introduction of "neutral" peacekeeping forces,
- the institutionalization of a "political status" to the east bank of the Dniester river by the Moldovan parliament, and ultimately,

- the conduct of bilateral negotiations on the withdrawal of Russia's 14th Army (Lamont, 1993, p. 591).

Undoubtedly, all these points aimed at filtering the power gap, as this had become apparent and proved at the battlefield, through institutional means, establishing Transdniestria's regional political preferences within Moldova's new institutional equilibrium, as this would emerge as soon as the critical juncture period would be terminated by the adoption by the Moldovan state of its new Constitution on August 27, 1994.

On July 6, a CIS meeting in Moscow agreed to the deployment of a force between 2,000 and 10,000 soldiers from Russia, Ukraine, Belarus, Romania and Bulgaria under the umbrella of a Joint Peacekeeping Forces (JPKF). Its mission would be to uphold a ceasefire in the region and keep the troops of the two embattled apart (Lamont, 1993, p. 591).

Accordingly, on July 7, a ceasefire was signed, when the head of CIS General Purpose Forces, Vladimir Semenov, met in Moldova with the Moldovan First Deputy Defense Minister, Pavel Creanga, and Transdniestria's Defense Minister Ştefan Chiţac (Lamont, 1993, p. 591). The ceasefire became effective at midnight on July 8, only to realize twenty-four hours later that the Moldovan side had honored its signature, in contrast to Transdniestria, which had committed multiple violations; even more, its supreme soviet had declined an offer by the Moldovan side for four government seats to be filled by representatives of Transdniestria, suggesting, instead, that Russia and Ukraine were to represent it, since they were the only actors to which it entrusted its protection and security (Lamont, 1993, p. 591). It is obvious that Transdniestria, having its status significantly reinforced after the critical victory achieved at Bender and the de facto alliances that the latter gave birth to or further solidified (with Ukraine and Russia respectively), it would not compromise with anything short than the full institutionalization of its regional political preferences (i.e., federalization of the Moldovan state). [15]

A peace agreement was finally drawn up on July 21, in the presence of Presidents Yeltsin (Russia), Snegur (Moldova), and Smirnov (Transdniestria).

On the Principles of Peaceful Settlement of the Armed Conflict in the Transdniestrian Region of the Republic of Moldova," July 21, 1992

1. A special status (autonomy) along with the right of self-determination should Moldova change its statehood (i.e., unification with Romania)
2. A security zone was established, guarded by Moldovan, Russian and Transdniestrian peacekeeping forces (approximately six thousand),
3. The command and supervision of the aforementioned has been placed under a Joint Control Commission (JCC) (Chinn and Roper, 1995, p.

309; Lamont, 1993, p. 592; Roper, 2001, p. 109; Sanchez, 2009, p. 163).

This agreement was not signed by Smirnov in a clear indication of the high level of polarization that had taken place between the two embattled. The violence of summer 1992 was codified as a war for the independence of the Transdniestrian fatherland, and as such became mythologized. Memorials were erected outside key institutions of the emerging de facto republic, such as the Supreme Soviet/Parliament in Tiraspol, whereas medals were given and other awards were made to people who fought under the umbrella of the "Dnestr Guards" for "liberating" the region from the Moldovan fascists (King, 2000, p. 197). This narrative passed also to the younger generations, with schoolbooks and historical accounts to refer to the 1992 hostilities as a war for national liberation, and present Transdniestria in a direct line of succession to the MASSR of the interwar period (King, 2000, pp. 196–198, 206). In this manner, the mental-cultural foundations for the continuation of the polarization and the establishment, as firm as possible, of Transdniestria's rising de facto statehood had been set.

On March 6, 1994, the Moldovan government conducted a referendum, during which it was affirmed the volition for drawing up a Constitution. In this Constitution, neither the 1989 Language Law was repealed, nor was any revision of the Transdniestria-discarded 1992 ceasefire agreement. Certainly, there were provisions for the use of the Russian Language and the preconditions for awarding a regime of autonomy to Transdniestria, but as shown earlier, these fell far short of bridging the gap between the two, trust-deficient, sides.[16]

POST-CONFLICT REGIONAL POLITICAL PREFERENCES

On August 27, 1994, a new constitution was adopted by Moldova and a new institutional equilibrium was struck. In Article 111, a "special status" for the southern Moldova was stipulated, but a final arrangement was pending. In the elections conducted in 1994, pan-Romanians lost to centrist candidates, who highly prioritized political stability over national ideals (King, 2000, p. 218). The emphasis on the upgrading of district councils and local government paved the way for considering the devolution of political power to distinct entities, such as Gagauzia. The Agrarian Democrats government, headed by the Andrei Sangheli, along with President Snegur, fostered for Gagauzia's special status (Batt, 1997, p. 43; King, 2000, p. 218).

Gagauzia constituted a rather complex case as far as population is concerned; with the Gagauz to outnumber the Moldovans and the Bulgarians in only two of the five raions, in particular in the Ceadîr-Lunga raion (64.2%)

and Comrat (63.8%), the issue of allocating political, economic, and cultural powers to the Gagauz called for a very delicate handling (King, 2000, p. 218).[17]

As earlier mentioned, the Gagauz call for "self-determination" was qualitatively different from that of Transdniestria, seeking mostly control over local resources and the upgrading of the regional culture. The erstwhile declaration of independence of the "Gagauz Republic" or the endorsement of plans for federalizing Moldova served, primarily, as a means of survival and security against the rising tide of the Moldovan nationalism. In reality, it lacked solid grounds and opposed any prospect of power-sharing with the central authorities at Chisinau (federalization), much less, separate from Moldova should federalization failed. Proving the case further, in 1994, the President of the so-called Gagauz Republic, Stepan Topal, was not in position to even draw up a map demonstrating the territorial extent of the alleged Gagauz Republic (King, 2000, p. 217).[18] Any mobilization around ethnic attributes, such as the language, and adoption of symbols implying independent statehood, had defense connotations and aimed at extracting secondary concessions from the central government. Imitating the way that the Moldovans had claimed back the republic's political system from the Moscow-supported Russian speakers, the Gagauz targeted at a "greater share of the local control that Chisinau had begun to wrest from Moscow" (King, 2000, p. 217). As a result, a local autonomy law was drafted, which was executory of the Moldovan Constitution (King, 2000, p. 217). Should any changes be brought upon the main text, a 3/5 enhanced majority in the Moldovan parliament was required along with Comrat's consent (Socor, 1995).[19]

The draft law became a state law in December 1994. Drawing on paradigms such as those in Spain (Catalonia), Italy (Tirol), Finland (Aaland Islands), and Belgium's ethnolinguistic regions, where autonomous regional formations had been designed to combine the minority groups' demands with the international principles of territorial integrity and inviolability of borders, the Gagauz are treated as a distinct, territorially concentrated, ethnic group (Socor, 1995). Moreover, next to the civil rights which are stipulated for all Gagauz by the Moldovan Constitution, there are also collective rights attached to ethnic identity and representation, which, nevertheless, are implied, given that the law avoids references to terms such as "collective rights" and "ethnic-territorial autonomy" (Socor, 1995). Gagauzia constitutes a special "territorial autonomous unit" within Moldova, with the latter's Constitution to fully apply on it.[20]

As far as the main institutional framework of this unit is concerned, a governor (Başkan), an executive committee (Bakannik Komiteti), and a legislative assembly (Halk Topluşu) are provided for, with the governor to serve also as deputy prime minister of Moldova, and the citizens of Gagauzia to participate in Moldova's parliamentary elections in addition to those for the regional legislature (Socor, 1995). Furthermore, the law devolves numerous powers to Gagauzia and sets clear lines between them and those held by the organs of the central government (Socor, 1995). The latter decide on the policy-areas of citizenship, foreign policy, defense, currency, finance, and customs, whereas Gagauzia is fully responsible on issues limited to the region and revolve around the areas of economy, education system, cultural life, labor relations, social welfare, land use, town planning, administrative-territorial organization, institutions and organs, elections and referenda, budget and tax-revenues allocation (Socor, 1995). Even further, when it comes to foreign policy, despite the exclusive jurisdiction of the central government, Gagauzia participates "in the formation and execution of Moldova's foreign policy on matters involving (its) interests"; this provision reflects Gagauzia's sensitivity towards contacts with Turkey and other Turkic countries, and, on these grounds, the presence of Gagauz representatives in diplomatic missions to these countries is highly likely, if not institutionalized outright (Socor, 1995). In addition, this provision proves that collective rights attached to the ethnic identity have been well taken care of, despite their implicitness in the official formulation of the law.

Finally three languages—Gagauz, Moldovan, and Russian—were institutionalized in Gagauzia, with the most apparent intention to alleviate all survival and security fears that had been associated with Moldova's 1989 language law.[21] Moreover, it was stipulated that in the occasion of a "change in the status of the Republic of Moldova," the most probable being that of unification with Romania, the Gagauz upheld the right to self-determination, choosing their own course of action (King, 2000, p. 219).[22]

The "local autonomy law" acquired solid foundations and resonance within Gagauzia; it laid, first and foremost, the groundwork for a "Gagauz cultural renaissance," whereas second, it epitomized this by satisfying the core demands of the local elites (King, 2000, p. 219). The latter were given the possibility of a more sufficient organization at the local level and a more significant involvement in the local government, being, concurrently, entitled to funding from the central budget (King, 2000, p. 219). Thus, not only the cultural platform was thoroughly guaranteed, but the central authorities in Chisinau managed to convert the, once rival, local elites into their allies in their effort to control the Gagauz independence movement. Unlike the case of Transdniestria, where both the administration and the armed irregulars were beset with their regional political preferences and power-sharing considerations, in Gagauzia, the armed irregulars, albeit a nominal threat to the local law enforcement agencies, were easy to handle; the Moldovan ministry of internal affairs, instead of just breaking up the "Bugeac (Budjak) Battalion," it formed, in its place, the "Military Unit 1045," a special task force, which was comprised of the Battalion's ex-members. Their gear was registered, new uniforms were provided, and new salaries were given, in an indication of both their compliance with and loyalty to the central government, and their desire to become legitimized (King, 2000, p. 220). In fact, the accession to the Military Unit 1045 once more corroborates that the main concern for the Gagauz was the protection and conservation of their cultural identity. Once this had been thoroughly achieved by the local autonomy law, the armed irregulars were deprived of their cause of mobilization.

On the contrary, Transdniestria remained locked in its regional political preferences that, at their core, had power-sharing considerations within the internationally recognized borders of the Republic of Moldova. As earlier argued, Transdniestria was primarily interested in establishing as firmly as possible its political power next to the Moldovan one, in a political landscape who had experienced for more than fifty years a zero sum power game between the Moldovan and Transdniestrian elites. The Moldovans managed to gain the upper hand in the political affairs of the republic in 1989, only to realize that a workable peace plan between them and Transdniestria would be discussable upon the principles of a federalized republic.

On May 8, 1997, the Moscow Memorandum was signed between the Republic of Moldova and Transdniestria, unraveling, gradually, the Transdniestrian regional political preferences as well as the Moldovan authorities' elasticity towards them; in particular, the memorandum stipulated in Point 3 that "Transdniestria shall participate in the conduct of the foreign policy of the Republic of Moldova—a subject of international law—on questions touching its interests," whereas any decision made were subject to unanimity (OSCE, 1997). Furthermore, Transdniestria was granted the right to "unilaterally establish and maintain international contacts in the economic, scientific-technical and cultural spheres, and in other spheres by agreement of the Parties" (OSCE, 1997). These points, similar to that offered to Gagauzia with regard to Turkey, served, prima facie, to respect any sensitivities Transdniestria may have had in relation to neighboring Russia and Ukraine, but more fundamentally, they aimed at defusing security concerns, which had been gravely exacerbated following an all-out war (OSCE, 1997). Staying tuned with the "security issue," Point 9 mentioned the commitment by both signatories to the 1992 peace agreement to respect and facilitate the activities carried out by the JPKF in the Security zone in order to preserve the peace (OSCE, 1997). Finally, Point 11, took the whole "security issue" a step further, engaging the power-sharing considerations of Transdniestria, and calling for both parties to "build their relations in the framework of a common state within the borders of the Moldavian SSR as of January of the year 1990" (OSCE, 1997). This point caused friction between the two parties, with each one to try to maximize its possible gains from the formulation "common state," but ultimately, usher the bilateral relations to yet another dead end that further aggravated the incumbent lack of trust and sense of insecurity. Even more, it paved the way for the thorough articulation of

Transdniestria's perception towards a resolution, which came in the form of the Kozak Memorandum, named after Putin's closest confidant, Dmitri Kozak, who was sent to directly negotiate between Chisinau and Tiraspol.

THE KOZAK MEMORANDUM: KEY POINTS

1. The Republic of Moldova and the Transdniestrian Moldovan Republic, being aware of their responsibility for the unification of the state and guaranteeing the civil peace and the complete democratic development, agree that the final settlement of the Transdniestrian problem shall be based on the transformation of the government structure of the Republic of Moldova according to the federal principles, so as to build a unified, independent, democratic state within the boundaries of the Moldavian SSR, defined on January 1, 1990.
2. The Federal Republic of Moldova is a democratic, sovereign federal state, founded upon the principles of territorial unity and unified state power, and having a single defense, customs and monetary space. . . . The people are the holders of sovereignty and the only source of state power.
3. The federation is a neutral, demilitarized state. . . . Before the full demilitarization, the Armed Forces are formed and operate on the basis of guaranteeing the territorial integrity (against foreign threats), with their deployment for purposes of law enforcement and security at the domestic (federal) level to be ruled out. The command of the Armed Forces of the Federation fully lies within the executive branch (of government).
4. The TMR is subject of the federation, a sovereign entity within the federation, that forms its own legislative (the Supreme Council of the TMR), executive (president of the TMR, and government of the TMR), and judiciary branches; it has its own constitution and legislation, its own government, independent budget and tax system, as well as its own state symbols and other attributes related to its state status.
5. The constitutional-legal status and boundaries of the territories of the Subjects of the federation cannot be changed without their consent.
6. The subjects of the federation may be members of international organizations, regional and global, where an international legal personality is not a prerequisite; they can also maintain international relations, clinch international agreements on issues of their interest, and establish missions on other states, which, however, do not relish the status of a diplomatic or a consular one.

7. The subjects of the federation uphold the right to exit the federation only in cases of a decision to unite the federation with another state, or total loss of sovereignty.
8. The acts by all state institutions, central and local-administration ones, shall be issued in both the Moldovan and the Russian language.
9. For the preparation of the draft Constitution of the Federation, the parties formed a Joint Constitutional Commission, comprised by plenipotentiaries of each of the sides; supplementary, international experts from the guarantor states, the OSCE, the EU, . . . and the Council Europe, are invited to participate with the status of observer.
10. The parties shall address suggestions on the provision of security guarantees, and the conditions for the unification and territorial integrity of the Federal Republic of Moldova, stipulated for within the current memorandum, to the Russian Federation. For a transition period till the full demilitarization is complete, but not later than 2020, the Republic of Moldova shall sign and ratify agreement with the Russian Federation on the deployment in the territory of the future federation of peacekeeping forces by the Russian Federation, drawn up of no more than 2000 soldiers, and without heavy weaponry. The agreement is put into force concurrently with the adoption of the Constitution of the federation. In the occasion of non-fulfillment of the condition provided for in this paragraph, this Memorandum is considered invalid (Regnum, 2005).[23]

All above points serve the power-sharing aim of Transdniestria, which insisted on the ratification of its final status by a state-to-state treaty, and not by a law, as it had happened with Gagauzia (Roper, 2001, p. 119). Taken the Kozak Memorandum's points one by one, nowhere was made reference or implied the prospect of secession or separation; on the contrary, a unified, independent, democratic state within the 1990 boundaries of the Moldavian SSR was fundamentally provisioned, with the federal set up of the government to fulfill Transdniestria's demands and build bridges between the two parties.

In particular, the formation of a federation, with its main attributes being that of territorial unity, unified state power, and single defense, customs, and monetary space, would open up the way for Transdniestria to participate in the government as a constituent part (Point 2). Furthermore, it would be awarded the right to its own constitution, its own legislation, government, judiciary, symbols, budget, and tax system (Point 4). Thus, the institutionalization of its political status would be accompanied by freedom to handle its quite critical for the whole republic economic situation as it saw fit. Next to that, the Moldovan and the Russian language were designated as official languages of the administration (Point 8), a fact of utmost importance, given the earlier mobilization and the power connotations which the language issue had been associated with.

Addressing the "security issue" in all its aspects, demilitarization stood atop (Point 3); with the bilateral relations to have been gravely rattled by the 1992 war, and any trust to have been seriously impaired, if not outright evaporated, it was stipulated the that the Armed Forces of the newfangled republic would be oriented towards foreign threats, holding no role to the developments at the domestic level. Moreover, their command would be assigned to the government of the federal republic. In this manner, any possible threat from one side on the other would be neutralized, given the balance of power emerging by the joint ownership. Further to this argumentative line, it was stipulated that the constituent parts of the federation could not change their borders unilaterally (Point 5), whereas any possible decision for uniting the federation with another state would empower the other part to unilaterally withdraw from the federation (Point 7). The same provision had also been offered to the Gagauz, and, here most probably reference is made to the "Romanization" fears of the early mobilization period (late 1980s), when the Moldovan authorities were more actively discussing unification prospects with Romania. The memorandum called for Russia to guarantee the territorial integrity of the Federal Republic of Moldova (Point 10). In fact, it appealed to the Moldovan government to sign and ratify an agreement with Russia, which would allow for the deployment of Russian, light-armored, peacekeeping forces at the territory of Moldova for a period not exceeding 2020, so as for the demilitarization to be completed. This point well indicates the trust-deficient and insecurity-permeating environment of the post-war period; in essence, the security concerns were so alarming and vital, that should this provision was not put into effect, the whole memorandum was null and void.

To this direction were also the rights awarded to Transdniestria, as far as its international profile is concerned (Point 6); by being able to become member of international organizations that did not require the status of a state, it could pursue closer cooperation with states which it did share interests with, and primarily security ones; drawing the parallel with the Gagauz case, just like the Gagauz were enabled to participate in Moldova's diplomatic missions on issues relating to Turkey and other Turkic countries that ranked high in their preferences, in the same manner Transdniestria had the opportunity to nurture its rapprochement with states like Russia, which had an increased osmosis with its cause. Yet, this rapprochement would not undermine the unity of the provisioned federal state, with any mission sent to fall short of the status of the diplomatic one.

Finally, the preparation of the Constitution would be observed also by international experts from the guarantor states, the OSCE, the EU and the Council of Europe, aiming at its thorough and all-encompassing setup.

All in all, the Kozak memorandum was a Russia-mediated effort to reestablish Moldova upon a federal structure with two equal, power-sharing, constituent units: the Moldovan government and Transdniestria. It largely fulfilled Transdniestria's regional political preferences, and when leaked, it met the vehement criticism on behalf of the EU, USA, and OSCE. Nevertheless, the Moldovan President, Vladimir Voronin, who had been elected with the Party of Communists in February 2001, was just about to sign the deal, when, at the last moment before the arrival of Putin at Chisinau, decided to reject it (Johansson, 2006, p. 510); this did not only terminate the Kozak memorandum per se, but it also reverberated on the Moldovan-Russian relations, which had been experiencing an upsurge from the moment that Voronin's administration rose to power.

With an outright solution to the Transdniestrian issue to be unattainable, a "step-by-step" process within the context of the OSCE would be followed, aspiring at the spillover of trust and security from the confidence-building measures.

In particular, on September 26–27, 2005, the "5 + 2" format was set up, and the "Permanent Conference on Political Issues in the Framework of the Negotiations Process for the Transdniestrian Settlement in the "5 + 2 format" (hereinafter referred to as "Permanent Conference") has ever since become the official, resolution-seeking, institution.[24] Within its context, a settlement on the Transdniestrian conflict based on the sovereignty and territorial integrity of the Republic of Moldova within its internationally recognized borders with a special status for Transdniestria has been pursued (OSCE, 2005, 2016a). However, such a process has encountered certain difficulties, such as that of the removal of Russian arms and equipment from Transdniestria. On November 13, 2006, the OSCE staff gained access to Russia's ammunition depot at Colbasna, near the Moldovan-Ukrainian border in northern Transdniestria, only to witness that no withdrawals had been made, despite the multiple agreements between the Russian and the Moldovan government in the 1990s and the OSCE's last inspection in March 2004; as a matter of fact, more than 21,000 tons of ammunition remained stored in the region, eroding the prospects for a settlement (OSCE, 2006). Maneuvering around this impediment and pursuing a "step-by-step" process, a milestone was reached on June 2–3, 2016, at Berlin, when the respective (Berlin) protocol was signed, with the Moldovan government and Transdniestria to agree that:

1. the apostilisation of diplomas issued in Transdniestria would further be refined following the European experts' recommendation from 2014,
2. the inclusion of vehicles with number plates issued in Transdniestria would further be elaborated in accordance with the EU-Border Assistance Mission (EUBAM) Technical Opinion Paper from 2015,[25]

3. the telecommunications and the overall connection would be addressed properly,
4. a protocol in the area of meteorology and protection of natural resources in the Dniester River basin would be signed in the following days pursuant this (Berlin) protocol (OSCE, 2016b).

Next to that, issues on the functioning of the Moldova-administered Latin Script Schools in Transdniestria, the use of farmlands in Dubasari region, the freedom of movement for people, goods and services, and the opening of the bridge across the Dniester River between the villages Gura Bicului and Bychok, were added, constituting, in total, the so-called "package of eight," aimed at confidence-building between the two sides (OSCE, 2017b, 2017c). As the special representative of the Austrian OSCE Chairperson-in-Office for the Transdniestrian Settlement Process, Ambassador Heim, stated, "a little political will could go a long way in making tangible progress in the settlement process, resulting in immediate improvements to people's quality of life" (OSCE, 2017b).

With all previous efforts towards a direct resolution to have proved of limited resonance, the "step-by-step" process has been prioritized as means of creating wider synergies, maximizing the spillover of trust, alleviating the intractability of regional political preferences and, ultimately, laying the groundwork for the resolution of the Transdniestrian conflict.

CONCLUSION

Summarizing and drawing the main conclusions with regard to the conflict in Transdniestria, Table 2.1 is of particular assistance.

Transdniestria's regional political preferences towards federalizing the Republic of Moldova are substantiated through comparison across different periods of the historical continuum and through their juxtaposition with the

Table 2.1. Anatomy of the Conflict in Transdniestria: Substantiating Causality

	Transdniestria	Test case: Gagauzia
Pre-war period	*Regional political preference:* Federalization of the Moldovan State	*No regional political preference:* Demand for cultural autonomy
War period	*Regional political preference:* Federalization of the Moldovan State	*No regional political preference:* Demand for cultural autonomy
Post-war period	*Regional political preference:* Federalization of the Moldovan State	*No regional political preference:* Local autonomy law (1994)

test case of Gagauzia, which, although it did embark on the same conflictual path as Transdniestria in late 1980s early 1990s, it ended up as a part of the Republic of Moldova. This happened due to the different demands posed by it, i.e., cultural versus political (power-sharing) by Transdniestria. The anatomy of the conflict includes also the seeds for its resolution, so as a solid socio-political ground to be laid and development to follow suit. In fact, this development will be, first and foremost, reflected on the citizens' national identity type, which starting from the rudimentary one of "atomized," will be gradually transformed into "ethnic" and "hybrid," reaching, finally, the most advance type of "civic," which stands for citizens/actors who put rationality ahead of ethnic attachments and xenophobia.

Of course the facts on the ground point towards a different direction. Moldova ranks 103 out of 174 as far as corruption is concerned with a score of 35 on a scale from 0 (highly corrupt) to 100 (very clean) (McDevitt, 2015, p. 22). Corruption is among the top five concerns of citizens, with insufficient checks on government power, impunity of government officials as far as misconduct is concerned, and government intervention in the delivery of civil and criminal justice, to affect the overall balance of power among the state's main institutions to the detriment of democracy (McDevitt, 2015, p. 22). Political parties have not adequately developed internal democratic procedures, whereas the funding of parties as well as the electoral campaigns suffer from transparency. Finally, civil society remains largely politically controlled, with the phenomenon of Government Organized NGO (GONGO) to account for ex-ministers and political figures reallocating funds, theoretically earmarked for Civil Society Organizations (CSOs), to public bodies founded by them (McDevitt, 2015, p. 23). In this manner, not only the political elite's inbreeding is nurtured, but also critical funds are withheld from society, leading to its further compartmentalization. Indicative is the fact that 15.6% of the citizens of the Republic of Moldova has trust in people in general, with approximately the same value (18.8%) to hold for the citizens of Transdniestria (Berg, 2012, p. 1285; Tudoroiu, 2011, pp. 251–252).[26] Of course, such a lopsided political situation has also impacted on the economic sphere, with the GDP per capita, PPP and the unemployment level, two indicators tied to the very essence of the quality of life, to hover around alarming figures (World Bank, 2018).[27]

Such a hardly promising socio-political reality could backfire even in cases which, for many years, have been considered "settled." Gagauzia, albeit having its culture-oriented autonomy institutionalized since 1994, has regularly been airing complaints regarding the enfeeblement of its cultural rights as well as its control over tax and revenue. The Moldovan Law on Local Finance became a point of friction, given that it would allocate fewer funds to the Gagauz from the national budget, whereas the Moldovan-Gagauz relationship soon acquired a geopolitical dimension; the Moldovan side coveted an association agreement with the EU as a result of the EaP Summit set to meet at Vilnius on November 28, 2013, while the Gagauz saw a rapprochement with the Putin-promoted Customs Union as an economic and security necessity. To elaborate, the Moldovan authorities' intention created the fear to the Gagauz that a European integration might bring about a union with Romania, which, in turn, may result in the "loss of Gagauz autonomy similar to that of Hungarians in Romania" (Tudoroiu, 2016, p. 384). On the eve of the EaP Summit, a referendum was decided by Gagauzia, and was, finally, conducted on February 2, 2014; 70% of the Gagauz took part, with 98.4% qualifying closer relations with the Putin-promoted Customs Union, 97.2% opposing the EU integration plan, and 98.9% upholding Gagauzia's right to resuscitate its late 1980s position of declaring independence as a means of survival and security, should Moldova forfeit or give up its sove- reignty and unite with Romania (Tudoroiu, 2016, p. 384). Providing a clearer picture of these percentages, Gagauzia's governor, Mihail Formuzal, stated the next day of the referendum:

> We want free markets in both Europe and the Russian Federation. We, Gagau- zians, a small minority, are telling the central government [of Moldova]—stop all of political integration [with the EU]; take care about economic integration. Who can guarantee that we will manage to jump on the last cart of the train speeding towards Europe and the EU will not end up like the Soviet Union? Is there such a guarantee? No, there isn't. (RFE/RL, 2014)

The analysis, so far, proves a series of points: (a) should any integration project be initiated, the once cultural autonomy would revert to the regional political preferences of independence as the only means of survival and security in Moldova's perpetuating trust-deficient socio-political environ- ment of "atomized" rational actors, (b) economic issues play an equally critical role, being inextricably linked with the very essence of the quality of life, and (c) the Gagauz, perceived the "Russia factor" in the affairs of the Moldovan republic in survival and security terms, a fact that also emerges from Formuzal's caution against any prospect might resemble that of the USSR.

All in all, regional political preferences, embedded within an ethnicized Moldovan national identity, comparatively weak economic growth, and un- employment served as the prime movers beyond the frozen conflict at Transdniestria. Russia, despite its direct involvement in the early 1990s, it has been dealt with as a contextual factor to allow for the primacy of state- level analysis.

NOTES

1. For a map on these developments, see http://romaniatourism.com/romania-maps /wallachia-moldavia-transylvania-map. html.

2. Before elected to the Presidency, Snegur had served from July 29, 1989, until April 27, 1990, as Chairman of the Presidium of the Supreme Soviet of Moldavia, and from April 27, 1990, until June 23, 1990, as Chairman of the Supreme Soviet of the Moldavian SSR. During that time, the Supreme Soviet embarked on an attempt to steadily uproot the Communist control from the republic; at first, in May 1990, multiparty democracy was instituted to succeed the monopoly of the Communist Party as the fundamental organization principle of the political life. Second, on June 23, 1990, state sovereignty was declared, clearly signaling the primacy of the national legislation over the supranational all-union laws, issued by the central institutions of the USSR (King, 2001, p. 148).

3. At this point consider the influx of Russian immigrants during the Soviet period as well as the russification policies that came to supplement these influxes. For more on the issue, see the beginning of this chapter and Chinn and Roper, 1995, p. 294.

4. As previously mentioned, this competition in the declaration of independence is far from symbolic and is related to the international law principle of *Uti possidetis* ("as you possess"); according to this, the possessor of a specific territory or property at the end of a conflict (i.e., critical juncture period where institutional fluidity, if not gap, prevails) becomes the rightful owner, unless there is a treaty providing otherwise. Simply put, the *de facto* (i.e., the acquired by force during the war), becomes *de jure* (i.e., legally recognized). For more on the issue, see Shaw, 1997, pp. 491–492.

5. Bender is two-thirds the size of Tiraspol, which, according to the 2004 census, is mostly inhabited by Russians (43.35%), Moldovans (25.03%), and Ukrainians (17.98%). Interesting is the fact that according to a referendum conducted in 1990 in Bender, over 90% of the population approved of forging an alliance with the breakaway republic of Transdniestria, thus providing fertile ground for the latter's overall mobilization across the Dniester (Chinn and Roper, 1995, p. 309).

6. Dubăsari had two bridges connecting it with the western bank of the Dniester river. During the fighting in the first semester of 1992, they were destroyed.

7. The OMON (Отряд Мобильный Особого Назначения) belongs to the Russian Ministry of Internal Affairs, and was created in 1988 as the special forces of the Soviet Police. Subsequently, it got extensively involved in multiple armed conflicts that erupted during the USSR's dissolution (Beissinger, 2002, p. 338).

8. To prove the case, in early 1992, Lieutenant General Gennadii Yakovlev, the 14th Army's commander, defected to lead Transdniestria's forces, and Ştefan Chiţac, the 14th Army's chief of staff, also left for the position of TMR's Defense Minister (King, 2000, p. 192).

9. For more on this, see the chapter on Georgia's "frozen conflicts."

10. The Commonwealth of Independent States (CIS) is a loose confederation of nine member states (Armenia, Azerbaijan, Belarus, Kazakhstan, Kyrgyzstan, Moldova, Russia, Tajikistan, and Uzbekistan), and two associate members (Turkmenistan, Ukraine), which formed during the dissolution of the USSR with the aim to coordinate issues pertinent to trade, finance, lawmaking, and security, given the high level of interdependence during the Soviet period (SNG, 2018). Moreover, it could be considered as an umbrella-international organization, comprising other organizations, such as the Collective Security Treaty Organization (CSTO), the Eurasian Economic Union (the Eurasian Customs Union and the Eurasian Economic Space included), and the Union State (between Russia and Belarus), all varying as far as membership and level of integration are concerned (EEC, 2016; CSTO, 2002).

11. In terms of inclusion, however, public statements by leading figures of the Russian political scene of the time, such as the Russian Foreign Minister Andrei Kozyrev should be mentioned. Asked by the French newspaper, *Le Monde*, if Moldova's Dniester area "would someday become part of Russia," he answered that he "would not rule that out," whereas when he commented on the situation in Ukraine, Moldova and the Baltic states, he argued that these states should consent to the creation of certain regions within their territories "which would

have a special status and very close links, privileged links, with Russia" (Lamont, 1993, p. 589).

12. Discussing the importance of the "Transdniestrian case" to the Russian political system, the Transdniestrians held the central position within a diverse group of minorities placed under the label "Russian-speakers," having, traditionally, exhibited their allegiance to the Soviet state, and even more significantly, to the "Great Russian culture" (King, 2000, p. 195). This fact increased the sensitivity of the Russian administration when issues of security were becoming hard-to-escape.

13. In the mayhem of the time, military spokesmen in an interview on Russian TV, who kept their anonymity and were quoted by the *Washington Post*, claimed that "Russian soldiers had been ordered out of the barracks to 'defend' Russian-speaking areas." In the same direction, commanders on the ground claimed that part of the five thousand soldiers of the 14th Army stationed at Bendery had individually and unofficially engaged the May fighting. At the official level, nevertheless, on May 19, Major General Yurii Netkachev, commander of the 14th Army, revoked previous statement that he was unable to keep his troops under control (Lamont, 1993, pp. 587, 590).

14. As far as casualties are concerned, there were different estimations, with the Moldovan side to mention a few dozen and the Transdniestrian almost seven hundred. For more, see King, 2000, p. 194.

15. It is noteworthy that during the agreements on July 6th among the CIS member-states for the deployment of JPKF and the promotion of separateness, certain provisions met the support of states, such as Romania, that during the conflict had showed their intimacy with the Moldovan cause. This volte-face poured water on Transdniestria's windmill.

16. In fact, Transdniestria, experiencing this wider context of intransigence and seeing no way out of the imbroglio, approved, in a referendum in 1995, of its new Constitution by 98.5%. This course was once more corroborated in 2006, when a similar referendum was conducted (97.1%) (Sanchez, 2009, p. 160).

17. The other three raions were dominated by Moldovans or Bulgarians, shaping a reality where the ethnic Gagauz amounted to 47.2% of the total population, and certainly impacted on the "self-determination" calls on behalf of the latter.

18. It is noteworthy that the local leaders as well as the local committees had continuously been funded by the state budget (King, 2000, p. 217).

19. Komrat is the administrative center and the capital city of the autonomous region of Gagauzia.

20. Each village, regardless of a Gagauz majority or not, would decide in a referendum to decide whether it would join the special "territorial autonomous unit." In the referendum conducted on February 5, 1995, as well as in others in March, an ethnically homogenous Gagauz land ("Yeri") was formed in one larger and one smaller part of land, divided by a few mixed and non-Gagauz villages (Socor, 1995).

21. There were also other, more culture-related, reasons beyond the official status of each of these languages. Thus, the Moldovan were also serving to accommodate the residents of the mix villages in the Gagauz Yeri, the Gagauz were meant to reverse a long period of underdevelopment and marginalization, whereas, finally, the Russian, to address the consequences that a protracted period of Russification since the 1940s had implanted in the region (Socor, 1995).

22. This provision had also been offered to Transdniestria, as a repellent of survival and security fears, in the peace-agreement negotiations conducted in 1992.

23. The translation from Russian has been made by the author, and responsibility for any mistakes rests solely with him.

24. The participating states in the "5 + 2" format of the OSCE are Moldova, Transdniestria, Russia, Ukraine, OSCE, plus the EU and the US.

25. In December 2005, the EU institutionalized the EUBAM, surrounding Transdniestria with two fronts, Ukraine (East) and Moldova (West); at first, in the eastern front, monitoring the 450km Transdniestrian part of the Ukrainian-Moldovan border would assist in countering smuggling and other criminal activities, thus gravely constricting Transdniestria's illegally possessed economic resources (Sasse, 2009, p. 377). At second, in the western front, the collaboration between Moldovan and Ukrainian authorities, according to which the former's

goods would be transited to the latter's soil only if carrying the official Moldovan customs stamp (with Moldova to have provided for easy access to this stamp by registered Transdniestrian companies) would propel Transdniestria towards rapprochement with the Moldovan government, sowing, concurrently, the seeds for a resolution of the conflict (Sasse, 2009, p. 377; Dias, 2013, p. 347).

26. Likewise, Transdniestria has been on the same tracks, with the Smirnov administration (1991–2011) to have been accused by political parties, journalists and civil society to have been utilizing the Ministry of State Security (MGB), the de facto state intelligence service, and his personal security guards to build an authoritarian regime, downgrading the parliament to a decorative role, far from a functional one (Sanchez, 2009, p. 159). In fact, anti-Smirnov organizations, media, and politicians had hardly been found in Transdniestria, whereas according to human rights groups, more than two hundred residents of Transdniestria are missing or presumed dead for having engaged into actions against Transdniestria, and by extension against the regime (Sanchez, 2009, p. 169). Smirnov and his family were allegedly behind "Sheriff," the second-largest company base in the region, owning a chain of petrol stations, supermarkets, a TV Channel, a publishing house, a construction company, a Mercedes-Benz dealer, etc., while they had also expanded to the sports sector, owning even a football team (Sanchez, 2009, p. 169). All these made the regime, or the governing alliance controlling the biggest part of the local economy, thrive at the expense of the local population. Transdniestria's economy at large has been suffering from structural deficiencies, such as population decrease due to migration and depopulation, lack in qualified personnel, intra/inter-sectoral imbalances, both within the industry and between the industry and the agriculture, with latter to experience a protracted period of stagnation (CISR, 2010, p. 1). As a result, dependence on imports of raw materials, energy resources and foodstuffs has gravely increased (CISR, 2010, p. 1).

27. It is indicatively mentioned that the average (1994–2017) GDP per capita, PPP (current international $) is $2,949, whereas the same number with regard to unemployment (% of total labor force) (modeled ILO estimate) is 7.37% (World Bank, 2018a).

Chapter Three

The Case of Crimea (Ukraine)

UKRAINE AND THE EU EAP SUMMIT AT VILNIUS:
"THE TIP OF THE ICEBERG"

If the EU EaP summit at Vilnius impacted on Moldova, Ukraine could not have escaped that influence; almost twenty-two years after it had its independence established, Ukraine had not succeeded in building a socio-political reality which would convert its citizens from rational actors beset with the "atomized" type of national identity to ones approaching the "hybrid" or, ideally, the "civic" type of national identity, thus having survival and security concerns minimized, if not eradicated.

In November 2013, Ukraine reached another turning point in its tumultuous post-soviet history; the EU EaP summit at Vilnius provisioned the signing of political and free-trade agreements between the EU and Ukraine. The whole procedure came to a standstill, when the then President of Ukraine, Viktor Yanukovych, did a *volt face* on previous political pledges, yearning for the Customs Union among Russia, Belarus and Kazakhstan (Herszenhorn, 2013). Widespread mobilization swept Ukraine, with survival and security concerns, similar to those of the early independence period, to come to a crescendo, and the country to gradually become intractably divided between pro-EU and pro-Russia parts (Sakwa, 2015). This situation quickly acquired a geopolitical dimension too, sinking the EU-Russia relations into the lowest point since the end of the cold war. In view of these, the dynamics within the Ukrainian society call for particular attention, since beyond this intractable divisiveness, long-submerged and unaddressed regional political preferences could be discerned. Much more when these regional political preferences had been embedded within a diachronically ailing nation-building process, that resulted in the prevalence of the "atomized" type of national identity among the citizens. In such conditions, regional political preferences would be expressed in a rather assertive manner, in an effort to maximize the power of those allied under them, and ensure their survival and security in an anarchy-returning socio-political environment that had started to have a striking resemblance with that of the early independence period.

Taken from there, the 2013–2015 crisis is analyzed within a comparative historical continuum, that places prime emphasis on two critical periods of post-Soviet Ukraine, i.e., the early independence period versus the 2013–2015 crisis period, and on the mostly affected regions of the eastern part, primarily Crimea, and far secondarily Donbass (Luhansk and Donetsk) (Sotiriou, 2016, p. 2). Any identification or similarity in terms of regional political preferences, then and now, could establish them, according to Mill's "Method of Agreement" as the key causal factor lying behind the 2013–2015 crisis (Skocpol, 1979, p. 36). Of course, next to regional political preferences, quality of life also takes its toll on citizens' preferences (Bakke et al., 2014); thus, narrowing it down to two principal variables, the GDP per capita PPP and unemployment, their contextual impact is examined throughout the post-Soviet period by connecting the two periods *via* time series. In further detail, these two variables are juxtaposed for both Ukraine and Russia, since the latter had been a weighing factor in the Ukrainian politics and got heavily involved in the 2013–2015 crisis. Any impact is corroborated by the correlation of a widening point difference between the two countries as far as the variables in point are concerned with the deterioration of the socio-political situation within Ukraine, and by extension, of its bilateral relations with Russia.

The Critical Juncture Period of the Late 1980s to Early 1990s and Regional Political Preferences

Ukraine proceeded to its declaration of independence on August 24, 1991. From that point until June 1996, when the constitution was adopted and a new institutional equilibrium came to succeed the critical juncture period, multiple efforts had been made on behalf of the authorities, so as to address the issue of nationalities. To begin with, on November 1, 1991, the parliament adopted the "Declaration of the Rights of Nationalities of Ukraine," to be supplemented by the law "On National Minorities in Ukraine," passed a few months later, on June 25, 1992 (Solchanyk, 1994, p. 64). Next to these and being aware of the "automated" way that the country's nationalities could be associated with the "Russia factor," at first for survival and security reasons, the Ukrainian authorities were cautious to assure that the Ukrainian statehood posed "no threat to the Russian and Russian speaking population" (Solchanyk, 1994, p. 64).

Crimea, which twenty-three years later would become the bone of contention between Russia and Ukraine, constituted the sole sizeable administrative sub-division of Ukraine, where ethnic Russians outnumbered Ukrainians (Solchanyk, 1994, p. 50). In fact, in 1989, 65.5% of the region's total population was Russian as opposed to 26.7% that was Ukrainian (State Statistics Committee of Ukraine, 2004). In 1990 and early 1991, when Kiev was seriously suspected of declining Gorbachev's initiative towards a new Union Treaty which could give a new lease of life to the thus far cumbersome USSR, numerous voices among the Crimean population called for the region's 1945–1946 abolished republican status to be reinstated (Solchanyk, 1994, p. 51). To this direction, the Crimean Soviet spoke out on the restoration of statehood in the form of an Autonomous Soviet Socialist Republic (ASSR), "subject of the USSR and a party to the Union Treaty" (Solchanyk, 1994, p. 51). A referendum came to seal these dynamics and prove the mobilization among the citizens of Crimea on January 20, 1990, when 93.3% of the participants threw their support behind the question "Are you for the restoration of the Crimean ASSR as a subject of the USSR and a party to the Union Treaty?" (Belitser, 2000, p. 3). The Ukrainian parliament, shaken by the steadfastness beyond Crimea's regional political preferences as the only means of survival and security in the anarchy-resembling socio-political environment of late 1980s early 1990s, passed, on February 12, 1992, the law "On the Renewal of the Crimean ASSR," reinstituting Crimea's autonomy "within the borders of the Ukrainian SSR" (Belitser, 2000; Solchanyk, 1994, p. 51).

That law, however, would prove of limited capacity to defuse the distrust-laden and security-lacking environment, which had reached an apex after the collapse of the USSR, and Crimea would project an ever firmer profile; with Crimean Tatars and other ethnic groups to repatriate *en masse* for the first time since their deportation during WWII, and the interethnic relations to walk a tightrope, three possible scenarios, ranked by preference, were examined: (a) a complete autonomous status within Ukraine, as provisioned by the moribund Constitution of the Crimean Republic of May 6, 1992, (b) a creation of an independent Crimean Republic, and (c) secession from Ukraine and accession to Russia, a scenario highly likely among the pro-Russia forces inside and outside the region (Belitser, 2000; Lazzerini, 1996, pp. 427–433).

Face à Face such a situation, the Ukrainian parliament fell back, and tried to assuage Crimea's security and trust issues by adopting the law "On the Delineation of Power between Ukraine and the Republic of Crimea." Before the ink was dry, the law was renamed in its final form "On the Status of the Autonomous Republic of Crimea," eliminating, in this manner, Crimea's hopes for being treated in its relations with Ukraine as an equal partner (Solchanyk, 1995, p. 55). In no time, widespread unrest broke out again, followed by Crimea's parliament declaring independence, subject to a refe-

rendum, set for August 2, 1992 (Schmemann, 1992). By June 30, 1992, both
parties consented to Crimea's full-grown autonomy within Ukraine, and the
law "On the Delineation of Power between the Organs of State Rule of
Ukraine and the Republic of Crimea" passed by the Ukrainian parliament
(Solchanyk, 1994, p. 56). This, however, would be nothing more but a temporal stop in the tumultuous course in the bilateral relations that reached an
end in 1996 and 1998, when both the Ukrainian and the Crimean Constitution were adopted respectively, and a kind of arrangement seemed to be at
work.[1]

To make the argument more measurable, the joint analysis of both Constitutions below is of particular assistance:

The Constitution of Ukraine (1996) and the Constitution of Crimea (1998): Key Points

1. The Autonomous Republic Crimea is inalienable part of Ukraine and
   within the limits of plenary powers certain by Constitution of Ukraine,
   decides the questions attributed to its knowing (Constitution of
   Ukraine, 1996, Article 134)
2. The legal foundation of the status and powers of the Autonomous
   Republic of Crimea, the Supreme Rada (Parliament) of the Autonomous Republic of Crimea and the Council of Ministers of the Autonomous Republic of Crimea shall be the Constitution of Ukraine, Ukrainian laws and the Constitution of the Autonomous Republic of Crimea
   (Constitution of Crimea, 1998, Article 2, par. 1)
3. The Autonomous Republic of Crimea has Constitution of the Autonomous Republic of Crimea, which Supreme Soviet of the Autonomous
   Republic of Crimea adopts and Supreme Soviet of Ukraine more no
   less as by a half from constitutional composition of Supreme Soviet of
   Ukraine asserts (Constitution of Ukraine, 1996, Article 135)
4. The legal normative acts of Supreme Soviet of the Autonomous Republic of Crimea and decisions of Council of Ministers of the Autonomous Republic Crimea cannot conflict with Constitution and laws of
   Ukraine and are accepted in accordance with Constitution of Ukraine,
   laws of Ukraine, acts of President of Ukraine and Cabinet of Ministers
   of Ukraine (Constitution of Ukraine, 1996, Article 135, par. 2)
5. The Council of Ministers of the Autonomous Republic Crimea serves
   as the Government of the Autonomous Republic Crimea. The Chairman of Council of Ministers of the Autonomous Republic Crimea is
   assigned for and removed from position by the Supreme Soviet of the
   Autonomous Republic of Crimea in agreement with the President of
   Ukraine (Constitution of Ukraine, 1996, Article 136, par. 3)

6. Authority of the Supreme Soviet of the Autonomous Republic Crimea and Council of Ministers of the Autonomous Republic Crimea, is determined by the Constitution of Ukraine and laws of Ukraine, and by legal normative acts of Supreme Soviet of the Autonomous Republic Crimea on questions attributed to its jurisdiction (Constitution of Ukraine, 1996, Article 136, par. 4)

7. The Autonomous Republic of Crimea carries out the normative adjusting on questions:

   • agriculture and forests
   • land-reclamation and quarries
   • social works, handicrafts and trades
   • labor, labor remuneration, conditions and protection, social issues and employment of population, social protection of population
   • interethnic relations (securing application and development of Official language, Russian, Crimean Tatar and other Ethnic Groups' languages in the Autonomous Republic of Crimea)
   • town-planning and housing economy
   • tourism, hotel business, fairs
   • museums, libraries, theaters, other establishments of culture, historic-cultural preserves
   • transport, communication and road construction
   • hunts, fishing
   • sanitary and hospital corps (Constitution of Ukraine, 1996, Article 138; Constitution of Crimea, 1998, Article 10, 38, par. 2)

8. Pursuant to the Constitution of Ukraine and Ukrainian laws, the Autonomous Republic of Crimea shall determine the structure and priorities of development of its economy and fix taxes and tax benefits under Ukrainian laws (Constitution of Crimea, 1998, Article 18, par. 11; Article 26, par. 8)

9. The financial self-sufficiency of the Autonomous Republic of Crimea shall be guaranteed through steady assignment, by Ukrainian laws, to the budget revenue of the Autonomous Republic of Crimea of the national taxes and fees, fully entered into the budget of the Autonomous Republic of Crimea, sufficient for the exercise of powers of the Autonomous Republic of Crimea and ensuring that the living standards of citizens and population in general should not be below the social standards and needs as determined by Ukrainian laws (Constitution of Crimea, 1998, Article 18, par. 14)

10. The Autonomous Republic of Crimea shall participate in the building and implementation of the fundamental principles of the domestic policy, foreign-economic and foreign policy activity of Ukraine in

what concerns the Autonomous Republic of Crimea (Constitution of Crimea, 1998, Article 18, par. 3)

11. The call of regular elections for members of the Supreme Rada of the Autonomous Republic of Crimea, approval of members of the election committee of the Autonomous Republic of Crimea and solution of any and all other matters of organization and holding of elections abides by the Ukrainian legislation (Constitution of Crimea, 1998, Article 18, par. 6)

12. The powers of the Supreme Rada of the Autonomous Republic of Crimea may be terminated by the Supreme Rada of Ukraine before the expiry of its term on the grounds and in accordance with the procedure determined by the Constitution of Ukraine (Constitution of Crimea, 1998, Article, 22, par. 1)

13. Justice in the Autonomous Republic of Crimea is carried out by courts which belong to the unique system of courts of Ukraine (Constitution of Ukraine, 1996, Article 136, par. 5)

14. The local self-government in the Autonomous Republic of Crimea shall be exercised under the Constitution of Ukraine and Ukrainian laws (Constitution of Crimea, 1998, Article 42, par. 1)

15. The Supreme Rada of the Autonomous Republic of Crimea may, following an advisory republican (local) referendum, make motions on alterations regarding the limitation of the status and powers of the Autonomous Republic of Crimea, the Supreme Rada of the Autonomous Republic of Crimea and the Council of Ministers of the Autonomous Republic of Crimea, as determined by the Constitution of Ukraine and Ukrainian laws (Constitution of Crimea, 1998, Article 48, par. 2).

As emerges from the joint analysis of the Constitutions of Ukraine and Crimea, the kind of settlement that was finally reached between the two sides had more to do with a thorough institutionalization of a cultural autonomy, similar to that granted to the previously examined case of Gagauzia, than with a political considerations-inclusive one. The latter could have served as the starting point of an all-inclusive state, where anarchy-associated security concerns would have been constrained, and in which all the formerly suppressed (Soviet era) and embattled (critical juncture period) citizens-ethnic groups could participate on an equal basis. Moreover, it could lead to the gradual reinstatement of social trust, both *vis-à-vis* the state institutions as well as throughout the society, setting the foundations for the upgrading from an "atomized" perception of living towards a "civic" one. What Crimea was offered, instead, was, qualitatively different. Although there was indeed a Constitution providing for the fundamental structure of government, this was seriously curtailed, with the Ukrainian side to retain the final say in every development (Points 3–6, 10–13). As earlier noted, the powers granted to the Crimean side, albeit a major step towards a permanent settlement, focused primarily, if not solely, on the cultural sphere and on issues of "low" politics, with any reference made to the participation of Crimea in issues of "high" politics, such as the foreign policy, to be constrained only to those issues that concerned the "Autonomous Republic of Crimea" (Point 9). Consequently, they did not take into account situations which may have had serious repercussions on Crimea and the Eastern parts of the country; such a situation has diachronically been the (geo)political orientation of Ukraine, with the EU and Russia to exert major influence on the country's domestic politics.

In parallel, aside from issues of "regional political preferences" that the settlement was lacking, the economic ones were also lagging; the establishment of a firm, and ideally self-standing, economic basis, holds an important role, as has already been shown in the cases of Transdniestria and Gagauzia. Crimea's economic self-sufficiency and development fell within the approval of the Constitution of Ukraine and the laws of Ukraine (Points 8, 9). Issues relating to investments, incentives to (foreign) investors, establishment of free economic zones, exports of local products, foreign economic activity, development of science and technology, all were dependent upon endorsement by the Cabinet of Ministers of Ukraine (Constitution of Crimea, 1998, Article 18, par. 11). Nevertheless, doing justice to this bilateral settlement, a reference should be made to the right of the Supreme Soviet of the Autonomous Republic of Crimea to advance demands for revisions concerning the status and the powers of the Autonomous Republic of Crimea and its state institutions, pursuant a local referendum.

Like in Crimea, the Ukrainian independence impacted negatively on the people of Donbass and the remainder of the south-eastern regions. With Russians far from being a negligible part of the local population (44% and 23%, respectively), the Ukrainian independence stood little chances, if any, than being viewed as an act of "nationalism and separatism" (Solchanyk, 1994, p. 59; State Statistics Committee of Ukraine, 2004). Consequently, sentiments of regionalism reactively erupted, allying otherwise "atomized" rational actors upon fundamental elements of the "ethnic" type of identity (i.e., non-inclusive perception of ethnicity and language, hoping, first and foremost, for survival and security).

Numerous local movements were formed in pursuit of two goals. First, the preservation of the USSR by all means.[2] Should this prove unfeasible, autonomy within a (federated) Ukraine would be the ideal scenario. The regional political leadership, nevertheless, while it did endorse this course of action, it paid particular attention to keeping the balance between its true demands and what it could, indeed, be attained, so it did steer away from maximalist positions such as the federalization (Solchanyk, 1994, p. 60). Truth be told, the main concern of the south-eastern regions, and Donbass, in particular, had to do less, if at all, with politics, and more, if not exclusively, with economics. Having, diachronically, been Ukraine's "industrial heart," a stronger say in the economic affairs of the nascent independent country was above critical (State Statistics Service of Ukraine, 2010, p. 26). As portrayed by the words of the leader of the Donetsk Miners' Strike Committee in 1993:

> We're interested in greater regional self-determination for the Donbass, not separatism nor ever the type of autonomy the Crimea has. We contribute a large proportion of revenue to Ukraine and get almost nothing in return. Now we want to decide how much to give Kiev, not vice versa. (Solchanyk, 1994, p. 61)

Assessing, in brief, what has been so far discussed, it becomes apparent that the eastern part of the country exhibited a far more acquiescent profile in terms of autonomy, compared with Crimea's "tie-breaking" one. The latter pushed for an autonomy that, in essence, was a power-sharing within a feder-ated Ukraine, whereas the former called for an autonomy focused, primarily, on economics, seeing decentralization and upgrading of local self-govern-ment as the best guarantee. (Sotiriou, 2016, pp. 3–4)

Once the collapse of the USSR and the Ukrainian independence became facts, the sensitivity of the abovementioned regions to the "Russia factor," either this being in terms of language and ethnicity, or just security provision by Russia or broader organizations it did oversight, such as the CIS, acquired particular significance.

Accounting for and further substantiating this sensitivity, a concise histor-ical-political elaboration on the region's past is rather illuminating. To begin with, the lands of south-eastern Ukraine have been presenting an intimacy with the Russian lifestyle since the last quarter of the eighteenth century, when the then Tsarist Russia annexed them from the Zaporozhian Cossacks, the Crimean Khanate, and the Ottoman Turkey, and onward the Russian influence started to spread throughout (Canadian Institute of Ukrainian Stud-ies, 2001). In 1812, they would be trisected to the Katerynoslav, Kherson and Tavriia provinces for administrative purposes, only to be expanded further until 1917, with the inclusion into their borders of the Stavropol region and the provinces of Bessarabia and that of the Don Cossacks (Canadian, Insti-tute of Ukrainian Studies, 2001). As soon as the USSR was officially formed in 1922, the biggest part of these lands was incorporated into the Ukrainian SSR, with Crimea, however, remaining within the RSFSR until 1954, when it would be, finally, transferred to the Ukrainian SSR as well (Solchanyk, 1994, p. 47).

Having said that, the question that plausibly emerges is: how did the "Russia factor" reverberate across the Ukrainian society in the post-soviet period, and what dynamics were at play? Below, a set of issues was examined throughout the country, allowing for polarization tendencies to come to the fore (table 3.1).

In particular, "place of residence," "nationality," "language," and "religion" were the most critical variables affecting polarization between the western and the eastern parts of the country. When the impact of the "Russia factor" was examined, either directly (items 2, 4, 5) or indirectly (items 1, 3), "place of residence" along with "religion" had the highest polarizing effect. Consequently, the eastern parts of the country, where 61% of the residents espoused the Ukrainian Orthodox faith (Kievan), had a high sensitivity towards the "Russia factor."

EN ROUTE TO THE 2013–2015 CRISIS: SOCIO-POLITICAL DEVELOPMENT AND QUALITY OF LIFE

With these dynamics on the ground, it is essential to see how critical variables, besides regional political preferences, for a population's mobilization, such as socio-political development and quality of life, turned out in the

Table 3.1. Degree of Item Polarization in Ukraine across Regions and Demographic Categories, 1995

Items	Geographic region: east/ west (%)	Nationality: Russian/ Ukrainian (%)	Language most frequently used: Russian/ Ukrainian (%)	Religion: Orthodox Kiev/Greek Orthodox (%)
1. Ukrainian language only for public business	-55.7	-21.2	-26.5	-63.7
2. Ukraine should join federation with Russia	38.3	27.2	19.5	25.4
3. Ukraine alone should control Black Sea Fleet	-32.5	-25.1	-21.6	-42.7
4. Ukrainians and Russians have basically the same culture	23.6	22.3	18.3	40.8
5. Russian immigrants should have full rights	20.9	27.0	24.0	42.3

Note: Percentage point difference in levels of agreement between categories

Source: Hesli, Reisinger, and Miller, 1998, p. 241

country. Measuring the former in terms of national identity type and the
second in terms of unemployment and GDP per capita, PPP, Ukraine exhibited a rather feeble profile; in fact, this was reflected on alarming incidents,
such as the country-dividing Orange revolution in 2004, that someone could
argue that it had served as a forewarning of the imminent critical juncture of
2014, should the course of the country continued unabated (Gorenburg,
2011; Kuzio, 2007).[3]

In further detail, table 3.2 provides a thorough examination of Ukraine's
socio-political development, or, better, the ailing situation of it.

Among the major ethnic groups (Ukrainians and Russians), the type of
national identity that was dominant was the "atomized," with 51.3% of
Ukrainians and 53.7% of Russians feeling as rational actors in a condition
pretty much resembling that of the anarchy-like early independence period.
The "ethnic" type of national identity ranked far lower, with only 25.1% of
Ukrainians and 27.7% of Russians experiencing a sense of ethnic kinship,
while the "civic" type, which is met in mature democracies with efficient
institutional structures, held the third place, with very low percentages for
both Ukrainians and Russians (15.5% and 13.8%, respectively). The prevalence of the "atomized" and the "ethnic" type of national identity, which
cumulatively reached 76.4% for Ukrainians and 81.4% for Russians, signaled the absence of social trust as a result of a feeble and inefficient institutional structure (Paraskevopoulos 2001, p. 259; Putnam, Leonardi, and Nanetti, 1993). Moreover, it indicated that from the early independence period
up to 2013, the alignment of "atomized" rational actors under regional political preferences as a means of survival and security remained intact.

Passing, now, to the fundamental economic variables related to the quality of life, below, "unemployment" and "GDP per capita PPP" are analyzed
in a manner that juxtaposes Ukraine and Russia (figures 3.1 and 3.2), given
that (a) the eastern parts had a diachronic sensitivity to the "Russia factor"
and (b) Russia would become heavily involved in Ukraine's anew critical

Table 3.2.   National Identity Types within Ukraine's Major Ethnic Groups

Ethnic group	Atomized (%)	Ethnic (%)	Hybrid (%)	Civic (%)
Ukrainians	51.3	25.1	8.0	15.5
Russians	53.7	27.7	4.8	13.8
Crimean Tatars	23.6	41.2	26.1	9.0
Hungarians	53.0	14.0	6.5	26.5
Roma	49.4	7.6	2.3	40.7

Source: Hansen and Hesli, 2009, p. 7

juncture of 2013–2015, capitalizing on existent perceptions and forging new, *de facto*, dynamics. The lines in figure 3.2 are the same as figure 3.1 (L to R, Ukraine, Russia, Trend Line (Ukraine), and Trend Line (Russia).

To begin with, the examination of unemployment between the two critical junctures in the country's post-soviet history is quite revealing. Although Russia was in worse condition throughout the 1990s, and only from 2000s onward seemed to bounce back, the truth is that the prospects of the two economies were antithetic from the very beginning.

Assessing Ukraine's and Russia's trend lines, it becomes apparent that from the early 1990s all the way to the crisis period of 2013–2015, the two countries had been following a diverging course. Russia, despite its comparatively worse scores, had been moving in a positive trajectory, and every year the problem of unemployment was being constrained. On the contrary, Ukraine, despite its comparatively better scores, had been pursuing a negative trajectory, with the problem of unemployment to expand year by year. Proceeding one step further and judging from the slope of each line, it could also be argued that the progress in the case of Russia was drastic, further highlighted by the expediting deterioration in the case of Ukraine.

Proceeding the "GDP per capita, PPP," the situation between the two countries had been clear from the early independence period onward, both in terms of figures and trend lines.

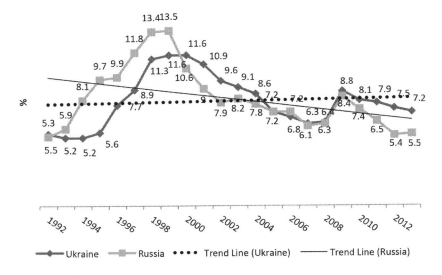

Figure 3.1.   Total unemployment (% of total labor force) (modeled ILO estimate). Source: World Bank, 2018a.

Citizens in Russia had been in a much better and promising economic situation compared to those in Ukraine, since not only the incomes were way higher, but also the prospects, as emerge from the trend lines, were far more optimistic. Focusing on the trend lines, and particularly to the slope of each one, it is apparent that in the case of Russia progress in the increase of the GDP per capita, PPP is occurring in a very accelerated pace, surpassing by far that in the case of Ukraine, where the slope of the line, albeit upwards, is very slight.

All of that having been said, and having substantiated Ukraine's protractedly weak and compartmentalized statehood between the two critical junctures in the country's post-soviet course, below, the 2013–2015 crisis is in the spotlight. In essence, the latter corroborates the thus far argumentation that, in a crisis, such as that of 2013–2015, where Russia would extensively intervene, (lasting) regional political preferences, embedded in a fragmented and porous national identity framework, unemployment, and weak economic growth, would serve as catalysts of overall destabilization in the eastern parts of the country, and primarily in Crimea. Donbass, nevertheless, and particularly Donetsk and Luhansk, would not follow in Crimea's footsteps, given that their preferences lacked a solid and steadfast political claim, being mostly focused on economic parameters.

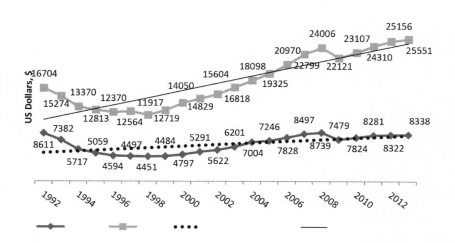

Figure 3.2. GDP per capita, PPP (constant 2011 international $). Source: World Bank, 2018a

THE CRISIS OF 2013–2015 AND REGIONAL POLITICAL PREFERENCES

Crimea

The second critical juncture in Ukraine's post-soviet history took a more radical turn on February 21, 2014, when President Yanukovych and the leaders of the opposition signed an agreement, which, *inter alia*, provided for the raging mobilization to come to an end, for the government shake up with the aim of forming an interim national unity one, and, finally, for new elections by the year end (Meyers, 2014; Walker, 2014). Although that agreement could have mollified the all the more widening and deepening standoff, Yanukovych had already been in a plight; with its legitimacy to plummet, members of his own political party, the Party of Regions, sought their survival and security by distancing themselves, a stance also upheld by the army. At the same time, the mobilization was persisting in defiance of the agreement (Sotiriou, 2015, p. 216). Before the ink was dry, Yanukovych fled Kiev towards an unknown destination (Walker, 2014).

Not losing a minute, the opposition initiated impeachment proceedings and expedited elections for May 25, 2014 (Walker, 2014). In particular, by a 328/450 majority, the law-makers decided to impeach the President on charges of leaving office and being responsible for the death of 80 protesters (Sindelar, 2014). This majority, however, was in violation of the Constitution of Ukraine, which stipulates a three-fourths majority, i.e., 338 votes (Constitution of Ukraine, 1996, Article 111). Regardless of the objections by the Yanukovych side on a coup d'état, and Russia's denial to approve of any political action taken, the opposition proceeded in appointing Oleksandr Turchynov as Ukraine's interim President until May 25, 2014, with his temporal mandate to include also further rapprochement with the EU (Pravda.ru, 2014; Zabrodina, 2014).

From that point onward, the events acquired an irreversible flux. Domestically, the fighting started to exhibit the features of a civil war, with pro-EU groups to be more assertively positioned against pro-Russian ones and *vice-versa*. In Crimea, Kiev's *contra constitutionem* actions were perceived as a reality to steer clear from and maintain order, a stance which would also be adopted by many cities of the eastern parts, namely Kharkov, Donetsk, Luhansk, and Dnipropetrovsk (Agamalova and Raibman, 2014; Interfax.ru, 2014a; Raibman, 2014; Salem et al., 2014). Internationally, the EU and the US were appealing to Russia for quadrilateral negotiations with the Turchynov administration, at the same time that Russia was abstaining from any recognition of the latter on grounds legitimacy (RIA Novosti, 2014; *Rossiĭskaia Gazeta*, 2014).

Russia, caught between the hammer of the illegitimate, according to Ukraine's Constitution, west-leaning and west-recognized Turchynov administration, and the anvil of a profoundly divided and polarized society between pro-EU and pro-Russia insurgents, decided, unilaterally, to resort to military action as *ultima ratio* (Sotiriou, 2015, p. 217). In particular, following a referendum which was conducted in the peninsula on March 16, 2014, in the presence of Russian soldiers, the green men with their insignia hidden as they became widely known, and qualified the accession of Crimea to Russia by 96% of the votes, Russia annexed Crimea on March 18, 2014 (Lally, 2014; Sneider, 2014).[4]

The instant reaction to these military advances was an international outcry, followed by the UN Security Council unsuccessful efforts to adopt a text prompting member-states to abstain from any recognition of these actions (United Nations, 2014). With no middle ground to have been left, Russia and Crimea set also the legal foundations for their reunification (Interfax.ru, 2014b).

While Russia's involvement in Ukraine's domestic affairs during the 2013–2015 crisis is a fact and holds a role in the overall course of events, this should not overshadow the striking resemblance of the events in point with those of the early post-soviet period (first critical juncture). Thus, scratching under the surface, the role of (lasting) regional political preferences and how they evolved all the way up to the 2013–2015 crisis acquire particular interest.

Table 3.3 shows that midway to the 2013–2015 crisis, Crimea's political preference of seceding from Ukraine and unifying with Russia (item 1) was the dominant one as far as the region's political future is concerned. Following suit, the preservation of the current status of autonomy within Ukraine with expanded, however, rights and powers (item 2) was endorsed by 54.7% of Crimea's Ukrainians, 53% of Crimea's Russians, and 57.6% of the Crimean Tatars. This item refers to the moribund 1992 Constitution, as can plausibly be inferred from its juxtaposition to item 5, and it is noteworthy that it was one of the two choices offered during the referendum on March 16, 2014.

Finally, Russian national autonomy as a part of Ukraine (item 3), and independence (item 4), scored lower in the preferences of the citizens of Crimea, with the upholding of the current status quo (item 5) to meet the least support.

Taking a closer look, the approval ratings of the major ethnic groups (Russians and Ukrainians), as illustrated in items 1 and 2, call for particular attention; while 55.2% of Ukrainians put its weight behind item 1, the very same moment another 54.7% qualified item 2. Similarly, 75.9% of Russians singled out item 1, with a 53% advocating also item 2. On the basis of these overlaps and divisiveness certain inferences can be made:

Table 3.3. Political Preferences in Crimea as of 2008 (% of Polled)

Would you like Crimea to . . . ?		Nationality (Crimea)		
		Ukrainians	Russians	Crimea Tatars
1. Secede from Ukraine and join Russia	Yes	55.2	75.9	13.8
	No	29.7	13.6	68.5
	Hard to say	15.1	10.5	17.7
2. Preserve its current status of the autonomy as a part of Ukraine with expanded rights and powers	Yes	54.7	53.0	57.6
	No	22.8	28.3	29.7
	Hard to say	22.5	18.7	12.7
3. Become Russian national autonomy as a part of Ukraine	Yes	32.3	40.1	5.9
	No	40.7	33.7	75.5
	Hard to say	27.0	26.2	18.6
4. Secede from Ukraine and become an independent State	Yes	35.2	34.7	30.1
	No	43.4	35.5	46.8
	Hard to say	21.4	29.8	23.1
5. Preserve its current status of the autonomy as a part of Ukraine with existing rights and powers	Yes	27.9	17.9	28.3
	No	42.7	51.5	53.3
	Hard to say	29.4	30.6	18.4

Source: Razumkov Center, 2008, p. 20

- the demand for the 1992 Constitution (item 2) indicates, first and fore-most, the strained relations with Kiev as well as the limited success of nation-building process throughout the post-soviet era. But, secondly, next to this negative picture, the federation-leaning prospects lurking within the provisions of the 1992 Constitution were perceived as a satisfactory means which could assuage survival and security concerns, laying the ground-work for a functioning state, and for the gradual accumulation of social trust in the place of the prevalent "atomized" national identity throughout the country.
- Should this course of events within Ukraine proved fruitless, the "Russia factor" could serve as a luring outlet to foster for the political and econom-ic security of the region.

All in all, "opinions of Crimeans, regarding the desired future of their region were rather controversial and unsteady, which made them vulnerable to inter-nal and external influences" (Razumkov Center, 2008, p. 19). Undoubtedly, the March 2014 referendum, which would go ahead in the presence of Rus-

sian soldiers who operated in the framework of a pro-Russia public dis-
course, would corroborate the veracity of the aforementioned assumption
(Zabrodina, 2014b).

Even further, almost a year before Crimea's *de facto* annexation by Russia and six months prior Ukraine entered the 2013–2015 crisis, in May 2013,
63% of Crimea's Russians prioritized the "Russian" attribute of their identity, 29% "Crimean," and 3% "Ukrainian" (IRI, 2013). Likewise, 66% of
Crimea's Ukrainians prioritized the "Ukrainian" attribute of their identity,
19% "Crimean," and 10% "Russian." Both cases further affirm the preservation of the above-mentioned inferences, that of strained relations with Kiev
and the need for an "eleventh-hour" federation-leaning restructuring of the
Ukrainian state, and that of the progressively mounting effect of the "Russian
factor," turning critical in case of physical presence (IRI, 2013).

Reaching, now, the crisis period and "pausing" the time two days before
the referendum on March 16, 2014, not much of a change was observed out
there; the endo-Ukrainian developments remained stagnant, sinking, all the
more, into intractability, while Russia started to weigh more and more in the
course of events. In this context, political preferences in Crimea adopted their
radical and uncompromising version.

Seeing table 3.4, the course towards Russia had been put primary emphasis on, whereas any desire to reinstate the 1992 Constitution, as a means of
rebooting relations with Kiev, had been evaporated. In particular, item 1
shows that 70.6% of Crimea's citizens would choose unification with Russia
in the referendum set for March 16, 2014, with the option of restoring the
1992 Constitution to score as low as 10.8%. While a couple of years ago
(2008) (table 3.3), the 1992 Constitution could have been an option upon
which to build a common future within Ukraine, in the years that ensued any
faith in reversing the souring relations with Kiev had been lost. To this
direction points also item 2, with 67% of the respondents to have been
complacent with the either/or structure of the upcoming March 16, 2014,
referendum. Finally, items 3 and 4 complete the picture, with the part of
Crimea's citizens which prioritized the "Ukrainian" attribute of its identity to
have been constrained to 21.3%, and the course towards Russia to pose as
irreversible, since the break down in the relations between Kiev and Crimea
was so irrevocable, that nothing could talk Crimea's citizens out of it, not
even the presence of the Russian troops.

In a nutshell, table 3.4. corroborates and concludes the so far argumentation, closing the circle by sort of reproducing the findings of table 3.3, this
time, however, presenting the dominant option in its "highly likely" form.
Truth be told, that option was confirmed by the events that ensued (96%
voted for the unification in the March 16, 2014, referendum), thus showing
that in a crisis, such as that of 2013–2015, where Russia would extensively
intervene, (lasting) regional political preferences, embedded in a fragmented

Table 3.4. Political preferences in Crimea (March 12–14, 2014)

Items asked	Answers	%
1. Which option on referendum on Sunday will you choose?	• Joining Crimea with the Russian Federation as a subject of the Russian Federation	70.6
	• Restoration of the 1992 Crimean Constitution and Crimea's status as a part of Ukraine	10.8
	• Don't know/No opinion	12.9
2. This referendum will offer voters only the above two choices. Would you prefer the referendum offer more choices?	• Yes	25.6
	• No	67.0
	• Don't know/No opinion	7.5
3. How do you feel most comfortable describing your identity?	• Russian	54.8
	• Ukrainian	21.3
	• Tatar	9.9
	• I have no mixed/more than one identity	7.1
	• None of these describe me	4.7
	• Hard to answer/Refuse	2.3
4. Do you think the presence of Russian troops is likely or unlikely to influence how freely people vote in the referendum?	• Highly likely	13.4
	• Somewhat likely	9.9
	• Somewhat unlikely	15.6
	• Highly unlikely	49.3
	• Don't know/No opinion	11.7

Source: GfK Ukraine, 2014

and porous national identity framework, unemployment, and weak economic growth, would serve as catalysts of overall destabilization in the eastern parts of the country, and primarily in Crimea. Below, the case of Donbass takes its turn in the spotlight.

Donbass

Parallel with Crimea, general mobilization and heavy fighting was taking place also in other regions of the eastern part of the country, and particularly in numerous cities of Donbass. Brutal encounters between Pro-EU and Pro-Russia groups were the main theme, with the latter to take hold of government buildings in the cities of Donetsk, Luhansk, and elsewhere, in April 2014, and transform them into self-styled People's Republics (Felgenhauer,

2014; Herszenhorn and Roth, 2014b). In addition, they appealed to Russia's President, Vladimir Putin, to dispatch troops as a peacekeeping force, while, at the same moment, they were committed to going ahead with a referendum on May 11, 2014, on secession from Ukraine and unification with Russia, following the example of Crimea (Chivers and Herszenhorn, 2014).

The authorities in Kiev were taken by tension and uneasiness; perceiving the developments as a Russia-orchestrated effort to repeat the Crimean precedent, they sent the Ukrainian forces to claim back the occupied administration buildings, terminating self-proclaimed People's Republics, such as the "Kharkiv Republic" (Herszenhorn and Roth, 2014a; TCN, 2014). Adding a comparative perspective, interesting is the fact that in the case of Crimea no such radical mobilization on behalf of Kiev had taken place (Bugriy, 2014). But, Russia's reactions were different too.

In talks held regarding Ukraine's possible federalization as means of defusing the crisis, Putin maintained on May 7, 2014, that he would "ask the representatives of South Ukraine [who] support federalization to delay the referendum planned for May 11, to create conditions for dialogue" (Felgenhauer, 2014).[5] In this manner, Russia kept a distance from the undergoing developments in the eastern regions of the country. As a result, the pro-Russia insurgents got isolated; to provide but an example, Vyachislav Ponomaryov, the self-appointed mayor of Slovyansk, while insisted on conducting the referendum as planned, he made clear that "for now, we should just specify for ourselves that we should definitely secede from Kiev. Then we'll decide for ourselves which path to take further" (Chivers and Herszenhorn, 2014; Interfax.ru, 2014c).

As in the case of Crimea, these lines reveal a deep-seated discontent towards Kiev, which the crisis facilitated to come to the surface. As a matter of fact, the regions of the eastern part of the country had been the most industrialized and those with the largest industrial turnover on a national scale (State Statistics Service of Ukraine, 2010, p. 26). In more detail, Donetsk held the first place with 19.1%, followed by Dnipropetrovsk with 15.6% (State Statistics Service of Ukraine, 2010, p. 26). Luhansk occupied the fourth place with 6.9%, with the rest of the eastern regions to tag along. In view of these and taking into account that the regional preferences of the early post-soviet focused primarily on autonomy on the economic sphere, it plausibly arises that the 2014 explosive ambiance was most probably connected with the same issues. This argument is further pursued later on, when the Minsk agreements, aimed at settling the 2013–2015 crisis, are in the limelight.

Meanwhile, while Russia, *prima facie*, seemed to abstain from the realities being created on the ground, in reality, its troops operated in Ukraine's eastern parts within the context of the "Operation Russian Spring" (Sutyagin, 2015).[6] Moreover, after having responded to the July 2014 advances of the

Ukrainian forces by artillery fire from within the Russian soil, in the middle of August, they assumed active combat roles (Sutyagin, 2015). Nevertheless, by that time, pro-Russia separatists had become further alienated, both socially and militarily, having been accused by angry residents since May 2014 for the violence and instability in the region.[7]

Tense as the overall situation could have possibly got, the first landmark as far as the mobilization in the eastern parts is concerned was reached on September 1, 2014, when the Minsk agreement was signed by the representatives of Ukraine, Russia, and the OSCE.

Minsk Agreement: Key Points

1. Provide monitoring and verification on behalf of the OSCE of the ceasefire.
2. Provide permanent monitoring at the Ukrainian-Russian state border, and verification by the OSCE, with creation of a safety zone in the areas adjacent to the border in Ukraine and the Russian Federation.
3. Conduct decentralization of power, including through the approval of the Law of Ukraine "On temporary order of local self-government in certain districts of the cities of Donetsk and Luhansk (Law on special status)."
4. Conduct early elections in accordance with the Law of Ukraine "On temporary order of local self-government in certain districts of the cities of Donetsk and Luhansk (Law on special status)." (OECD, 2014)

The main points of the Minsk agreement revolve around three pillars: (a) the return to normality, with the termination of hostilities between the two belligerents and the implementation of a credible ceasefire (point 1), (b) the monitoring of Russia's role in the developments by controlling the Ukrainian-Russian state border and setting up a safety zone in the neighboring areas of the common border (point 3), and (c) the decentralization of power (points 3 and 4).

A closer look, allows the inference that the core demand slipping through the provisions of the Minsk agreement had to do with the decentralization of power; that would pave the way for the re-establishment of the relationship between the regions of the eastern part and Kiev upon a more balanced basis, especially as far as economic relations are concerned. The "Russia factor" holds a marginal role and is referred to indirectly (point 2), just to keep the prospects of a powerful neighbor affecting the crisis in check. The Mink agreement had also been signed by the Russian ambassador to Ukraine, a fact that reveals Russia's awareness of the endo-Ukrainian structural discrepancies, the power struggles among regions, as well as the role it could hold in these fragile power dynamics, much more when these were materializing in an anarchy-resembling socio-political environment, rife with the "atomized" type of national identity.

Despite the early hopes arising from the agreement, these soon proved futile, with the hostilities to continue unabated, particularly in the cities of Donetsk and Luhansk, as a result of Kiev's inelasticity towards implementing key-provisions (points 3 and 4) (Fedyakina 2014). Russia, on its side, witnessing the atrocities prolonging, increased its troops in the field to approximately 10,000 in December 2014 (Sutyagin, 2015). The conditions for a second Minsk agreement were already in place.

On February 11, 2015, the second Mink agreement was signed, with its core demand remaining that of the decentralization of power.

Minsk Agreement II: Key Points

1. Ensuring effective monitoring and verification of the ceasefire regimes and of the withdrawal of heavy weapons by the OSCE.
2. Conduct of constitutional reform in Ukraine with a new Constitution entering into force by the end of 2015, providing for the decentralization as a key element (including a reference to the specificities of certain areas in the cities of Donetsk and Luhansk, agreed with the representatives of these areas), as well as adopting permanent legislation on the special status of certain areas of the cities of Donetsk and Luhansk.
3. The organs of local self-government of Donetsk and Luhansk are entrusted with the power to participate in the appointments of the heads of the prosecutor's office as well as of the courts in certain areas of Donetsk and Luhansk.
4. The organs of local self-government of Donetsk and Luhansk are entrusted with the power to clinch agreements with the organs of the central authorities as far as issues of economic, social and cultural development of certain areas of Donetsk and Luhansk are concerned. (Minsk soglasheniya, 2015)

In particular, a more concrete basis was set, according to which the adoption of a permanent legislation on the special status of certain areas in Donetsk and Luhansk, would become part of a new Ukrainian Constitution, due for the end of 2015 the latest. Elaborating on the context of the special status, points 2.1 and 2.2 are of particular assistance. Initially, point 2.1 indicated the heavily distrustful environment that had been created between the regions of the eastern part and the Ukrainian authorities, which it aimed at alleviating by stipulating for the participation of the organs of local self-government in Donetsk and Luhansk in the appointment of the heads of the prosecutor's office and of regional courts by the organs of the central authorities. A step further, point 2.2 entrusted the organs of local self-government of Donetsk and Luhansk with the power to conclude agreements with the organs of the central authorities, as far as economic, social, and cultural issues of certain areas of Donetsk and Luhansk are concerned. In this manner, security concerns were addressed, and the region's preferences were thoroughly illuminated; in essence, the demands sought for a reboot of the eastern parts' primarily economic relations with Kiev, exhibiting no vital political demands, as it had happened in the case of Crimea. Drawing the parallel, an analogy could be made, parallelizing, *mutatis mutandis*, Crimea with Transdniestria and Donetsk and Luhansk with Gagauzia.

Summarizing the gist of everything that has been so far discussed, a nation-wide poll that was being intermittently conducted from 2006 to 2012 is rather insightful; in particular, in the question "Is Ukraine threatened by. . . ?" the answer that each time ranked first was "Ukrainian authorities," endorsed by 40% of the respondents in 2006, 50.6% in 2009, 33.4% in 2011, and 35.3% in 2012 (Razumkov Center, 2014).

CONCLUSION

The main takeaway from the latest "frozen conflict" in Eurasia is the anatomy of the crisis in Crimea (substantiating causality). The second major eruption period (critical juncture of the Crisis period) was 2013–2015.

Regional political preference: Federation-leaning restructuring of the Ukrainian state / if not, unification with Russia

No regional political preference: Greater self-administration, focus on economic issues / included as a core-clause in the Minsk agreements

The collapse of the USSR created an abrupt pass from a fully regulated environment to a fully deregulated one, where former Soviet citizens would have to strive as "atomized" rational actors, primarily, for their survival and security. In this effort, human nature-connected attributes, such as family, language, ethnicity, would serve as connective strands for an alliance that would see the institutionalization of its political standing (i.e., the right to exist as a governable entity) as the most fundamental means of survival and security. In this context, post-soviet Ukraine would have to deal with the cases of Crimea and the regions of the eastern part of the country from the early independence period. Crimea, on the one hand, strove towards the reinstatement of its 1945–1946 abolished republican status in the form of a federation-leaning full-grown autonomy, with referendums and a Declaration of Independence by the Crimean Parliament in August 1992 to indicate its determination. Donbass, on the other hand, and particularly Donetsk and Luhansk, sought greater self-determination, considering their big input to the country's budget; as a matter of fact, multiple regional movements called for autonomy, especially with regard to economic issues.

The solidification of the new institutional equilibrium, with both Ukraine's and Crimea's Constitutions to be enacted in 1996 and 1998 respectively, typically ended the critical juncture period of the early post-soviet years (1991–1996), without, however, intercepting early efforts towards top-down integration of the nationalities. It is a hard to deny fact, that these efforts bore very little success, since as data of 2009 showed, a few years prior the 2013–2015 crisis period was initiated, the dominant type of national identity across the country had been the "atomized." This type exhibits the evaporation of social trust as well as the inefficiency of state institutions as far as an inclusive nation-building process is concerned. Moreover, in this protractedly inauspicious situation, the economic hardships of the country were also included, given that the first thing a population highly values, following the institutionalization of its political standing, is the quality life, reflected primarily on the variables "GDP per capita, PPP" and "unemployment." On this basis, the analysis demonstrated that in a crisis, such as that of 2013–2015, where Russia would be heavily involved, (lasting) regional political preferences, embedded within a fragmented and porous national identity framework, unemployment, and weak economic growth, would function as catalysts of general destabilization, primarily in Crimea. Donbass, and Donetsk and Luhansk in particular, although affected by the overall mobilization, would not follow in Crimea's footsteps, given that their preferences lacked a solid and steadfast political claim.

So it happened. The 2013–2015 crisis brought to light the simmering regional political preferences of the early-post-soviet period following a circular pattern. In Crimea, the trust in state institutions was in a freefall, with citizens seeing the repeated calls for the upgrading of Crimea's autonomous status within Ukraine to fall on deaf ears. With no extra rights and powers to be on the table for Crimea, the citizens, weeks before the region was annexed by Russia, had started to become more Russia-oriented, perceiving the region's unification with Russia as a "gateway" from an otherwise insecure and sub-functioning state, where a stagnant social, political, and economic situation was thriving.

In the Donbass region a similar circularity was observed. Just like in the early post-soviet years, the region called for the decentralization of power (or upgrading of the self-administration status) in particular districts of the wealth-producing cities of Donetsk and Luhansk, demanding also the implementation of the Law on Special Status and the codification of the all these changes in a new Constitution. The demands were heard, as they were included as core-clauses in the Minsk agreements of September 2014 and February 2015.

Adopting a more detached look at the issue of decentralization, the truth is that it permeated the very structure of the Ukraine's socio-political edifice. The state-periphery relations in the country were once established in the 1996 Constitution, and ever since remained unchanged all the period leading up to the 2013–2015 crisis. The institutional structure at regional (*oblast*) and sub-regional (*rayon*) level was comprised by directly elected assemblies and regional and sub-regional state-administrations. The latter functioned as "dual feedback" executive bodies, representing both the assemblies elected at the local level and the central government in Kiev (Shapovalova, 2014, p. 3). Their leadership was fully and exclusively accountable to the President, who appointed or dismissed them, following a proposal by the cabinet of ministers (Shapovalova, 2014, p. 3). To make their power far more conceivable, it is mentioned that the 80% of the national revenue that constituted the state budget was channeled back to the regions and sub-regions solely via these state administrations (Shapovalova, 2014, p. 3). Consequently, there was a "top-down" institutional structure, which deprived the local authorities of any flexibility and adaptability to the local needs, since any resources for the provision of basic services remained reliant on the central government and the President (Shapovalova, 2014, p. 3). Such an institutional arrangement in conditions where regional political preferences were strong, the "atomized" type of national identity was rife, and diachronic structural deficiencies were challenging the economy, more expedited the course towards the critical events of 2013–2015, than hedged the country's bets. It also in this logic that the "Russia factor" was included in the current analysis as a contextual variable, which functioned more as a "turn-on" that reactivated in the most uncompromising and *de facto* manner long-lasting structural deficiencies of the Ukrainian political system, and less as an "aggressor."[8]

NOTES

1. In March 1995 the parliament of Ukraine abolished the 1992 Constitution of Crimea, and from June until September 1995, the whole region was governed by a direct Presidential administration decree issued by the then Ukrainian President, Leonid Kuchma. In October 1995, the parliament of Crimea adopted a new Constitution, which, after many back-and-forths between the Crimean and the Ukrainian authorities, was, finally, ratified by both sides in 1998 and came into effect on January 12, 1999. For the ratification of the Constitution of the Autonomous Republic of Crimea, as well as for the relations that were established between the two parties, see: (Constitution of Ukraine, 1996, Article 1, 2; Constitution of Crimea, 1998). The phrase "a kind of arrangement" in the main text serves to highlight the fact that, when the Crimean crisis broke out in 2014 and Ukraine seemed to sink back into an era of institutional fluidity similar to that of the late 1980s early 1990s, the 1998 Crimean Constitution was repealed by Kiev in the aftermath of a disputed referendum on Crimea's status, conducted in March 2014.

2. For these local movements in the regions in point, see Solchanyk, 1994, pp. 59–61.

3. The Orange revolution seriously divided Ukraine between its western and eastern parts, but in a far more moderate and reversible way, given that all demonstrations, strikes and

various other acts of civil disobedience resulted in no deaths (expect for one man who died of a heart attack). Moreover, the whole crisis was defused through institutional means; in particular, the country's Supreme Court ordered a revote between the two main candidates, the eastern parts-preferred Viktor Yanukovych and the western parts-preferred Viktor Yushchenko, only to declare the latter as winner with 52% of the vote. In contrast, in the critical juncture of 2014, that strikingly resembled that of the early independence period, the events entered an irreversible death spiral, which not only would leave numerous dead as a result of an intractable civil war, but would also culminate in the institutional dead-end of Crimea's accession to the Russian Federation.

4. That referendum posed two questions, neither one providing for the continuation of the state of affairs as they were (Saideman, 2014). In particular, the questions were "Are you in favor of the reunification of Crimea with Russia as part of the Russian Federation?" and "Are you in favor of restoring the 1992 Constitution and the status of Crimea as part of Ukraine?" Whereas the first question calls for no further clarification, the second one makes reference to Crimea as a political entity being sufficiently and substantially strengthened within Ukraine (Sneider, 2014). In essence, the 1992 Constitution vested the Crimean authorities with broad powers, a fact which would allow them to set independently ties with whichever state they preferred, in the case in point with Russia (Sneider, 2014). Taking this argumentative line a bit further, the 1992 Constitution could be resembled to the demands of Transdniestria and the Kozak Memorandum, in particular, which was, more or less, pushing for the federalization of Moldova. Even more, the fact that the 1992 Constitution was selected over the arrangement that had been codified in the Ukrainian and Crimean Constitution of 1996 and 1998, respectively, indicates that Ukraine's nation-building attempts had been proved of limited success, failing to alleviate the survival and security concerns of the citizens of Crimea and start rebuilding social trust, both fundamental elements of establishing a constantly improving functioning state.

5. For a detailed account on how Russia viewed the prospect of Ukraine's federalization, on the one hand, and how Ukraine considered Russia-orchestrated projects, such as the Customs Union among Russia, Belarus, and Kazakhstan, on the other, see Kommersant.ru, 2014, and Kylymar, 2014.

6. The Russian military operation in Ukraine followed Gerasimov's Doctrine of "Ambiguous Warfare" (Sutyagin, 2015, p. 1).

7. In the same line of reasoning, the influential businessman of the eastern parts, Rinat Akhmetov, accused the separatists of attempting the "genocide of Donbass" (Herszenhorn and Roth, 2014b).

8. Parts of this chapter appear in Stylianos A. Sotiriou (2016), "The irreversibility of history: The case of the Ukrainian crisis (2013–2015)," *Journal of Southeast European and Black Sea Studies*, Vol. 16(1): 51–70.

Chapter Four

The Cases of South Ossetia and Abkhazia (Georgia)

THE REAWAKENING OF UNDERCURRENT DYNAMICS

On August 1, 2008, South Ossetia experienced a new wave of violence, when separatists from the region ceased the opportunity of resumed tensions between South Ossetia and Georgia to blow up a Georgian military vehicle, injuring five Georgian peacekeeping troops (*Financial Times*, 2008). Avenging this action, the Georgian forces hit back, killing six South Ossetian militiamen and leaving others wounded (Olearchyk, 2008). Each side incriminated the other for inciting violence in the mountainous region adjacent to Russia, expediting, in parallel, its evacuation in polar opposite directions; South Ossetians were transported to Vladikavkaz, capital of the North Ossetian republic, in Russia, whereas Georgians fled for other, safer places in Georgia (Amnesty International, 2008, p. 8).

A Russian initiative to convene a UN Security Council emergency meeting on the quickly worsening situation did not succeed in getting the two belligerents to agree against the use of force (Amnesty International, 2008, p. 9). As a result, the initial skirmishes soon revealed their tidal dynamics, with a five-day war to break out at 11:30 pm on August 7, when the Georgian offensive pounded South Ossetia's capital, Tskhinvali (Avaliani et al., 2008). The war quickly soared into a major international incident, enmeshing regional and global powers; Russia, the US and the EU became integral parts, each in its own manner.

Russia, operating within the legal framework that had been created in the aftermath of the first major eruption of the Georgian–South Ossetian conflict, in 1991–1992, dispatched its 58th army in South Ossetia to support its peacekeeping forces there (Izvestya.ru, 2008). The US, which at the time stationed

130 military advisers in Georgia, found itself in a diplomatic predicament; on the one hand, it denied that it had sanctioned the action against South Ossetia, and, on the other hand, it was charged with not doing more to intercept the crisis (*Financial Times*, 2008). Rather illuminating is the statement by Strobe Talbot, the former US deputy secretary of state: "I am quite convinced there was no green light. There was definitely a problem with an insufficiently red light" (*Financial Times*, 2008).[1] Finally, France, then at the helm of the EU rotating presidency, managed, on August 13, to bring the presidents of Georgia and Russia around a six-point peace plan that would stop the war, the second major eruption in the Georgian–South Ossetian conflict in the post-soviet period (Kramer, 2008).

Aside from the international outcry, the 2008 five-day war added numerous internally displaced people (IDPs) to the numbers from the brief civil wars of early 1990s. Resorting to the estimates by the Georgian government and the UN refugee agency, 192,000 IDPs were the immediate outcome. Included in this estimate were 2,500 people displaced from the Georgia-controlled Upper Kodori valley in Abkhazia, Georgia's second breakaway region; in fact, the Abkhaz authorities sought to capitalize on the eruption in South Ossetia to force the remaining Georgians to flee (Amnesty International, 2008, p. 51). Even though most of the IDPs in the end returned to their place of residence, 31,000 people have not (UNHCR, 2008).

Putting things into perspective, Georgia was already hosting 223,000 IDPs from the early 1990s. The extra 31,000 from the August crisis brought the total to 254,000 in the fall of 2008, a number which was revised upward to 289,000 in December 2017 (UNHR, 2008; IDMC, 2018). This upheaval affected the very foundations of the Georgian society, with a displaced woman at the Dila camp on the outskirts of Tbilisi to summarize the pervasive despair as follows: "Why do we need this fighting and the atrocities? Why are they killing us?" (Fawkes, 2008).

With this question in mind, below, the August 2008 crisis is put in a comparative historical continuum which juxtaposes it with the other equally critical period in Georgia's post-soviet history, that of early independence, as far as regional political preferences in South Ossetia and Abkhazia are concerned. An identification, then and now, could substantiate "valid associations of potential causes" through Mill's "method of agreement" (Mill, 1950, p. 344; Skocpol, 1979, p. 36). Moreover, these regional political preferences are assessed in the context of a fragmented, porous, and artificially ethnicized national (Georgian) identity framework. Next to these socio-political factors, economic ones that reflect the quality of life in the country, primarily GDP per capita, PPP, and unemployment, are also included in the analysis, since, as earlier, shown, weigh much in the preferences of the citizens (Bakke et al., 2014). In fact, they are presented in time series, comparing Georgia with Russia for all the years that lie in-between the two major eruption periods (i.e., critical junctures). In this manner, Russia is included in the analysis as a contextual factor, given that it held a role in the developments in both regions. Any impact is confirmed by the correlation of a widening point difference between the two countries as far as the variables in point are concerned with the deterioration of the socio-political situation within Georgia (breakaway regions), and by extension, of its bilateral relations with Russia.

CRITICAL JUNCTURE OF LATE 1980S EARLY 1990S AND REGIONAL POLITICAL PREFERENCES IN SOUTH OSSETIA AND ABKHAZIA

Regional political preferences in South Ossetia and Abkhazia crystallized long before independence, during the Soviet times. In brief, the USSR could be portrayed as a Russian "nesting doll" (матрёшка), comprised by the fifteen SSRs, the highest unit in the administrative hierarchy, and their subunits (ASSRs; autonomous okrugs and autonomous oblasts), each aimed at representing the "fatherland" of a respective nationality (Wheatley, 2009, p. 120). In the case of the Georgian SSR there were two subunits, Abkhazia and Adjara with the status of ASSRs, and a third, South Ossetia, that relished the status of an autonomous oblast (Wheatley, 2009, p. 120).[2]

South Ossetia was an autonomous oblast of the Georgian SSR from 1936 until 1991. During that period, it never ceased to be a separate minority, primarily in the identity-critical element of language; the Eastern Iranian language that was dominant among Ossetians, was not compatible with that of Georgians, thus bringing about a reality, that as of 1988, 86% of Ossetians could not communicate with Georgians (Nielsen, 2009, p. 174). For their part, Georgians perceived the designation of a South Ossetian territory within Georgia as a RSFSR-orchestrated attempt to "divide and rule," thwarting Georgian independence (Birch, 1995, p. 44; Nielsen, 2009, p. 176). This "never-converging" and distrustful co-existence took the downturn in late 1980s, when the Ossetian Popular Front, dubbed Ademon Nykhaz (popular shrine), heavily affected by the "tide of nationalism" that at the time was sweeping across the Soviet territory, condemned what it perceived as Georgianization policy against the Ossetian identity (Nielsen, 2009; Beissinger, 2002). Moreover, it resurfaced the almost seventy-year-old demand (since 1925) for the reversal of the Stalin-era federal structures—which had artificially divided Ossetia into North (within the RSFSR) and South (within Georgia)—thus paving the way for the unification of the two regions, even if this would happen "under the protective wing of Russia" (Birch, 1995, p. 44).

In like manner, Abkhazia, following a period in which it held the status of a SSR and was united with Georgia by treaty, was an ASSR inside the

Georgian SSR from 1931 until 1991 (Nielsen, 2009, p. 175; SSR, 1925). The onset of this co-existence, and particularly the first twenty years, witnessed the suppressing and discriminatory policies of Lavrentii Beria, a Mingrelian born near Sukhumi (Abkhazia's capital), when at the helm of the Communist Party in Transcaucasia. The Abkhaz cultural identity was put at great stake, first, by the in-migration of large numbers of Mingrelians and other Georgians, as well as Russians, and Armenians, that gravely curtailed the representation of the Abkhaz people in the Abkhaz Communist Party (from 28.3% to 18.5%). The Abkhaz-language media were closed down, Russian or Georgian schools replaced all those that offered curriculums in the Abkhaz language, while the Georgian alphabet replaced the Latin script (Slider, 1985, pp. 51–54). These policies, although reversed after the Stalin era, they left their identification mark: the Russian language had risen to the status of *lingua franca*, with the Abkhaz and the Georgian languages to constitute a point of division; 75% of the Abkhaz declared fluency in Russian, and numerous Abkhaz students moved to the RSFSR to attend a university; 56% of the Georgians in Abkhazia claimed the same capacity (Slider, 1985, p. 55). On the contrary, only 1.4% of Abkhaz spoke Georgian, and a meager 0.3% of Georgians living in Abkhazia spoke Abkhaz (Slider, 1985, p. 55). This cleavage within Georgia, "one of the most nationalistic of the Soviet republics," reawaken the Abkhaz nationalist orientation, which since 1930s had been more in favor of "separation from Georgia rather than Russian domination" (Beissinger, 2002, p. 223; Nielsen, 2009, p. 176). As a result, in late 1980s, in tandem with the rise of "Ademon Nykhaz" in South Ossetia, the Abkhaz nationalists allied under their own Abkhaz Popular Front, "Aydgylara," which, although there was no "northern Abkhazia" in Soviet Russia to turn to, appealed to Moscow to protect the Abkhaz interests (Nielsen 2009, 175).[3]

The two cases taken together, the "never-converging" and distrustful environment between the South Ossetian and the Abkhaz, on the one hand, and the highly ethnicized Georgians, on the other, had left very narrow margins of co-existence, if any.[4]

South Ossetia

Shortly before the critical juncture period of early 1990s (1991–1995) and the outbreak of extensive fighting in South Ossetia, Georgia engaged in some policies that polarized political attitudes in the "about-to-explode" regions; in short, in August 1989, its Supreme Soviet passed a language policy that enhanced the status of Georgian, the official language of the SSR, across the public sphere, relegating minority languages such as the Ossetian and Abkhaz, which up to that time relished equal status in minority areas, to the sidelines (Cvetkovski, 1999). Even more, in August 1990, on the eve of the first democratic, multiparty elections for the Supreme Council (Parliament) of the Republic of Georgia, an election law was adopted that banned the participation of area-constrained parties, such as the Ademon Nykhaz or the Aydgylara, in the elections (Cvetkovski, 1999).

Within this canvass of the ethnic type of nationalism on behalf of Georgia, the South Ossetian oblast council gave a new lease of life to its prior demand for more political autonomy by being upgraded to an ASSR, further declaring on September 20, 1990, that South Ossetia was an "Independent Soviet Democratic Republic" within the USSR (HRW, 1992, p. 7). Intensifying the polarization, on October 28, 1990, Zviad Gamsakhurdia's Round Table, a coalition of parties that shared extreme nationalistic views, won the parliamentary elections circulating the slogan "Georgia for Georgians"; this, in turn, made South Ossetians to further realize that there was middle ground as far as a political solution is concerned, and the road towards independence should be more resolutely followed. In this spirit, elections were organized for the region's Supreme Soviet (HRW, 1992, p. 8). In fact, it would not take long for a political gridlock to be reached, when on December 11, the Supreme Council of the Georgian Republic would abolish even South Ossetia's incumbent status of an Autonomous Oblast (Nielsen, 2009).

On December 12, the Georgian government, pointing to the murders of two Georgians (with gun permits) and one Ossetian in Tskhinvali, declared a state of emergency (HRW, 1992). When the USSR Interior Ministry troops (MVD) arrived on the scene aiming at smoothing things out, the Georgian government strongly opposed what it perceived to be Moscow's intervention in Georgian affairs, and proceeded with the deployment of 3,000–4,000 militiamen to Tskhinvali. South Ossetians, in turn, considered this move as an act of "occupation" (HRW, 1992, pp. 8–9). On January 7, 1991, Mikhail Gorbachev cancelled both South Ossetia's Declaration of Independence and Georgia's state of emergency, demanding all armed units except the Soviet MVD troops to withdraw from South Ossetia (HRW, 1992). Georgia, nevertheless, rebuffed Gorbachev's decrees due to uninvited third-party intervention in internal affairs (HRW, 1992). The spreading of the conflict on a large scale was "at the gates."

So it happened. On the night of January 5, Georgia's belatedly assembled "National Guard" under the command of Tengiz Kitovani, one of the two fighting forces that were filling the gap that the absence of a ministry of defense had created, came into Tskhinvali and committed atrocities in the attendance of the Soviet MVD troops (Cvetkovski, 1999; HRW, 1992, p. 9).[5] Over the remainder of 1991, the conflict was kept in check. A May 31 protocol issued by a Joint Commission on behalf of Georgia, North Ossetia, the USSR, and the RSFSR, identified the conflict as a hurdle to the reestablishment of Georgian Independence and appealed to the Georgian government for the resolution of the conflict by political means (HRW, 1992).

Eventually, the Joint Commission proved of very limited efficiency as a result of the Georgian parliament's nonparticipation, and violence found its way back in South Ossetia in early winter 1991 (HRW, 1992).

This time, however, in a far more ethnicized, intractable, and methodical manner; first, in November 1991, the state of emergency, eleven months after it had been imposed, was revoked by the Georgian parliament, stripping the USSR MVP troops that were protecting the South Ossetians of their cause of existence (Birch, 1995). Then, Georgia's President Gamsakhurdia called on "all Georgians who can carry a gun" to advance to Tskhinvali to finish off South Ossetian aspirations for independence or unification with Russia's North Ossetia (Birch, 1995, p. 44). In view of such a mounting *zero-sum* Georgian "tide of nationalism," the South Ossetians coalesced behind the declaration of independence as the sole means of survival and security (Beissinger, 2002, p. 29).

Having already exhausted all the low-mobilization institutional "tools" on hand for purposes of addressing issues of political autonomy, namely the Supreme Council of Georgia and the oblast council, now, the high-mobilization institutional "tool" of the referendum was resorted to, seeking to firmly establish regional political preferences. On January 19, 1992, South Ossetia's *de facto* authorities headed by Znaur Gassyev, who temporarily was serving as both prime minister and President, organized a referendum with two questions (table 4.1.).

Not only did the referendum mobilize the population with an overwhelming 97% of voters taking part, but it also further solidified the intentions of South Ossetia's *de facto* authorities, since it articulated the region's regional political preferences in a far more explicit and unequivocal manner. The results showed the continuing separateness that the South Ossetians felt within a highly nationalistic Georgia, with almost all voters (99.9%) being convinced that there was no middle ground to be worked out and the independence was the only option. Moreover, in response to the second question in the referendum, which examined the possibility of unification with Russia, again almost all voters (99.8%) put their weight behind it. The secondary placement of this question was a move of high symbolism as far as political preferences are concerned; in view of the perpetuating deadlock in its co-existence prospects within Georgia, South Ossetia prioritized independence, and then unification with North Ossetia, seeing the prospect of its inclusion within Russia more on security terms. The latter could provide for the primary needs of survival and security of the South Ossetians in the anarchy-resembling conditions of Georgia's early independence period, which had pushed the essentially "atomized" Georgians to assemble under a rather assertive and nationalistic banner.

This argumentation is further substantiated by the ceasefire agreement signed on June 24, 1992, following a period of small-scale regional clashes

Table 4.1. South Ossetia Referendum on Independence and Unification with Russia: January 19, 1992

Question	Right to vote	Voting Partici-pation	Valid	Yes	No
1. Do you agree that the Republic of South Ossetia becomes independent? [Согласны ли Вы, чтобы Республика Южная Осетия была независимой?]	55151	53441 96.9%	53356 99.8%	53308 99.91%	48 0.09%
2. Do you agree with the decision of the Supreme Soviet of the Republic of South Ossetia of 1 September 1991 on reunification with Russia? [Согласны ли Вы с решением Верховного Совета Республики Южная Осетия от 1 сентября 1991 г. о воссоединении с Россией?]	55151	53441 96.9%	53348 99.8%	53291 99.89%	57 0.11%

Source: Müller, 2005

and Russia's last-resort military engagement of South Ossetia *via* the Roki tunnel, the only route connecting North and South Ossetia. The head of the State Council of Georgia, Eduard Shevardnadze and the President of Russia, Boris Yeltsin, endorsed in Dagomys, Russia, the Sochi Agreement on the Settlement of the Georgian-Ossetian conflict; it stipulated:

- the withdrawal of forces,
- a 14km-wide buffer corridor along the border between Georgia and South Ossetia,
- the deployment of a JPKF comprised by Russian, Georgian, and Ossetian troops and,
- the assignment of that JPKF under the command of a JCC. (Thomas, 2009, p. 37)

South Ossetia's prime minister Oleg Teziev and many other Ossetians, "despite retaining their ultimate (if not inescapable) goal of a unified Ossetia within Russia," they did not stop sort of recognizing the JPKF, and the Russian forces in particular, more as a security necessity to put up with rather than as a preference (Birch, 1995, p. 48).[6]

Abkhazia

In parallel, Abkhazia, following in the same footsteps, declared its independence from Georgia in reaction to the August 1990 election law (HRW, 1995a, p. 16). As violence kept raging on the South Ossetian front, the Abkhaz authorities sought, in November, to forge a wider alliance as a means of strengthening their status, coining an agreement of confederation with "thirteen peoples of the North Caucasus, located within Russia" (HRW, 1995a, p. 16). This agreement met the Georgian government's rejection, which announced, instead, that it would restrain to a grave level the status of increased autonomy that Abkhazia was relishing (as an ASSR within the Georgian SSR during the Soviet era, and subsequently as an autonomous republic within the independent Georgia) (HRW, 1995a, p. 16). In no time, polarization and separation spread within Abkhazia's state institutions, with Abkhaz and Georgians to form two distinct and adversary parliaments, each of which denied the other's legitimacy (HRW, 1995a, p. 16). Even more, in summer 1992, Abkhazia's 1925 Constitution (according to which Abkhazia was a SSR associated with the Georgian SSR) was restored by the Abkhaz parliament, which, then, declared independence (HRW, 1995a, p. 16).

A wide-ranging confrontation was imminent. On the night of August 13–14, 1992, the solidly armored Georgian "National Guard" advanced on the Gali region of Abkhazia (HRW, 1995a, p. 17). With the Abkhaz immovable from their demand for expanded autonomy within Georgia, and should this was attainable, then, full independence from Georgia, the polarization and division within the Abkhaz state institutions proliferated in the streets: Georgians of Abkhazia and Abkhaz pitted themselves against each other in a concerted effort to oust the rival ethnic group from key-areas for their own ethnic group (HRW, 1995a, p. 5). Whole villages were taken captive in a confrontation where ethnicity, one of the fundamental attributes of the human nature, served as a connective tissue for a wider alliance to be forged among otherwise "atomized" rational actors as means of survival and security in an anarchy-resembling socio-political environment.

In this context are also placed the violence and the abuses committed by the belligerents (regular and irregular forces alike), the pattern of which showed a willingness to cross the boundaries of the laws on waging war, in support of maximizing ethnic gains (HRW, 1995a, p. 6). Russia's role in the conflict exhibited a whole spectrum of actions, ranging from neutrality bolstered by force if necessary, intervention, to mediation along with humanitarian aid (HRW, 1995a, p. 37).

Following an ephemeral effort towards a ceasefire in mid July 1993, the governments of Georgia and Abkhazia endorsed in Moscow, in May 1994, the "Agreement on a Ceasefire and Separation of Forces" (UN, 2006). That agreement paved the way for the presence in the region of 136 military observers representing the UN Observer Mission in Georgia (UNOMIG) and 1,600 Russian peacekeeping troops within the framework of the CIS (UN, 2006). As a result, the tension was de-escalated, but the seeds for a lasting peace settlement had not been sown; the bone of contention, namely the political status of Abkhazia, remained outside the scope of the agreement. In reality, the Abkhaz and the Georgian authorities held irreconcilable positions, since the former's regional political preferences, after hostilities had broken out and any trust had plummeted, were for full independence, in the best case scenario, or for a confederative status within Georgia, in the worst case scenario (HRW, 1995a, p. 8). Russia, just like in the case of South Ossetia, did not affect the Abkhaz political preferences, being primarily viewed in security terms, as a protector of Abkhaz interests through the peacekeeping force.

Pursuing the case further, on November 26, 1996, the Abkhaz parliament dropped a bombshell by declaring anew its independence, this time upon the solid foundations of a new Constitution. Thus, the prospects of co-existence within Georgia were further torpedoed, and the region's *de facto* status was further solidified (HRW, 1995a, p. 7).[7]

EN ROUTE TO THE EVENTS OF AUGUST 2008: SOCIO-POLITICAL DEVELOPMENT AND QUALITY OF LIFE

Since the time that the two breakaway regions had begun to exist as a *de facto* states, in 1992 and 1994 respectively, during Georgia's critical juncture period, three elements had crystallized: (a) their political preference for independence should no other political solution that would allow for co-existence within Georgia was feasible, (b) their aversion to the Georgian polity, and (c) their acceptance of the Russian presence, mostly in security terms (JPKF) rather than as a political preference. Given these, Georgia and Russia figure as two critical elements that, next to their direct involvement in the course of the conflict, may have also exerted an indirect and enduring (contextual) impact on political preferences in both South Ossetia and Abkhazia *en route* to the events of August 2008; in essence, they could have propelled their manifestation in a more assertive manner, bordering on consolidation.

For this to happen the following should be assumed: first, the "atomized-turned-ethnicized" national identity of the early independence period in Georgia should have been retained, and second, Georgia and Russia should have been following quite dissimilar paths with regard to two central variables of the quality of life, that of GDP per capita, PPP, and unemployment. As earlier argued, the economically perceived quality of life is an essential part of human thinking, especially so after an embattled situation had given birth to *de facto* independence.

To begin with, and to assess whether the "atomized-turned-ethnicized" national identity in Georgia had been retained since the early independence period, a fact which, in turn, would bring to the surface anarchy-related connotations, the item, or better indicator, of "corruption" comes in handy. With the term "corruption" to define a situation where it is observed "the abuse of entrusted power for private gain," it becomes rather apparent how it is connected with the "atomized-turned-ethnicized" national identity.[8]

Drawing on the World Bank to explain this indicator, "control of corruption captures perceptions of the extent to which public power is exercised for private gain, including both petty and grand forms of corruption, as well as "capture" of the state by elites and private interests. As shown in figure 4.1, estimates gives the country's score on the aggregate indicator ranging from approximately –2.5 to 2.5 (Kaufmann et al., 2010). From 1996 up to 2007, months before the second major eruption breaks out, (far) more than 50% of the citizens of Georgia felt the "ego-centric" functioning of the state and its "capture by elites and private interests," a fact which shows that the fragmented and porous national identity framework had persisted all the way up to the second critical juncture, with the "atomized-turned-ethnicized" operating scheme of the national identity to have remained the dominant one. Even when perceptions had started to improve two years before the second critical juncture, in 2006 and 2007, these did not fall below 50% of the citizens. To make things worse, corrective and non-delicate policies by the government targeted vital economic activities of South Ossetia, a fact which, as shown

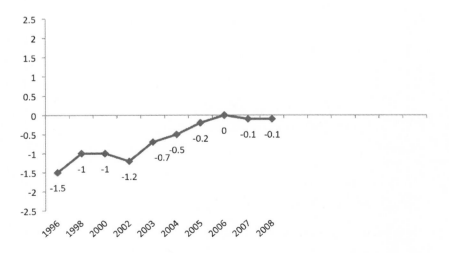

Figure 4.1.   Control of Corruption: Estimate, Georgia. Source: Kaufmann et al., 2010.

later on, increased the possibilities of backfiring rather than of building a sustainable socio-political environment.

With not so much distance to have been covered between the anarchy-resembling early independence period and an efficient state, below, Georgia is juxtaposed with Russia in terms of unemployment and GDP per capita, PPP.

During the 1990s, Georgia and Russia were comparable in terms of un-employment (figure 4.2), at least according to the data that are available for both, with Georgia being in a better place in 1998 (12.4%), the year that Russia suffered a major setback, that of the financial crisis (Kyrkilis, 2010, pp. 91–95).

This trend, however, was reversed in the years that ensued, with the gap constantly widening from 1999 onward, until it reached its maximum value in 2008, with a point difference of 10.3 favoring Russia. Next to this, it should also be taken into account the comparison that emerges from the trend lines of the two countries; whereas in the case of Georgia there are negative prospects, indicated by the upward trend of the line, in the case of Russia it is exhibited a course of stability associated with positive prospects, indicated by the downward trend of the line.

Passing, now, to the examination of the GDP per capita, PPP (figure 4.3), the same inferences can be made. From the onset (1992) of the post-soviet era, the two countries were on parallel, but qualitatively different, paths; in fact, the gap separating them notably widened after 2000, reaching a maxi-mum value in 2008 with a point difference of $14,000.

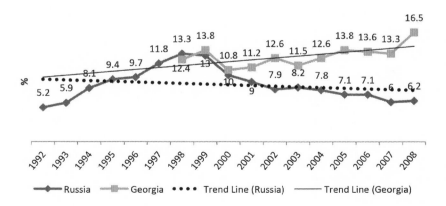

Figure 4.2.   Unemployment, total national estimate (% of total labor force).
Source: World Bank.

Pursuing the argument further by making reference to the trend lines of Georgia and Russia, again here becomes apparent the difference between the two economies as far as prospects are concerned; Georgia's was moving in slightly upward trajectory, that at times could also correlate with stagnation, the very same moment that Russia's was following a strikingly upward trajectory, highlighting in a rather clear-cut manner the positive prospects of its economy.

In this context, an intensification of regional political preferences took place. For instance, in a referendum in 1999, the Abkhaz approved by 97.7 % a new Constitution as a means of solidifying their independence (Volkov, 2017).[9] In parallel, sporadic ethnic-instigated fighting kept erupting in both breakaway regions, e.g., in Abkhazia's area of Kodori in 2001.[10] In January 2004, Mikheil Saakashvili succeeded Eduard Shevardnadze in the Georgian presidency, with the latter to have been toppled in the bloodless "Rose Revolution" of the previous November (Welt, 2006). Anti-corruption and democratization reforms stood atop his priorities, while he also tried to restore the Georgia's territorial integrity by promising "broader autonomy" for both Abkhazia and South Ossetia in the form of guaranteed language and education rights and representation quotas in government structures (Saakashvili, 2005; George, 2009, p. 148).

These promises, nevertheless, did not find fertile ground among South Ossetians and Abkhaz, who, against a background that was being challenged by hostilities and distrust, were seeing a contradiction between words and deeds: Georgia's goal of joining NATO, and by extension the Western military system, contradicted the 1990s situation on the ground in both break-

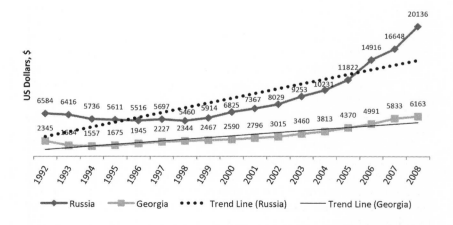

Figure 4.3.   GDP per capita, PPP (current international $). Source: World Bank.

away regions, that had their *de facto* independence safeguarded by Russia (Fuller, 2004a; George, 2009, p. 149). Moreover, in spring 2004 a crisis flared up in Adjara, an autonomous republic mainly inhabited by ethnic Georgians, which resulted in the removal of its leader, Aslan Abashidze, on corruption charges and the restoration of Tbilisi's control.[11] This had negative repercussions on the already distrustful views of South Ossetians and Abkhaz (George, 2009, p. 149; Geostat.ge, 2002).

In fact, Saakashvili perceived the issue of Georgia's restoration of territorial integrity in terms of agency, not structure. In his view, leaders such as Eduard Kokoity (South Ossetia) were kept in power *via* their networks of corruption, and once those were wiped out, democratization and territorial integrity would spring up (Fuller, 2004b). In this spirit, Saakashvili, in summer 2004, engaged a major contraband market at Ergneti, on the border with South Ossetia, and attempted at establishing customs control on goods flowing across the Russian border (*Georgia Times*, 2012). Yet, such actions came to add up to South Ossetia's economic anguish, rekindling violence for the first time since the 1992 ceasefire, and attracting bitter criticism from both Russia and the local leadership; even more, they propelled the South Ossetian population towards uniting around those leaders rather becoming isolated from them, as Saakashvili had expected (BBC, 2012a; George, 2009, p. 149). To make things worse, at the time, the gap between Georgia and Russia in terms of unemployment and GDP per capita, PPP, was becoming wider, and such disparities, as perceived by South Ossetians, were contributing to the intensity of regional political preferences.

In a context of almost no trust and enhanced suspicion, South Ossetians headed toward their November 12, 2006, Presidential election. The Kokoity regime planned to link the vote with a referendum asking whether the republic of South Ossetia should "retain its current status as an independent state, and be recognized by the international community." This move, however, was met with a political counteroffensive, when the South Ossetian town of Eredvi served as the headquarters of a competing electoral campaign for a Tbilisi-supported Presidential vote and referendum, that focused on Georgian-populated and mixed Georgian-Ossetian villages with population not more than 14,000 (Fuller, 2006; Landru, 2006). Their referendum question was "Should South Ossetia engage in discussions with Tbilisi concerning a federal state uniting it with Georgia?" (Landru, 2006).

Polarization between the two rival ethnicities rose to crescendo again; indicative were the competing advertisements in the streets of Tskhinvali. For example, a piece calling for the rebuilding of the "Grand Alani" provided the following reasoning: "if all peoples of the Caucasus have the right to a state, why not us—the Ossetian Nation? . . . Such an independence for North Ossetians is currently impossible in Russia. We must show them the way" (Landru, 2006). The Tbilisi-supported candidates, on the contrary, stood for peace within a multi-ethnic South Ossetia reunited with the Georgian state (Landru, 2006).

The two sets of presidential and referendum results corroborated the raging division between the two ethnicities, albeit not recognized by members and institutions of the international community, Russia and Georgia included (NATO, 2006).[12]

Eduard Kokoity received 98.1% of the vote, and his referendum on keeping hold of *de facto* independence and being recognized by the international community as such met an overwhelming approval by 98.8% (table 4.2). In fact, that was the second referendum on regional political preferences since the 1992 ceasefire, and it was conducted, according to Kokoity, "in order to give the younger generation of voters, who did not participate in the previous referendum in 1992, a chance to register their views" (Fuller, 2006).

In the parallel election, Kokoity's rival, the Tbilisi-favored candidate, Dmitrii Sanakoev, won 80% of the votes among the Georgian residents of South Ossetia. These results attested to the persistence and polarization of regional political preferences across the examined continuum, embedded in a highly ethnicized Georgian national identity, in conditions of comparatively weak macro-economic growth and unemployment as demonstrated by the juxtaposition of Georgia against Russia. With these facts on the ground, the second critical juncture was coming up fast.

Table 4.2.   South Ossetia Referendum on Independence: November 12, 2006

Question	Right to vote	Voting Participation	Yes	No
Should the republic of South Ossetia retain its current status as an independent State, and be recognized by the international community? [Согласны ли вы с тем, чтобыРеспубликаЮжн аяОсетиясохраниласв ойнынешнийстатуснез ависимогогосударства ибылапризнанамежду народнымсообщество м]	55163	52163 (94.5%)	51565 (98.88%)	60 (0.11%)

Source: Tsentral'noi Izbiratel'noy Komissii, 2006

THE AUGUST 2008 FIVE-DAY WAR

With the point spreads between Georgia and Russia in terms of unemployment and GDP per capita (PPP) to reach their highest values (10.3% and $14,000 respectively) in favor of Russia, the August 2008 Five-Day War consolidated South Ossetia and Abkhazia as two mono-ethnic *de facto* independent territories under the security provision of an enhanced Russian military presence (JPKF).

Close to midnight on August 7, 2008, Tbilisi had decided to take decisive action to reinstate "constitutional order in the entire region" (*Civil Georgia*, 2008). Citing the shelling of Georgian villages in the conflict zone by South Ossetians as a breach to a unilateral ceasefire called by Tbilisi, Georgia launched a large-scale attack on Tskhinvali at around 1:00 am on August 8 (*Civil Georgia*, 2008). South Ossetians did not leave these military advances unanswered, whereas Russia did not take long to assume its role in the eruption; at approximately 1:30 am, tank columns of the Russian 58th army were on the road to Georgia through the Roki tunnel, asserting their "responsibility to protect" (R2P) (ICG, 2008a, p. 28). At 6:00 am on August 8, the fighting had spilled over to Abkhazia, with its troops advancing on the Kodori Gorge, the sole part in its territory remaining under Georgian control (ICG, 2008a).

The hostilities raged for five days, during which the logic of mono-ethnic *de facto* independent territories dominated; South Ossetian ousted the last 14,000 Georgians, whereas Abkhaz expelled 2,500 Georgians from the area of the Upper Kodori, with a small number remaining at the Gali district (Amnesty International, 2008, p. 51). In this "no hold fire" environment, French President Nicolas Sarkozy drafted, on August 12, a succinct, six-point ceasefire document:

The Six-Point Ceasefire Agreement

1. No resort to the use of force
2. Permanent termination of hostilities
3. Free access to humanitarian aid
4. Return of the Georgian military forces to their places of permanent deployment
5. Return of the Russian military forces to their pre-conflict positions; pending an international mechanism, Russian peacekeeping forces would undertake additional security measures
6. Commencement of international discussion on the modalities for enduring security in Abkhazia and South Ossetia (Kramer, 2008)

On August 15–16, the document was endorsed and accompanied by a side-letter in which Sarkozy clarified a few critical points: to begin with, the term "security measures" in point 5 was provided with a specific content, calling for the delineation of an area around South Ossetia not more than several kilometers beyond the administrative border between South Ossetia and Georgia, so that no major urban center, such as Gori, be included (ICG, 2008a, p. 4). Moreover, the "measures" were confined to patrols by the Russian peacekeeping forces, as these had been provisioned by the 1992 ceasefire agreement, with all post-August 7 forces to withdraw to North Ossetia (ICG, 2008a, p. 4). Finally, the objection of both Russia and Georgia to the wording of point 6 led to the deletion of the words "the future status," thus underpinning the peacekeeping and security nature of the Russian intervention rather than the invasion-laden argumentation of Saakashvili (*Financial Times*, 2008).

Assessing the after-effects of the war as well as of the agreement, the next day found the relations between Georgia, on the one hand, and South Ossetia and Abkhazia, on the other, to go up in smoke, with the former to have completely lost control in both breakaway regions. The latter became further established as *de facto* states that were either fully mono-ethnic (South Ossetia) or nearly so (Abkhazia, especially its political elite) (Sotiriou, 2017, p. 10). To make things worse and far more difficult for Georgia to reverse, Russia, capitalizing on the loopholes set forth in point 5, increased the number of its troops in both regions, creating a reality whereby lasing regional political preferences dovetailed with security guarantees.[13] In fact, this reality was further facilitated by the Georgian Law on Occupied Territories (2008), which not only classified the South Ossetian and Abkhaz official as criminals, but also linked them to various Russia-coined plots against Georgia, terrorism included (Toal and O'Loughlin, 2013, p. 147).

A survey on attitudes conducted by Toal and O'Loughlin in 2010, two years after the August 2008 five-day war, is illuminating in this regard. When the item of trust in key individuals and institutions was examined, the South Ossetian and the Abkhaz presidents scored quite high, gathering the trust of more than 60% and 80% of the respondents respectively. In the same direction, the South Ossetian and the Abkhaz police were trusted by 50% in each case, while the Russian leadership figured as trustworthy for more than 80% in South Ossetia. The Georgian leadership, on the contrary, was heavily distrusted (90%) among South Ossetians on grounds of its inefficiency, or better said, the gap between words and deeds (Bakke et al., 2014, p. 597; Toal and O'Loughlin, 2013, p. 154). Moreover, this trust deficiency spilled over the whole society, with an overall 90% of South Ossetians reporting attitudes towards Georgians that ranged from neutral (23%), at best, to very bad (40%), at worst (Toal and O'Loughlin, 2013, p. 157). These attitudes were reversed when it came to Russians, with the overall acceptance touching 100%, ranging from very good (49%), at best, to neutral (9%), at worst (Toal and O'Loughlin, 2013, p. 157).

This rapprochement with Russia, while not departing from the security logic of the first major eruption period, had started to shift from the military to the economic aspect. The positive correlation between the widening gap separating Russia from Georgia in terms of unemployment and GDP per capita, PPP, and the intensification of regional political preferences (riots in Abkhazia in 2001 and 2004; the referendum in South Ossetia in 2006) attests to this shift. But next to this, there is also Russia's direct involvement, first in infrastructure projects such as the Sochi-Sukhumi railway in 2004, and second in mitigating the hardships inflicted by the August war by allocating $28,000 per person through the Russian Ministry of Regional Development (ICG, 2008b, p. 2; Toal and O'Loughlin, 2013, p. 146).

All things considered, South Ossetia and Abkhazia never dropped their aspirations for independence, should no political solution was feasible that would alleviate their survival and security concerns and allow for co-existence within the borders of Georgia. Quite the contrary, they carried on with determination, and when on August 26, 2008, Russia recognized their *de facto* statehood, both presidents welcomed the decision. President Kokoity stated: "Now we are an independent state, but we look forward to uniting with North Ossetia and joining the Russian Federation" (Toal and O'Loughlin, 2013, p. 148). His Abkhaz counterpart stated: "I think everybody in the world wants to be independent. Abkhazia is no exception. We want to build a small, democratic, law-abiding state of our own" (Wagstyl, 2008; Prezident Rossii, 2008).

Both Presidents emphasized the irreversible course towards independence, with South Ossetia hoping for unification with North Ossetia and restoration of the "Grand Alani" as a means of historical justification, and Abkhazia looking forward to the establishment of its independence, even if both would happen "under the protective wing of Russia." In the Abkhaz case, near to 80% stood for the status of independence and considered the region's *de facto* polity as a step in the right direction, with the option of integrating with either Russia or Georgia gathering less than 20% (Bakke et al. 2014, p. 596).

CONCLUSION

Considering the main takeaways from Georgia's "frozen conflicts," table 4.3 is of particular assistance.

The lasting regional political preferences held an independent role in the analysis, having been active long before Georgia declares its independence and enters the post-soviet era. The nuances of an ethnic type of nationalism

Table 4.3.   Anatomy of the Crisis in South Ossetia and Abkhazia: Substantiating Causality

	South Ossetia	Abkhazia	Test Case: Adjara
Soviet period	*Regional status:* • Autonomous oblast: moderate political autonomy	*Regional status:* • ASSR: Increased political autonomy	*Regional status:* • Autonomous oblast: moderate political autonomy
First major-eruption period (critical juncture 1991-1995)	*Regional political preference:* • Independence (should no increased, federation-leaning, political autonomy within Georgia feasible) • Georgian nationalistic attack • Russia's military involvement: Peacekeeping forces	*Regional political preference:* • Independence (should no increased, federation-leaning, political autonomy within Georgia feasible) • Georgian nationalistic attack • Russia's military involvement: Peacekeeping forces	*No regional political preference* • No Georgian nationalistic attack • No Russia's military involvement: Peacekeeping forces
Second major-eruption period (critical juncture of the August 2008 events)	*Regional political preference:* • Independence (should no increased, federation-leaning, political autonomy within Georgia feasible) • Georgian nationalistic attack • Russia's military involvement: Peacekeeping forces	*Regional political preference:* • Independence (should no increased, federation-leaning, political autonomy within Georgia feasible) • Georgian nationalistic attack • Russia's military involvement: Peacekeeping forces	May 2004: • Georgian President controls executive and legislative powers November 2007: • Russia's complete military withdrawal from Georgian soil: last military base in Batumi closes

had crept into Georgian SSR's engagement of both South Ossetians and Abkhaz throughout the Soviet period, but they did not reveal their true colors given the USSR's institutional equilibrium. Once this was tampered with by the collapse and the critical juncture period was initiated, the already existent South Ossetian and Abkhaz political preferences found their *cohabitation politique* with the Georgians hard to combine and irreversibly aggravated by the Georgian nationalist offensive. All these took place in a context, where the divergence in the quality of life between Georgia and Russia exerted an influence; in fact, this became rather strong after 2000, with the widening of the gap in Russia's favor to coincide with incidents that increased the intensity of regional political preferences in both breakaway republics. In the aftermath of the August 2008 five-day war, the interplay of these factors consolidated a *de facto* institutional equilibrium in South Ossetia and Abkhazia that had brewing since the time of the first major eruption in early 1990s.

Attempting an overall assessment, it could be argued that Georgia did not succeed in reading between the lines of the contradicting nationalisms at play in its territory. These "atomized-turned-ethnicized" nationalisms, especially on behalf of the two breakaway republics, had been beset with survival and security concerns. Should Georgia had been more perceptive and understood the value of accepting the South Ossetian 1980s demand for upgrading its status to that of an ASSR, like Abkhazia, along with securities for language and local autonomy for both regions, survival and security concerns would have been alleviated, laying the groundwork for co-existence within the Georgian territory. But as the currently employed historical continuum revealed, Georgia proved unresponsive to the lessons of history, a fact that resulted in the lasting regional political preferences becoming more and more firm over time.

On March 28, 2008, a few months before the hard-to-reverse became the *de facto* consolidated, President Saakashvili offered to Abkhazia an upgrading of its status, which provided for unlimited autonomy within a federal structure that would stipulate just representation in the bodies of the central government, and a right to veto laws regarding status, culture, language, and ethnicity; moreover, all this restructuring as far as political institutions are concerned would be accompanied by international guarantees and Russia's involvement in all conflict-resolution issues (ICG, 2008b, p. 18).[14] There is little doubt that such a plan could have alleviated survival and security fears and allow for co-existence within a common state and gradual accumulation of social capital, especially had it come at the beginning of the first major eruption period. But, by 2008, after almost twenty years of castles in the air and lost trust, it was declined by Abkhazia's *de facto* leadership in a reflex action on grounds of untrustworthiness (ICG, 2008b).[15]

NOTES

1. For more on the issue, see also Cooper and Shanker, 2008.
2. Oblasts enjoyed the lowest degree of political autonomy.
3. The opening to Russia by the South Ossetian and the Abkhaz was a watershed, since for years they had been opposing "both Russian and Georgian intervention in their internal operations" (Suny, 1994, p. 307).
4. The highly ethicized type of national identity among the Georgians once more corroborates what has been argued earlier in this analysis: that the Soviet state adopted top-down suppressive policies that more created reactive nationalism rather than an evolutionary course

towards the civic type of identity. The latter would allow for the peaceful and fruitful co-existence between the difference people of the USSR. As long as the institutional structure of the USSR was in place, these dynamics were in check. Once decomposed, the anarchy-resembling socio-political environment would push the erstwhile Soviet citizens to act as "atomized" rational actors who sought the formation of a wider alliance based on the fundamental attributes of the human nature as a means of survival and security in what they perceived as a raging, *zero-sum*, geopolitical competition.

    5. The other fighting force was Jaba Joseliani's "Mkhedrioni" (Horsemen) (HRW, 1995a, p. 17).

    6. The phrase "if not inescapable" has been added by the author. Thus, it is italicized.

    7. Adding to the thoroughness of the argumentation, it is reported that from 1996 to 1997, Russian agreed to a CIS-wide economic and arms embargo against Abkhazia as a means of taming its obduracy (Antonenko, 2005, p. 223).

    8. For the definition of the term "corruption," see https://www.transparency.org/what-is-corruption.

    9. Furthermore, in order to "securitize" independence, Abkhazia sought its incorporation into the Russian Federation as a "freely associated state" (Antonenko, 2005, p. 207).

    10. Providing an insight into this eruption, Georgian partisans, acting independently from the Georgian government, engaged the Abkhaz forces mostly in reprisal for the large number of Georgian refugees which was expelled from Abkhazia in 1993 (BBC, 2001b).

    11. For Georgian government's reinstatement of institutional rule over Adjara, see Rukhadze, 2013.

    12. At this point, of particular significance is the stance taken by the Russian President Vladimir Putin, who, on October 25, 2006, made clear that there were no incorporation plans of South Ossetia and Abkhazia on behalf of Russia, and urged them and the Georgian government to find a happy medium. Furthermore, he affirmed Russia's commitment to Georgia's territorial integrity (Fuller, 2006).

    13. Providing a thorough account on Russia's military presence in the wider region, it is reported that its troops in the North Caucasian Military District (Severo Kavkavskii Voennyi Okrug), or Southern Military District (Yuzhnyi Voennyi Okrug), as was renamed after 2010, amounted to 90,000 (ICG, 2008b, p. 9).

    14. For Russia's complete military withdrawal from the Georgian territory, see Antidze, 2007.

    15. Parts of this chapter appear in Stylianos A. Sotiriou (2017), "The irreversibility of history: The conflicts in South Ossetia and Abkhazia," *Problems of Post-Communism*, DOI: https://doi.org/10.1080/10758216.2017.1406310.

Chapter Five

The Case of Nagorno-Karabakh (Azerbaijan)

THE REGION OF NAGORNO-KARABAKH (NK): A SOURCE OF CONSTANT TENSION

"Dans la guerre sans fin du Haut-Karabakh" (Inside the war without end in Nagorno-Karabakh) had titled his article the special envoy of the French journal *Le Monde* to NK, Benoît Vitkine, on April 11, 2016, a few days after the biggest escalation since the 1994 ceasefire had taken place in the region (Vitkine, 2016). It would not be an exaggeration to argue that although this conflict falls within the phenomenon of "frozen conflict," tense and hostilities in the region never stopped; in fact, from 2006 until 2010, the number as well as the intensity of the violations of the ceasefire regime followed a steep upsurge (Newsru.com, 2017).

It was in this context that the April 2016 Four-Day War (or April War) broke out along the NK line of contact, enmeshing the Defense Army of NK, supported by Armenian Armed Forces, on the one hand, and the Azerbaijani Armed Forces, on the other.[1] The fighting took place in a mooted area between the *de facto* Republic of NK and Azerbaijan. The Azerbaijani forces went after regaining territory, a part of which was falling within the bounds of the Soviet-era Nagorno-Karabakh Autonomous Oblast (NKAO) (ICG, 2016, p. 21).[2] Moreover, there were allegations of atrocities committed by both sides as well as of usage of prohibited munitions, whereas numerous people had been left unaccounted for; indicative is the fact that according to the International Committee of the Red Cross (ICRC), more than 4,496 persons had gone missing (US Department of State, 2016, p. 3). Moreover, the overall fatality count reached 200, a score far surpassing the previous most horrible annual total (Broers, 2016, p. 14).[3] A ceasefire was finally reached on April 5, with both providing their own, "interests-fitting," explanation of the developments in this *zero-sum* geopolitical standoff; in particular, the Azerbaijani President, Ilham Aliyev, referred to the alleged recapturing of 2,000 hectares of land as a "great victory," whereas the Armenian President, Serzh Sargsyan, stated that out of the 800,000 hectares of land that functioned as a "safety zone" around NK, the four-day war resulted in the loss of 800 hectares that bore no tactical or strategic importance (Broers, 2016, p. 16; Panarmenian.net, 2016; RFE/RL, 2016).

The same fuzzy situation remained as far as which side was responsible for the instigation of such intense hostilities. Each put the blame on the other, with the Armenian defense ministry, first, to argue that Azerbaijan had employed aircraft, tanks and artillery in attempt to create inroads into NK, and thus "Azerbaijani authorities bear all responsibility for the unprecedentedly supercharged situation" (*The Guardian*, 2016). Azerbaijan, for its part, claimed that the fighting erupted when Armenian forces fired mortars and large-calibre artillery shells across the frontline. In further detail, the Defense Ministry spokesman, Vagif Dargyakhly, informed Associated Press that over 120 shots had been fired, some of which hit civilian residential areas (*The Guardian*, 2016).

Both Azerbaijan and Armenia have been buying arms from Russia; Azerbaijan has purchased at least $4bn worth of weapons, whereas Armenia, aside from counting for arms supplies solely on Russia, has been also Russia's strategic partner in the subsystem of Caucasus, hosting its only military base in the region.[4] This "two-doors" policy by Russia caused discontent within Armenia, since as the Armenian President, Serzh Sargsyan, stated: "The problem is not the quality of the weaponry, but the fact that an Armenian soldier standing at the border knows he could be killed by Russian weapons" (BBC, 2015a).[5]

Putting the developments in NK into perspective, the standoff between the two sides, the NK Armenians and the Azerbaijanis, started in late 1980s, and climaxed into all-out civil war in 1991 as the USSR was integrating, costing the life to approximately 30,000 people before a ceasefire was finally made possible in 1994 (BBC, 2016c). Azerbaijan lost swaths of territory, with over 600,000 ethnic Azerbaijanis from Karabakh and the adjacent areas to have fled for the outskirts of the capital Baku, where new housing compounds were gradually erected for the displaced families (BBC, 2015a, 2015b). In like manner, 300,000 ethnic Armenians, who resided elsewhere in Azerbaijan, were also displaced (BBC, 2015a). In total, Azerbaijan presents one of the highest percentages on a global scale as far as IDPs are concerned (BBC, 2015b). NK is deemed part of Azerbaijan, but its Armenian inhabitants, have long accused the Azerbaijani authorities of conducting forced Azerbaijanification in the region and of being loath to reach a political solution which would allow for co-existence within the borders of Azerbaijan.

Although it emits a sense of institutional normality by having its own flag, an international airport, police and armed forces, in reality, it is an isolated enclave within Azerbaijan, more often than not, challenged by hostilities. On the frontline with Azerbaijan serve regular Armenian soldiers, whereas its international airport stands empty due to Azerbaijani threats to shoot down any planes. As a result, it is an isolated region, financially and militarily dependent on Armenia (BBC, 2015a). As argued by the NK *de facto* foreign minister, Karen Mirzoyan, "when you withdraw NK from the negotiating table, it's very easy to say that it's not a conflict for self-determination, it's just a territorial problem. . . . But in reality this conflict is about self-determination" (BBC, 2015a).

Taking all these into consideration, below, NK's political preferences are examined within a historical continuum, which places primary emphasis on the two equally critical periods in Azerbaijan's post-soviet history, that of the major eruption in the early independence period and that of the four-day war in April 2016. This comparison between the two major eruption periods (i.e., critical junctures), however, does not stand alone, but is embedded within a fragmented and porous national identity context that permeated the Azerbaijani society in every nook and cranny.[6] Finally, Russia holds a contextual role, mostly that of arms supplier to both embattled. Any impact of regional political preferences that would establish them as the main driving force behind the conflict would be corroborated by their persistence in both major eruption periods, or in other words, through Mill's "method of agreement" then and now.

THE CRITICAL JUNCTURE OF THE LATE 1980S TO EARLY 1990S AND REGIONAL POLITICAL PREFERENCES IN NAGORNO-KARABAKH

A quick look back in history would reveal that, administratively, NK had never been part of Armenia in modern history (Panossian, 2001, p. 144). During the Tsarist empire, it constituted part of the Baku province, whereas in the critical juncture period that followed the collapse of the Tsarist empire, it came at the center of intense fighting between Armenia and Azerbaijan in late 1910s and early 1920, until the two republics got sovietized. In 1923, the region was granted the status of an autonomous oblast within the Azerbaijani SSR, being inhabited by both Armenians (70%) and Azerbaijanis (30%) (Jarosiewicz and Falkowski, 2016; Panossian, 2001, p. 144). Until the demise of the USSR, NK's critical policies and decisions, budget, and vital administrative choices, were all pending upon approval by the Azerbaijani authorities in Baku; as a result, although NK, nominally, relished the institutional structure of an "autonomous oblast," i.e., well-defined regional borders, a regional soviet, regional and local government agencies and various oblast-level institutions, in essence, that autonomy was completely devoid of any practical content (Panossian, 2001, p. 147). In these conditions, it did not take long for the co-existence between the two parties to be plagued by complaints about anti-Armenian discrimination, cultural degradation, economic sluggishness, and demographic shifts at the expense of the Armenian inhabitants of NK (HRW, 1995b; Panossian, 2001, p. 144).[7] Moreover, the intensity and the persistence of these grievances, along with the slim chance that any solution would be worked out, led to repeated demands on behalf of the neighboring Armenian SSR for the transfer of the region to it in 1929, 1935, 1963, 1966, 1977, and ultimately 1987 (Panossian, 2001, p. 144).

Such an action, however, was far from an easy task to accomplish during the Soviet era. Aside from informal institutions, such as ideas and perceptions, in Moscow that stood against any kind of border change throughout the USSR so as possible tidal effects to be kept in check, there were also the impediments posed by formal institutions, such as that of the constitution of the USSR. In particular, the 1977 USSR constitution stipulated that "the territory of a Union Republic may not be altered without its consent" and "the boundaries between Union Republics may be altered by mutual agreement of the Republics concerned," subject to ratification by the USSR's "highest bodies," i.e., the Supreme Soviet and Congress of the People's Deputies in Moscow (Constitution of the USSR, 1977, Article 73, par. 2; Article 78).

So, although the fermentation within NK was contained by the Soviet institutional equilibrium, the existence of all the oblast-based institutions, albeit nominal, assisted in the organization, and subsequent mobilization of the NK Armenians along ethnic lines. Experiencing a protracted socio-political suppression and economic destitution that more added to the "atomized" way of living than laid the groundwork for a "civic-tilting" transformation of the social co-existence, the NK Armenians viewed an "atomized-turned-ethnicized" recalibration of their national identity as an inescapable necessity should survival and security were to be guaranteed first. From this angle the repeated calls for unification with the Armenian SSR should be seen.

On the contrary, Azerbaijan did not see beyond the NK Armenians' initiatives survival and security concerns, but instead, interpreted them through a "Greater Armenia" spectrum (Panossian, 2001, p. 147). This suspicion would become further solidified when the Soviet state's institutional equilibrium would be disorganized and these dynamics would be reigning. The Azerbaijani answer to the NK Armenian's demands was to grant to the region the "highest level of autonomy," yet this was never defined so as to become known what it was consisted of and whether it could defuse the "about-to-explode" situation within the SSR; moreover, it created the impression that it was an empty promise not going a step further from what was already in place throughout the Soviet period, and for which the NK Armenian's were persistently objecting (Panossian, 2001, p. 148).

With this diachronically diverging co-existence on the ground, in February 1988, the NK Armenians took to the streets in Stepanakert, the capital of NK, calling for the region's incorporation into the Armenian SSR. This demand quickly found its institutional outlet, with the soviet of the NKAO to request from the USSR Supreme Soviet to sanction the transfer on February 20 (HRW, 1994, p. 1). Although not a day had passed before the Politburo in Moscow rejected the demand, this initial mobilization quickly spiraled and spread to the neighboring Armenia, where demonstrations swept Yerevan, the capital city, seeking to show the formation of a wider alliance along ethnic lines and to support the claims of their ethnic brethren (HRW, 1994, p. 1). That eruption would prompt waves of pogroms, with violent deportations of Armenians from Azerbaijan and Azerbaijanis from Armenia to become the rule rather than the exception. Moreover, in these conditions where allegiances were changing overnight and the power vacuum was becoming all the more contestable, the Soviet troops would recurrently intervene, making their presence felt in various forms.

Taking a closer look at critical "turns" of this first major eruption period, the spark of violence did not take long to enflame Sumgait, a small city of steel and petrochemical factories half-hour drive from Baku. With city officials to have received 3,500 out of the large number of Azerbaijani refugees from villages in Armenia, and with the local Azerbaijani population to long look with some resentment on the comfortable living of the local Armenians, it did take much for the appeals of a few young firebrands that were calling for vengeance to be heard (Keller, 1988). When on February 27, the Radio Baku broadcasted that two Azerbaijanis had been killed in a clash near Nagorno-Karabakh, a murderous crowd by young Azerbaijanis was instantly formed going on a window-smashing rampage that night (Keller, 1998). Anti-Armenian riots broke out, costing the lives to 32 people (26 Armenians and 6 Azerbaijanis), leaving hundreds more wounded, and deepening the fear of ethnic Armenians residing throughout Azerbaijan. That spasm of violence reserved a place for itself in the collective memory as the "Sumgait pogrom" (Keller, 1988). When the events cooled down, all the residents of Sumgait were taken aback, stating that a repetition of what happened was inconceivable, but for one occasion; in the words of Takhir Mamedov, a twenty-two-year-old Azerbaijani factory worker and a friend of Tale Ismailov who received fifteen years for murder, "it was a lesson for the people of Sumgait. But if another group of extremists tries something against the Azerbaijani nation, then everything could happen again" (Keller, 1998). These lines indicate how ethnicity, and particularly its ethnicized form, was instrumentalized so as to ally otherwise "atomized" rational actors under an umbrella for survival and security purposes in anarchy-resembling situations.

With the mobilization and the polarization to heat up, on June 15, 1988, the Armenian Supreme Soviet voted to accept NK into the Armenian SSR, a decision which met the Azerbaijani Supreme Soviet's antagonism, which voted not to give up on the region (HRW, 1994, p. 1). In July, the chairman of the Armenian Supreme Soviet, G.M. Voskanyan, further pursued his country's demand, visiting the Presidium of the USSR Supreme Soviet and pushing for the transfer of NK (Kaufman, 1998, p. 27). Gorbachev rebuffed, leading the soviet of NKAO along with Armenian crowds to embrace all the more ethnic nationalism as means of strengthening their "individual" status, and see independence from the USSR as the ultimate guarantee of survival, security and democracy.[8] Two month later, in September, 1988, another round of clashes between NK Armenians and ethnic Azerbaijanis broke out in Stepanakert, forcing almost all of the capital's Azerbaijani population out of the city (HRW, 1994, p. 1).

These events thickened the lines among Azerbaijanis, who on November 17, 1988, citing the unsanctioned construction of an allegedly (highly polluting) aluminum workshop in the natural preserve of Topkhana in NK, which was also sanctified by the Azerbaijanis as the place of a high-importance eighteenth-century battle against Iran, rallied in Baku; to them this action constituted a breach of the Azerbaijani sovereignty (Kaufman, 1998, p. 28). All the more people started to participate in the rallies on a daily basis, while a charismatic young machinist, Nemat Panakhov, appeared at the top of the nascent Azerbaijani popular movement (Kaufman, 1998, p. 28). Panakhov called for the reinstatement of Azerbaijan authority in NK and for the return of refugees in the region, endorsing, concurrently, perestroika and reforms on the spheres of social justice, human rights, culture, etc., and denouncing the Sumgait riots and the appearance of Islamic symbols (Kaufman, 1998, p. 28). This rhetoric notwithstanding, the brutality of violence and the population transfers were escalating.

With slogans such as "freedom for the heroes of Sumgait," nationalist mobilization and polarization had passed at grass-roots level (Kaufman, 1998, p. 29).[9] When on November 21, one of the Sumgait rioters was given the death sentence, Azerbaijani mobs targeted Armenians in the extensively segregated cities of Kirovabad (today's Ganje) and Nakhichevan, with protests to spread all over the republic. In a situation that pretty much resembled that of anarchy, troops appeared in the streets, enforcing a strict curfew and being as determined to uphold it as killing three people who acted against it in Kirovabad (Kaufman, 1998, p. 29). Armenia was also affected by similar events, with the death toll for Armenia's Azerbaijanis to be far higher than those for Armenians. Measuring the impact of the hostilities by the number of refugees, 180,000 Armenians left Azerbaijan (mostly from the cities of Kirovabad and Baku), and 160,000 Azerbaijanis fled Armenia (Kaufman, 1998, p. 29).

The USSR government, finding itself in this plight, placed NK under Moscow's direct rule, establishing a special commission in the region in January 1989 (Kaufman, 1998, p. 32). Yet, the clashes and the expansive situation of turmoil did not peter out; [10] in May 1989, during a general strike, in which the protesters again appealed for the NK unification with Armenia, and for new Azerbaijani settlements in the region to be stopped, the Soviet MVD troops along with tanks made an appearance in Stepanakert (HRW, 1994, p. 2). The NK Armenians accused the special commission of pro-Azerbaijani bias, whereas the intense mobilization on behalf of the Azerbaijani side and the chagrin caused by the loss of territory during the clashes, led to the rise of the Azerbaijan Popular Front (APF), the main opposition force, in July 1989 (Kaufman, 1998, p. 31). With its core demands revolving around democratization and sovereignty over NK, the APF rose quickly to prominence; two facts attest to this: first, the numerous rallies carried out under its banner in Baku in August and September 1989 that directly challenged the power of Abdulrahman Vezirov, first secretary of Azerbaijan's Communist Party, and, second, the well-targeted rail blockade against NK and Armenia that gravely impeded the recovery of the recently earthquake-struck Armenia, let alone the restoration of normal economic activity across the region (HRW, 1994, p. 2; Kaufman, 1998, p. 31). [11] In fact, the dynamic of the APF was such, that Vezirov's leadership appeared to succumb to it, when he prioritized the strengthening of Azerbaijan Republic's sovereignty in a set of laws, among which it was stipulated Azerbaijan's right to repeal NK's autonomous status, albeit ailing and repeatedly protested over long before the USSR entered the critical juncture period of the late 1980s and early 1990s. [12]

Vezirov's, and the Communist Party at large's, authority in Azerbaijan would not come in complete disarray until November 1989, when the USSR-drawn up special commission in NK would be disbanded and the region would be returned to Azerbaijani authority. Survival and security fears reached the red zone. Armenia responded with a proclamation of a "United Armenia" on December 1, 1989. Moreover, on January 9, the economic basis for such an endeavor was also attempted to be laid, when the Armenian Supreme Soviet in conjunction with the NKAO soviet discussed a 1990 budget for the Armenian SSR, in which economic and social development funds for NK were for the first time included (Croissant, 1998, p. 36). Azerbaijan did not leave these events unanswered, with the Azerbaijani Supreme Soviet to show its vehement opposition by unequivocally condemning all these actions on the grounds of "open interference in the internal affairs of Azerbaijan SSR, which is a sovereign republic" (Croissant, 1998, p. 36). In addition to that, this reply would be accompanied by an avalanche of violence during which, the anarchy-sinking socio-political environment would be exposed, the securitization of the interests of the involved parties would matter the most, whereas the whole standoff would culminate in the deaths of almost 137 people in a month which would be inscribed in the collective memory as "Black January."

In particular, on January 11, 1990, APF activists occupied government buildings in the city of Lankaran (280km south of Baku), calling for the dissolution of all government and Communist party institutions, whereas large rallies crowded the streets in Baku in a wider context of turmoil (HRW, 1995b; Kaufman, 1998, p. 31). Anti-Armenian rhetoric was prevalent, and Armenians themselves did not take long to be found at the center of massive attacks; on January 12, Armenians in Baku suffered major and extensive prosecution, whereas this anarchy-resembling situation accommodated material motivations, given that many insurgents appeared to be homeless refugees seeking to benefit themselves by taking possession of the Armenians' apartments right after the latter had been forced out (HRW, 1995a; Kaufman, 1998, p. 31). That was just the tip of the iceberg. On January 13, a second, and far more systemized, wave of anti-Armenian pogroms was materialized, costing the lives to 48 people (HRW, 1995b).

These pogroms, while not instigated by the government, were conducted under the tolerance of central authorities, including the local militia and 12,000 Soviet MVD troops in Baku, which did not engage in any decisive action to stop them (HRW, 1995b).[13] In fact, their indifference was that striking, that some journalists "pointed towards a conspiracy" (HRW, 1995b).

On January 15, in an attempt to keep the raging chaos at bay, a state of emergency was declared in various parts of Azerbaijan (the NK and the region at the Azerbaijani-Armenian border included), but not in Baku (HRW, 1994, p. 3). Nevertheless, the pogrom activity showed signs of de-escalation, allowing for the majority of the 27,000 Armenians that remained in Baku after the atrocities of 1988 to also leave the country (HRW, 1995b). Furthermore, the APF activists, seeking to guard their (expanding political) interests and maximize their power in that anarchy-sinking situation, proceeded to a blockade of Soviet military barracks so as to avert a possible military intervention (HRW, 1995b).

With the APF to have become the *de facto* dominant political force in numerous regions of Azerbaijan and poised to win Supreme Soviet Elections set for March 1990, Moscow had to come up with a solution to deal with the anti-Moscow APF and preserve the rule of the Communist Party in Azerbaijan. The raging hostilities between the Armenians and Azerbaijanis provided a fitting pretext. So the Kremlin, in the name of safeguarding the Armenian population, ordered the Soviet forces on January 19, 1990, to storm Baku and crush the APF, under the authority of a state of emergency decree which would be issued hours later from the events (HRW, 1995a).[14] The Soviet troops' deployment resulted in the deaths of more than 100 civilians, mostly

Azerbaijani, due to the unjustified and excessive use of force. Moreover, the military action hardly managed to intercept anti-Armenian attacks, "but also raised serious doubts about whether the Soviets wished to stem that violence" (HRW, 1995b). In the aftermath of the events, Communist Party politician Boris Yeltsin, commenting on the use of armed forces, stated that the East European socialism had become corrupted "because it was state socialism guarded by the military," indicating, in this manner, the top-down model of governance that had resulted in a deeply compartmentalized and atomized socio-political reality, which, when the USSR would enter its final stretch, would proper the once Soviet citizens to resort to fundamental attributes of the human nature such as the language (Moldova, Ukraine), or ethnicity (Ukraine, Georgia, Azerbaijan) as a means of individual power maximization and alliance formation so as to ensure survival and security (BBC, 1990).

Narrowing down to NK, by the summer 1990, the Soviet military appeared to control the entire region, having established checkpoints on all roads to Stepanakert, and keeping a close watch on any travel activity (HRW, 1994, p. 3). Nevertheless, armed encounters between bands of Armenians and Azerbaijanis, as well as raids on villages in the districts of Azerbaijan that border NK to the north, were numerous and repeated (HRW, 1994, p. 4). Indicative is the fact that for the period January–May 1991, 115 attacks were reported on almost every institution of law enforcement, civilian and military (HRW, 1994, p. 4).

Just like elsewhere in Azerbaijan that the Azerbaijani-Armenian relations had been subject to a *zero-sum* logic, in the same manner, NK would reach its own watershed, past which both Armenians and Azerbaijanis would seek to increase their relative gains by military means as a way of survival and security. That turning point became known as "Operation Ring," and was carried out in the spring and summer of 1991 by the Azerbaijani OMON in association with the 23rd Division of the 4th Soviet Army (HRW, 1995b). Theoretically, it appeared as a passport and arms check in the Armenian villages in NK, and the Khanlar and Goranboy (Shahumyan) districts of Azerbaijan, so as Armenian guerilla groups (fedayeen), which operated against an order to disband, to be disarmed (HRW, 1995b). In reality, no such groups' disarmament actually proceeded, with Armenian villages and the Armenian population in the area to be targeted and subject to various forms of harassment and abuse (e.g., forced relocation, imprisonment, beatings, etc.) (HRW, 1994, p. 5). Up to twenty-four Armenian villages were vacated "with unprecedented degree of violence and a systemic violation of human rights," whereas all actions were seen by the Armenians as being conducted under Gorbachev's orders in a socio-political environment where self-interest was standing atop (HRW, 1994, p. 5). The exerted brutality thickened the ethnic lines among the NK Armenians, who, on December 10,

1991, proceeded to a referendum on the region's declaration of independence, viewing the political status as the best guaranteed of their survival and security.

The referendum illustrated the unity which permeated the Karabakhi Armenians, with 99.89% (108,615) of those who participated in the voting to endorse independence (De Waal, 2013, p. 175), as shown in table 5.1. Given the protracted hostilities, any other political solution of co-existence had been rendered hard-to-achieve, if attainable.

This course of *de facto* separateness became far more solidified after the formal break of the USSR. Then, much of the soviet army equipment, i.e., heavy artillery, rocket-propelled grenades (RPGs), rocket launchers, tanks, armed personnel carriers, came into possession of combatants on both sides, and the Soviet successor states involved in the conflict were set to exhibit "the same violent, short-sighted approach to communal affairs as their Tsarist and Soviet predecessors" (HRW, 1995b). In more detail, from the outset of 1992, a full-scale civil war broke out, in which both sides perceived military activities and territorial gains as the only way to maximize their power and strengthen their relative advantage, thus ensuring their survival and overall security.

In February 1992, the NK Armenian forces, backed by soldiers from the 366th Motor Rifle Regiment of the Russian Army, captured the Azerbaijani-populated town of Khojaly, eleven kilometers north of Stepanakert, with

Table 5.1. Nagorno-Karabakh Referendum on Independence—December 10, 1991

Question	Right to vote	Voting Participation	Valid	Yes	No
"Do you accept that the proclaimed Nagorno-Karabakh Republic be an independent State independently determining the forms of cooperation with other States and communities?" "Согласны ли Вы, чтобы провозглашенная Нагорно-Карабахская Республика была независимым государством, самостоятельно определяющим формы сотрудничества с другими государствами и сообществами?"	132,328	108,736 82.2%	108,641 99.9%	108,615 99.89%	24 0.02%

Source: (MFA NK, 1991)

more than two hundred civilians getting killed (HRW, 1994, p. 6).[15] In May, the NK Armenians, again relishing Russian support, gained Shusha, a strategic place in the Karabakh mountains situated at a high altitude, and Karabakh's last Azerbaijani-populated town (HRW, 1994, p. 6). Once having their presence established there, the NK Armenian forces advanced to another strategic move: the capture of the Azerbaijani town of Lachin, which is only thirteen kilometers away from the Armenian border (Herzig, 1996, p. 262; HRW, 1994, p. 7). As a result, the so-called Lachin corridor was created, linking the mountainous Karabakh with Armenia, and assisting NK not only to strengthen and securitize its recently declared independence, but also forge a *de facto* alliance, further adding to its power and ensuring its position.

With the exception of a temporal invigoration by the Azerbaijani offensive in the summer of 1992, during which it claimed Goranboy and almost 80% of the Mardakert province, the NK Armenians' positions had been consolidated by September. Moreover, in February 1993, the NK Armenian offensive managed to recapture the Mardakert region, and, more importantly, to cut off the Armenia-adjacent (roughly thirty-one kilometers from the border) Kelbajar province from the rest of Azerbaijan, creating a second land corridor to Armenia and further reinforcing the *de facto* NK-Armenia alliance (HRW, 1994, p. 8). With the National Army of Azerbaijan to have been all the more bogged down by domestic political turmoil due to a power struggle between the political and the military leadership, itself instigated by the recurring losses in the geopolitical tug-of-war in the NK front, the NK Armenians expanded their control in a much wider area than the NK itself, considering it as a security zone; in fact, to the west lays Armenia, to the South the Lachin corridor, to the east the Mardakert province (the strategic Terter-Kelbajar road included), and to the north, the physical border of the Murov mountains. The latter host the Omar pass, the only connection of Kelbajar with Azerbaijan, which, although it remained unoccupied by the NK Armenian forces, geography (the altitude reaches as high as 3,048km) and weather conditions, especially during the winter time, make the pass highly impenetrable (HRW, 1994, p. 13).

Transforming all this geographic expanse into numbers, the NK Armenians consolidated their *de facto* rule, aside from NK proper which comprises 4,7% of the internationally recognized territory of Azerbaijan, to neighboring Azerbaijani areas, thus controlling 13,62% of the Azerbaijani land (BBC RUSSIAN.com, 2005).[16] Interesting is also to see what happens in terms of populations. With the population dynamics of the wider region affected by the conflict to be hard, if not impossible, to ascertain, the last conducted population census of 1979 could be of assistance; in particular, that time the NKAO was inhabited by 123,000 Armenians and 37,000 Azerbaijanis. Since the beginning of the conflict, all Azerbaijanis and many Armenians fled the region, with estimates by the staff of the international humanitarian missions to bring the population of Karabakh in 2000–2001 to 80,000 people (BBC RUSSIAN.COM, 2005). Yet this is nothing more but an approximate calculation, given that as of May 16, 2000, the then Prime Minister of NK, Anushavan Danielyan, stated that the population of the region is a "state secret" (BBC Russian.com, 2005).

With these facts on the ground, the involved parties in the conflict along with Russia proceeded to the ceasefire agreement of May 11, 1994. In particular, the conflicting parties agreed to the following:

The Four-Point Ceasefire Agreement

1. Implementation of a full cease-fire and cessation of hostilities from 00 hours 01 minutes of May 12, 1994.
2. The Minister of Defense of the Russian Federation would convene in Moscow no later than May 12 an urgent meeting with his counterparts from Azerbaijan and Armenia and the NK army commander, in which the lines of troops pullback and the deployment of an advance group of international observes would be agreed.
3. The negotiations would be completed in the next 10 days, and an Agreement on Cessation of the Armed Conflict would be concluded no past May 22, 1994.
4. That agreement would take effect as soon as authorized representatives from all opposing parties had endorsed it. [17] (MFA NK, 1994)

This agreement, and particularly provisions such as the second, which called for the exact delineation of the lines beyond which the troops would be withdrawn and for the guarantee of such process by the presence of international observers, paved the way for NKR's regional political preferences to put down roots, very hard to reverse. Much more after the collective memory had been tainted by the protracted atrocities, and the policies of the post-soviet Azerbaijan did little to avert the perpetuation of a fragmented and porous national identity framework. In this context, an atomized-turned-ethnicized transformation of the national identity, placed under the guarantee of an independent political status, would constitute the sole means of survival and security on behalf of the NK Armenians.

EN ROUTE TO THE EVENTS OF APRIL 2016

The years that ensued, the hostilities of the 1988–1993 period did not instigate too much of a change as far as the Azerbaijani policies towards building an inclusive state are concerned; many of the hardships that the Azerbaijani-NK Armenian relationship had encountered in the past remained intact, forging a seemingly irreversible course towards *de facto* separateness rather than greasing the wheels of a reversible course towards political co-existence within one state. Employing corruption as an indicator to evaluate the compartmentalization across the socio-political board, figure 5.1 is of particular significance.

With corruption to have already been defined as "the abuse of entrusted power for private gain" and the indicator "control of corruption" to measure the perceptions of the extent to which public power is exercised for private gain, including both petty and grand forms of corruption, as well as "capture of the state by elites and private interests" on a scale ranging from –2.5 to 2.5. Figure 5.1 showcases the persistence of compartmentalization in a socio-political environment that had little signs of progress from the end of the first major eruption all the way up to the second major eruption. In particular, the measurements exhibit that far more than 50% of citizens in Azerbaijan considered that the public power was exercised for private gain and that the elites along with private interests had been using the state institutions for their own, individual, goals. Consequently, the anarchy-resembling conditions of the early independence period never left the socio-political foreground, maintaining the artificial transformation of the national identity type from "atomized-to-ethnicized" as an inescapable means of forging a wider alliance, guaranteeing survival and security.

Putting these facts on the ground, since the ceasefire agreement of 1994, the outbreak of fighting along the 160-mile ceasefire line (also known as the

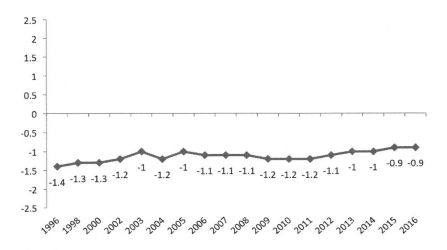

Figure 5.1.   Control of Corruption: Estimate, Azerbaijan. Source: Kaufmann et al., 2010.

"Line of Contact-LoC") never actually came to an end, with the aggregate number of violations to reach as high as 7,000 times (CSCE, 2017, p. 2).[18] Furthermore, as the epitome of the second critical juncture was closing by, i.e., the April 2016 Four-Day War, the breaches became far more intense and heavy as far as the deaths and the weaponry used are concerned.[19]

While up to 2013, there was occasional sniper fire, in November 2014, following a summer upsurge in the fighting that lead to the death of twenty soldiers on both sides, an Armenian helicopter was downed in the LoC, constituting the worst incident since the era of the first major eruption (De Waal, 2014; Reuters, 2014).[20] Three Armenians were killed, whereas the Azerbaijani official who downed the helicopter was awarded the medal of courage (De Waal, 2014). Initially, each side put the blame on the other, with the Azerbaijani to accuse the Armenian one for dispatching two helicopters over their positions, and the Armenian to respond that there was no danger posed since the helicopter was on a routine training mission (Reuters, 2014). A closer look, however, would shed light on an "eye for an eye" logic, retaliating the July 31, 2014 NK Armenians' incursion into Azerbaijani positions that led to the death of many Azerbaijanis (De Waal, 2014).[21] Throughout 2015, heavier weapons were employed, with mortars to be frequently fired and rockets to rain down on the Armenia-Azerbaijan border and on the LoC east of NK (De Waal, 2015).[22] While the pre-2013 small arms fire could be attributed to a local commander, the use of heavier weapons ran high in the chain of command, requiring the involvement of the political elites. All were precipitating the break out of the second major eruption.

In this about-to-explode for the second time setup, Russia would retain its contextual role; on the one hand, it had further tightened its long-term alliance with Armenia, signing a new lease on the Guymri military up to 2044 and inviting Yerevan into the brewing Eurasian Economic Union (EEU) (De Waal, 2015). On the other hand, it had also stiffened the military bond with Azerbaijan, scoring high as far as the country's heavy weaponry supplies are concerned (De Waal, 2015). But, certainly there is more to this; Armenia and Azerbaijan, themselves, did not count much on Russia, swaying between Moscow and the West. To begin with, Armenia had diachronically been balancing between being a formal ally of Russia, and seizing every opportunity to maintain warm relations with Georgia, the EU, NATO and the US.[23] Likewise, Azerbaijan, despite its wide and harsh crackdown on civil society, the media, and the opposition, facts which isolate it from the West and let it standing alone on Russia's south, its traditional alliance with Turkey, along with its energy interests, most of which bypass the dominant energy position of Russia in the Eurasia by providing outlets not controlled by Russian interests, did not allow it to be a full Russian ally, let alone count on its support in the paramount issue of the NK conflict.

All of these having been said, on November 10, 2015, it had been observed that "the latest Armenian-[Azerbaijani] fighting raise[d] the risk that a serious incident [would] precipitate, by miscalculation, a new small war that no one want[ed] but from which neither side would [be] prepared to back away" (De Waal, 2015). Indeed, the second major eruption period was *ante portas*.

THE "ZERO HOUR": THE APRIL 2016 FOUR-DAY WAR

With both Azerbaijani and Armenian Presidents, Ilham Aliyev and Serzh Sargsyan respectively, being in the US attending the Nuclear Security Summit, in the early hours of April 2, 2016, extensive fighting took place on the north-eastern, eastern, and south-eastern sectors of the LoC (BBC, 2016d).[24] By morning, the hostilities had claimed the lives of numerous civilians, with the NK Armenian artillery fire to be responsible for deaths in the Terter district, and the Azerbaijani rocket attacks for deaths in the town of Mardakert in NK (Broers, 2016, p. 11). As the first day of conflict came to an end, the Azerbaijani forces had managed to boost their relative military gains compared to the NK Armenian side, by taking over many, formerly NK Armenian, front posts in two areas: in the region of the Talish and Seysulan villages in the northeast, and in the mountainous region of Lale Tepe in the southeast, in close proximity to the Iranian border (Broers, 2016, p. 12). Nevertheless, these advances were hardly anything more than symbolic, since they moved the front lines in the conflict zones by more or less one kilometer (Jarosiewicz and Falkowski, 2016).

With these advances by the Azerbaijani army to constitute the most, if not all, of the April Four-Day War, the next days of intense fighting were constrained to the use of heavy weaponry and the pilling up of killed civilians. Although on April 3 a unilateral ceasefire was declared by the Azerbaijani Ministry of Defense, the atrocities on both sides kept raging, killing one Azerbaijani civilian in Terter and three Armenians in Talish (Haqqin.az, 2016; *hetq*, 2016).[25] On April 4, an "atomized-turned-ethnicized" mobilization took place on both sides of the almost anarchical socio-political environment, with the Azerbaijani to try to maximize its power by deploying suicide bombs and utter threats of strikes on NK's capital, Stepanakert, and the NK Armenian to promise a response of equal intensity in retaliation (Broers, 2016, p. 12). On April 5, both sides consented to a ceasefire in Moscow, pursuant Russian mediation, yet acts of aggression persisted throughout April, increasing the death toll (Broers, 2016, p. 12; Jarosiewicz and Falkowski, 2016; Harutyunyan, 2016).

During the period of open warfare, the Azerbaijani forces deployed next to the heavy weaponry of pre-war years, a renewed, and far more sophisticated, arsenal compared to the first major eruption; in particular, the Israeli-made Harop "kamikaze drone" made its first appearance, claiming the lives of nine people as a bus which was transporting Armenian volunteers from Sisian to Mardakert became the target of one such drone attack (Broers, 2016, p. 15; Eckel, 2016). Furthermore, the NK armed forces released photos of a Thunder B surveillance drone, which they claimed to have downed on April 2, whereas, in the same context, the Azerbaijani sources claimed to have destroyed "six enemy tanks" using Israeli-manufactured Spike missiles (Kucera, 2016).[26] Although discussing in detail the weaponry used in the war lies beyond the aims of the present analysis, there is some usefulness to it; the fact that Azerbaijan presented a sophisticated arsenal that had never before operated, much less owned, could serve as an indicator of two things: first, of the little progress made, if any, since the first major eruption concerning a political solution of co-existence with NK within a single state. Second, of the means by which the NK issue was to be addressed. Obviously, the "tit-for-tat" logic had taken the best of both sides, not allowing them to scrutinize the causes of the protracted hostilities of the first major eruption period, thus nurturing a shorter but far more acrimonious repetition, instead of creating the conditions in which truly rational actors would consent to an institutional setup, which would make the co-existence of the two communities, first and foremost secure, and then, viable.

The retaliatory attitude becomes more apparent if a closer look is taken at which party was the instigator of the brief war. At first sight, both sides put the blame on the other, with the Azerbaijani to accuse the NK Armenian of firing on areas away from the LoC, emphasis placed on a primary school, houses and factories, and the Armenian government to accuse Azerbaijan of unleashing a "massive attack" with tanks, artillery, and helicopters. But, putting things into perspective, there is little doubt that the 1994 ceasefire agreement had left the NK Armenians in charge of a territory far bigger than that of the NK proper, which was serving as a sort of sedative of their survival and security concerns and as a possibly expendable chip during a conflict-resolution negotiation. Moreover, Armenia, at large, posed as a militarily superior power. In contrast, Azerbaijan was the defeated side, with all the psychological and socio-political connotations such a situation may be associated with. In fact, these connotations would come to the surface after the April 5, 2016, ceasefire agreement by the Azerbaijani media, which emphasized a tactical Azerbaijani victory, that sort of readdressed the losses of the first major eruption period, by disproving the myth of the LoC impregnability, the superiority, if not invincibility, of the Armenian military, and the value of Armenia's alliances (Broers, 2016, p. 13; Jarosiewicz and Falkowski, 2016). In light of these, it is plausible to conjecture that the long-simmering psychological and socio-political implications could have functioned as motives, sufficiently propelling the advances of the Azerbaijani forces in the LoC.[27]

In the broader context, Turkey immediately sided with Azerbaijan, with Turkey's President Erdogan to state that Turkey backed Azerbaijan "to the end" in the clashes (BBC, 2016d). The same picture, however, does not hold for Armenia and its main ally, Russia. With the fact that 85% of Azerbaijan's weaponry for the period 2011–2016 was provided from Russia to be nothing more than an open secret, public demonstrations rife with anti-Russian sentiment flooded the streets of Yerevan right after the ceasefire (Broers, 2016, p. 13; Kucera, 2016). Moreover, the issue reverberated on a more structural level, when Khachatur Kokobelyan, the leader of the liberal and pro-European party "Free Democrats" drew up a draft resolution on Armenia's withdrawal from the EEU (Lragir.am, 2016).[28] As stated, the security component of the membership had been seriously compromised, since during the Azerbaijani advances against the NK, the member-states of the EEU abstained from the prime ministers' meeting set to take place in Yerevan, so as "not to insult Azerbaijan" (Lragir.am, 2016).[29] Consequently, the draft resolution concluded that the EEU is, aside from a barely helpful economic union, an "ineffective political and economic alliance" (Lragir.am, 2016). In this manner, it indicated that although economic considerations hold a principal role in the daily routine of both citizens and states, if the security uncertainties have not, primarily and essentially, been dealt with in the anarchy-resembling socio-political environment of the region, then the solid foundations of any further collaboration are gravely ailing. Yet, on April 7, 2017, during Russia's Prime Minister, Dmitry Medvedev, visit to Armenia, the President of the recently overpowered Armenia, Serzh Sarkisian, clarified that Russia remained a strategic partner of his country (Vzglyad, 2016). Moreover, Armenia's PM Ovik Abramyan asked Medvedev to expedite an agreement with Rosoboronexport, the sole state intermediary agency for Russia's exports of defense-related and dual use products, technologies and services (Vzglyad, 2016). The next day, Medvedev would visit Azerbaijan, corroborating, in this manner, Russia's contextual role in the NK conflict (Vzglyad, 2016).[30] Discussing in brief Russia's position in the regional developments, Russia not only maximized its cash-generating arms sales to both embattled parties, but also increased its relative gains *vis-à-vis* both Armenia and Azerbaijan, given their involvement and serious enfeeblement by the open socio-political wound of the protracted conflict in NK.

Overall, the next day of the April Four-Day War found both parties entrenched into their almost thirty years long positions; one the one hand, the Azerbaijanis rejected any confidence-building measures, linking any withdrawal of snipers or the establishment of an incident investigation mechanism to territorial withdrawals by the NK Armenian forces (Broers, 2016, p. 16). On the other hand, the NK Armenians, citing, first and foremost, survival and security reasons, saw the territory gained during the first major eruption period as a necessary (security) means in the absence of a political solution which would accommodate their regional political preferences, and thus set the foundations for moving ahead from the stagnant situation that the hostilities of the first critical juncture created and the April 2016 events reawakened and further deepened. On this basis, the NK Armenians accepted confidence-building measures without granting any of the extra territory gained before a political solution was reached. As argued by the NK Armenians themselves:

> It is impossible to ensure indivisible and equal security, focusing only on individual human rights and ignoring the collective rights of peoples. These two components of the Human Dimension are inextricably linked, as evidenced by the International Covenants of Human Rights. (EuCfA, 2016)

CONCLUSION

Considering the main takeaways from Azerbaijan's "frozen conflict," table 5.2 is of particular assistance.

During the Soviet era, the region of NK was granted the status of an autonomous oblast (similar to that of South Ossetia) within the Azerbaijani SSR. Although this status nominally stipulated for increased political autonomy, in reality, a situation of cultural discrimination, part of which was the non-provision of education in the native language, and economic degradation created a boiling magma of long-suppressed political preferences. With NK to have never been part of Armenia, the NK Armenians repeatedly called for the stipulated autonomy to acquire real essence and be abided by so as to make the co-existence within one (Azerbaijani) state possible. In fact, they were that determined to push forward with this demand that they also appealed to Armenia for unification as a means of highlighting the inescapability and intensity of their demand. In the Soviet period, however, such territorial changes were encountering high institutional barriers in their realization, if ever, thus NK's political preferences remained bottled up.

When the USSR reached the critical juncture period, and long established domestic alliances started to shift, the NK Armenians found a wide opening to resurface their demands, again in the same order: calls for a political solution that would allow for co-existence within one (Azerbaijani) state, with this political solution to refer to the federalization of the nascent Republic of Azerbaijan. In this manner, survival and security concerns on behalf of the NK Armenians would, first and foremost, be addressed. Then, the way would be wide open to try to regain the lost social trust of the Soviet years, operating within a system that would institutionally guarantee the domestic balance of powers. In this effort, the possibility of NK's unification with

Table 5.2. Anatomy of the Nagorno Karabakh Crisis: Substantiating Causality

	Nagorno-Karabakh	Test Cases
Soviet period	***Regional status:*** • Autonomous oblast: moderate political autonomy	**Gagauzia, Donbass,** **Adjara**: same background as NK (i.e. the Soviet State), No regional political preference
First major-eruption period (critical juncture 1988-1994)	***Regional political*** ***preference:*** • Independence (should no increased, federation- leaning, political autonomy within Azerbaijan feasible) • Azerbaijani nationalistic attack	
Second major-eruption period (critical juncture of the April 2016 events)	***Regional political*** ***preference:*** • Independence (should no increased, federation- leaning, political autonomy within Azerbaijan feasible) • Azerbaijani nationalistic attack	

Armenia stood as a means of increasing the heat to the Azerbaijani authorities by presenting a counterbalancing perspective. The NK-Armenia official
axis was never realized (and actually even as of today Armenia has not
recognized the NK *de facto* independence). Nevertheless, the Azerbaijanis
perceived the NK Armenians' mobilization, assisted by Armenia, as a move
towards reinstating the "Greater Armenia" at the expense of the emerging
Republic of Azerbaijan. In the anarchy-resembling socio-political environment of the time, ethnicity was employed as tool of forging wider alliances
by converting otherwise atomized rational actors into ethnicized. The NK
Armenian side expanded its territorial control to Azerbaijani lands, addressing by military means what it had not been made possible to be solved by
institutional means: its survival and security. But, following a protracted
conflict such as this which leads to a *de facto* outcome, any trust could have
left exiting the Soviet era was gravely minimized, if not eradicated outright,
whereas the prospect for a political solution that would allow for co-existence within one (Azerbaijani) state was almost evaporated. The NK Armenians would onwards prioritize self-determination (independence) as their
regional political preference, whereas the Azerbaijanis would be burdened by

the trauma of being unable to defend their own land, showing inferiority to the Armenian army.

With this almost intractably polarized atmosphere, the ensuing years, up to the second major eruption, did not witness any progress as far as the conditions of the early independence period are concerned. On the contrary, as the April 2016 Four-Day War revealed, the two embattled parties had remained locked in their erstwhile positions. Azerbaijan, considerably strengthened by the purchase of sophisticated weaponry by Russia and Israel, engaged NK Armenian posts in the LoC, managing to claim them back, and thus relieve, to a certain extent, the psychological and socio-political legacy of the first major eruption. An institutional arrangement, even at the very last moment, could have averted the seemingly irreversible from becoming further solidified, i.e., the *de facto* Republic of Nagorno Karabakh. Indeed, after the termination of hostilities, the NK Armenian side accepted confidence building measures as a gesture of goodwill, viewing, in parallel, its control over Azerbaijani lands as a "vital asset" in the absence of a political solution which could satisfactorily address the insurmountable survival and security concerns. This time, however, behind the term "political solution" was a far more consolidated call for independence.

In this context, Russia maintained a contextual role, supplying both sides with arms. In fact, such as situation not only added to its national economic interest, given the lucrative nature of the arms industry, but also increased its relative gains *vis-à-vis* the two Caucasian actors; the costly arms, instead of creating a deterrence based on the balance of power, and thus guarantee some sort of *de facto* security, underpinned the bleeding wound of NK that let no option to Azerbaijan and Armenia but to constantly reconfiguring their state budget by reallocating funds from critical public goods to armaments for the NK front.[31]

NOTES

1. The region of NK is called "Artsakh" by the Armenians.
2. For a detailed map of Azerbaijan and the key areas in the NK conflict, see CSCE, 2017, p. 2.
3. Unconfirmed sources increased this number to three hundred (Broers, 2016, p. 14).
4. This case is visited later on more extensively.
5. Discussing militarization in the region, indicative is the fact that in 2013, Azerbaijan's annual defense budget stood at $3.7bn, the very same moment that Armenia's rose to $447m. Moreover, according to the Global Militarization Index, issued by the German think tank Bonn International Center for Conversion (BICC), Armenia and Azerbaijan were, in 2015, among the top ten most militarized nations in the world (BBC, 2015b).
6. Leaders on both sides have been accused of dealing with the conflict as a tool to stay in power, thus avoiding any substantial efforts could contribute to its resolution (BBC, 2016a). By resorting to one of the fundamentals attribute of human nature, that of ethnicity, and capitalizing on the ethnic type of national identity, they have been seeking to forge alliances around it with them standing as "father figures" as a means of keeping their power unchecked and

unchallenged by otherwise "atomized" rational actors, who have been striving towards their survival and security through individual power maximization efforts and alliance formation. "Nationalist sentiment boosted by pro-government media in both societies had been at its height," especially prior to the Four-Day War (BBC, 2016a).

7. As far as demographic shifts are concerned, the Armenian population of the oblast was downsized from 95% in early 1920s to 76% in 1979, i.e., 123,000 out of a total of 161,000 (Panossian, 2001, p. 144). With regard to the quality of life within the Azerbaijan SSR that seriously impacted also on the residents of NK, the SSR ranked nearly last among Soviet republics in almost every indicator of standard of living, with the average per capita income and the consumer goods per capita which were consumed to reach only 62% and 59%, respectively, of the USSR's average (Kaufman, 1998, p. 22). Passing to the average monthly income, striking is the fact that it was below the wage level of 87% of the Soviet population, while the social funds which were added up were corresponding to only 65% of the all-union average per capita rate (Kaufman, 1998, p. 22). The general picture becomes far gloomier if considered that a big number of urban Azerbaijanis was residing in tenebrous run-down neighborhoods, rife with heavy pollution, a legacy of a century of oil production (Kaufman, 1998, p. 22). Overall, the Azerbaijani SSR was comparable with the traditionally lagging region of Central Asia, which was bogged down by the same, if not more, underdevelopment and country-wide pollution (Kaufman, 1998, p. 22). There is little doubt that such a diachronically accumulated socio-economic distress across the Republic would find the violence erupted in early 1988 a fitting outlet to pour out.

8. See also Kaufman, 1998, p. 27.

9. For the term "nationalist mobilization," see also Beissinger, 2002.

10. Nevertheless, doing justice to the argument, it has to be mentioned that 1989 was a far less violent and bloody year, compared to 1988, and even less to the years that ensued (Kaufman, 1998, p. 32).

11. Providing a complete picture of the Azerbaijani economic and transport blockades on NK and Armenia, it is mentioned that these were taking place periodically, until a full and permanent one was imposed in summer 1991 (HRW, 1994, p. 2).

12. See Kaufman, 1998, p. 31.

13. According to another account, the additional Soviet MVD troops in Baku reached 17,000 (HRW, 1994, p. 3).

14. To this direction of premeditated action on behalf of Moscow point also the documents of the military prosecutor's office in Baku, which show that the military action had been planned before the January 13, 1990, pogroms (HRW, 1995b).

15. Yeltsin's Russia became more pro-Armenian following the position upheld by Armenia and Azerbaijan in the 1991 coup; in particular, while Azerbaijan welcomed the coup, Armenia threw its weight behind Gorbachev, with its first post-soviet President and former leader of the Karabakh committee, Levon Ter-Petrosian, to also support the then new-fangled CIS (Herzig, 1996, p. 261).

16. In more detail, the neighboring former-Azerbaijani-now-occupied areas by the NK Armenians comprise the cities of Kelbajar, Lachin, Kubalti, Jebrail, and Zangelan, which are fully controlled by the NK Armenians, and the districts of Agdam and Fuzuli, which are partially controlled, i.e., 77% and 33%, respectively. Further to this, the NK Armenians have occupied two former village enclaves in Nakhichevan and Qazakh districts respectively, both bordering Armenia (BBC, 2017). On the other hand, Azerbaijan controls a former Armenian-populated enclave (BBC, 2017).

17. The text of the agreement was signed on behalf of Azerbaijan by M. Mamedov in Baku on May 9, on behalf of Armenia by S. Sargsyan in Yerevan on May 10, and on behalf of NK by S. Babayan in Stepanakert on May 11, 1994 (MFA NK, 1994).

18. Although the Azerbaijanis are "probably responsible for a greater quantity of ceasefire violations," the NK Armenians did not fall back in this *zero-sum* geopolitical game, also demonstrating their power (De Waal, 2014).

19. For a detailed table on civilian deaths and major military incidents for the period January 2014–March 2016, see Broers, 2016, p. 8.

20. In November 1991, an Azerbaijani helicopter transporting officials and mediators was downed by the NK Armenians not far from where this latest incident took place, critically heating up the rivalry between the two sides (De Waal, 2014).

21. The "law of retaliation" in the bilateral relations is also corroborated by the fact that the NK Armenians threatened a "painful" response to the downing of the helicopter (De Waal, 2014).

22. In particular, the Azerbaijani side started to bombard Armenian and Karabakh positions using MLRS brought in from its traditional ally in the region Turkey, whereas in late September 2015, it was also reported the use, for the first time since the onset of the conflict, of field artillery on the northeastern border of NK (Minasyan, 2017, p. 138).

23. Armenia could be placed in the same category with post-soviet states such as Belarus and Kazakhstan with regard to its balancing position between being a formal ally of Russia and the West.

24. For a map on the locations of the hostilities, see Broers, 2016, p. 4.

25. For the atrocities committed throughout the April Four-Day War, as well as during the period immediately after, each side presented its own account. For more, see Nagorno Karabakh Republic, 2016; MFA AZ, 2016.

26. In retrospect, such actions should, to a certain degree, be anticipated, given that in 2012, Azerbaijan had signed a dazzling $1.6 billion deal with Israel for arms supplies (Kucera, 2016).

27. In addition to these, it should also be mentioned that the Armenian side was so stunned by the eruption of the war that it accepted the ceasefire "with great relief" (Jarosiewicz and Falkowski, 2016). In more detail, on April 26, the Armenian President, Serzh Sarkisian, dismissed three senior Armenian military officials (Alik Mirzabekian, the Deputy Defense Minister, General Arshak Karapetian, the military intelligence chief, and General Komitas Muradian, the commander of the Armenian army's communication duties) amid severe criticism over poor and outdated supplies of weapons and ammunition to the Armenian army and wide disorganization attributed to the inefficiency of the communication units (Harutyunyan, 2016). Moreover, Sarkisian admitted that the Armenian military intelligence failed to get "precise information" about the upcoming Azerbaijani offensive (Harutyunyan, 2016). The opposition also joined the criticism, with the leader of the Armenian National Congress, Levon Zurabian, to take the issue a step further, linking the military setback with the nature of the Armenian state; in his words, "what we have now is a criminal-oligarchic, corrupt system which has demonstrated its inadequacy in the face of external threats" (Harutyunyan, 2016). In this manner, he highlighted that beyond the "atomized-turned-ethnicized" national identity in order to push for the NK regional political preferences as a means of survival and security in an anarchy-resembling socio-political environment, there is the prevalence of an egocentric (political) behavior that seeks to promote its relative gains *vis-à-vis* co-citizens and former allies, benefiting from the absence of an institutional framework that would arrange the socio-political relations in such a manner that the state would gradually and constantly progress towards Pareto's optimal outcome.

28. The political party "Free Democrats" was created in 2011 by Khachatur Kokobelyan. In the parliamentary elections of 2017 it did not manage to pass the threshold of 5%. For more on the party, see http://www.fdp. am/.

29. The same resentment was also expressed towards the Russia-led CSTO in which Armenia is a member. In particular, as stated by the head of the Armenian Institute of International and Security Affairs in Yerevan, Stepan Safarian, "[Russia] did not act as Armenia's strategic ally. And the CSTO also behaved . . . [like some] peacekeeping organization" (Baumgartner, 2018).

30. In fact, this course of action on behalf of Russia seems to indicate a pattern, since two years later, in 2018, in a meeting were the main topic was the region of NK, Russia's President, Vladimir Putin, would receive Armenia's President, Nikol Pashinian, a week after a meeting had taken place with his Azerbaijani counterpart, Ilham Aliyev (RFE/RL, 2018a).

31. From the outset of the conflict, Armenia stood by NK, providing it with aid, armaments, and volunteers (HRW, 1995b). As stated by the NK authorities, Armenia was responsible for an amount between 70% and 90% of the enclave's annual budget, providing it in the form of interest-free credits (HRW, 1995b). According to estimates by analysts, 7% to 9% of Arme-

nia's annual budget was channeled to NK (HRW, 1995b). After the Azerbaijani offensive bounced back in December 1993, Armenia's involvement in NK considerably increased, with conscripts, regular army and Interior Ministry troops to be dispatched to fight on the NK side. In fact, several active-duty Armenian Army soldiers were captured by the Azerbaijani forces (HRW, 1995b). While Armenia has not even up to day recognized the *de facto* independence of NK, its NK-descended first President, Levon Ter-Petrossian, stated, while in London in February 1994, that Armenia would not hesitate to intervene militarily should the NK Armenians were faced with "genocide" or "forced deportation" (HRW, 1995b). As far as the Azerbaijani budget is concerned, it is a fact that the military budget is considered to be a cornerstone in the country's capacity to overpower Armenia. Thus, when in 2016 there was a drop by 40% due to a plunge in the oil prices, fears started to spread over a military imbalance with Armenia, which could possibly be associated with grave dangers for the country's national security (Broers, 2016, p. 18).

Level II

International: Energy Politics in Eurasia

Chapter Six

The Clash of Interests across Eurasia's Underbelly

THE EURASIAN ENERGYLAND

The EU-Russia energy relationship has been confronted with multiple "critical junctures," particularly in the Black Sea region. Since the 2006 gas cutoff that endangered regular flows from Russia to the EU, the latter has conceived of policies to enhance its energy security; among these has been the plan for a "Southern Gas Corridor (SGC)" in the wider region of the Black Sea (European Commission, 2008; Sotiriou, 2015, pp. 83–88).[1] This plan calls for the supply of natural gas from Caspian and Middle Eastern sources to the EU through networks that will connect producer countries such as Azerbaijan and Turkmenistan with the EU market *via* transit countries such as Turkey (European Commission, 2008, p. 4; Tsygankov, 2016, p. 195).[2] In this manner, the EU aspires to rationalize or equilibrate its quantity and network dependency on Russia, which throughout the 2000s hovered around 35%, being mostly supplied *via* Russian networks (Eurostat, 2014, p. 69).

The SGC has identified the "Shah Deniz" offshore field in Azerbaijan's share of the Caspian Sea as its primary supply source (BP, 2016). Thus, on June 11, 2008, Bulgaria agreed to buy more than 1 billion cubic meters per year (bcm/y) of gas from Azerbaijan, signing the first natural gas supply contract from the Caspian Sea region (Dempsey, 2008). These shipments would be transported through Turkey once the then highly prioritized and EU-backed "Nabucco Pipeline" project became operational as the first "personification" of the SGC (Dempsey, 2008). Moreover, this project would supply Southeastern and Central EU with 25 bcm/y, a quantity at a fraction of the region's average natural gas needs of 150 bcm/y (BP, 2014; Gazprom, 2015).

Not much water had flown under the bridge until "Nabucco Pipeline" acquired a geopolitical perspective, being presented as rival to the Russia-backed "South Stream" project, which had been signed a year earlier, in the mid-2007, between Gazprom and the Italian ENI (*Scandoil*, 2007). It would connect the Russian and the Bulgarian Black Sea coasts with an underwater network supplying the same markets as "Nabucco" with a quantity, however, much larger, i.e., 50 bcm/y (totally 100bcm/y if the supplies via the incumbent "Blue Stream" network were included) (Gazprom, 2014).

The rivalry flared up with growing intensity, having, on the one hand, the "Nabucco Pipeline" been finally replaced in June 2013 by two other projects, the Trans Anatolian Pipeline (TANAP) and Trans Adriatic Pipeline (TAP), and "South Stream," on the other hand, proceeding apace (EurActiv.com, 2013; BP, 2015).[3]

With no signs of de-escalation, the EU and Russia squared off over the 2013–2015 Ukrainian crisis. "South Stream" soon became part of the bilateral standoff. Putin initially proclaimed, in December 2014, the redirection of the network from Bulgaria to Turkey and its renaming to "TurkStream." But, then, when a Turkish Air Force F-16 fighter jet downed a Russian Sukhoi Su-24M bomber aircraft near the Syrian-Turkish border on November 24, 2015, Russia's Economic Development Minister cancelled the whole project, albeit temporarily (Tomkiv, 2015; *Sputniknews*, 2015). This development, however, was perceived as a corroboration of the EU plans, which viewed the Russian networks as a "thinly veiled attempt by the Kremlin to cement its position as the dominant supplier in Europe" (Roth, 2014).

But, was this development as crucial as it seems at first sight? Could SGC's theoretical supplies of 25 bcm/y sourced only from Azerbaijan's "Shah Deniz" field, be satisfactory for an energy-intensive region of 150 bcm/y, thus rendering Russia a secondary Eurasian energy supplier? Before the "Nabucco Pipeline" was cancelled, it had been announced that "without Turkmen gas, Nabucco would not make any sense," an assessment that applies not only to the successor networks but also to any forthcoming (Comfort and Bierman, 2010). Given these, below is examined the feasibility of a trans-Caspian cooperation so as to enhance the EU energy security, as well as the impact of the Caspian Sea region on energy geopolitics in the Black Sea region, and across Eurasia's underbelly at large.

AT EURASIA'S UNDERBELLY: THE CASPIAN SEA REGION

The Caspian Sea is, first and foremost, a *sui generis* geophysical phenomenon, since it constitutes the largest enclosed body of salt water on Earth, and thus it cannot be classified either as a sea or as a lake. It contains an abundance of proven and probable oil and gas reserves, i.e., 48.2 billion barrels of oil (bbl) and 8269 bcm of natural gas (EIA, 2013). Comparing these with the proven world reserves, the Caspian Sea region contains 17–18% of the world oil reserves, and 12–14% of the world natural gas reserves (Rabinowitz et al., 2004, p. 26; EIA, 2013).

Allocating this natural resources-wealth among the five littoral states, striking is the fact that three littoral states, namely Azerbaijan, Kazakhstan and Turkmenistan produce significant quantities of crude oil in their Caspian Sea region (offshore and onshore combined), while the Caspian Sea region percentage of their total production reaches 100% for both Azerbaijan and Turkmenistan, and 92% for Kazakhstan (EIA, 2013). As far as natural gas production is concerned, Azerbaijan and Kazakhstan produce large quantities, with the Caspian Sea region being responsible for 100% and 74% of their total production respectively, while Turkmenistan ranks third with the Caspian Sea region holding a low position (12%) in the country's total production. Moreover, noteworthy is the fact that Kazakhstan's main production is in the onshore section of the Caspian Sea region (EIA, 2013).

Diachronically, the legal regime (division) of the Caspian Sea had long been among the most disputed issues in the region. In 1917, the then newly established Soviet government agreed with Persia to replace all previous agreements (1813, 1828) by the "Treaty of Friendship" (1921), which would, onwards, serve as the foundation of the bilateral relations (LNTS, No. 268; Janusz, 2005, p. 2). This treaty, although it did stipulate for equal rights of free navigation, it did not make any reference to a legal regime (Janusz, 2005, p. 2). Thus, the need for further elaboration brought about the 1935 "Treaty of Establishment, Commerce and Navigation," later to be replaced by the 1940 "Treaty of Commerce and Navigation" (Janusz, 2005, p. 2). The latter, albeit provided for many issues, avoided setting a clear boundary line, implying a condominium regime governing the "Soviet-Iranian sea" (Mehdiyoun, 2000, p. 180).

Following the collapse of the USSR, four newly independent states appeared on the shores of the Caspian, namely Russia, Azerbaijan, Kazakhstan and Turkmenistan, inheriting the legal situation that the aforementioned treaties had crystallized for several decades. Concurrently, the issue of whether these treaties should continue be legally binding or not, was addressed by the *Vienna Convention on Succession of States in respect of Treaties* (1978). In particular:

1. When a part or parts of the territory of a state separate to form one or more states: (a) any treaty in force at the date of the succession . . . continues in force in respect of each successor state so formed.
2. Paragraph 1 does not apply if: (a) states concerned otherwise agree (Article 34, pars 1–2).

In light of these, Russia, Azerbaijan, Kazakhstan, Turkmenistan and Iran adopted various policies that better served their national interest, clinching, finally, on August 12, 2018, a landmark agreement that gave the impression of a final division.

In particular, the five countries convened in the Caspian coastal city of Aktau (Kazakhstan), where they institutionalized a "special legal regime" for a body of water that was perceived neither as a sea nor as a lake, but as something "special" (*Le Monde*, 2018). Each party has been awarded a fifteen-nautical-mile (n.m.) zone of territorial waters, including also the respective air space, seabed, and underground (Prezident Rossii, 2018, Articles 6–9). In case of a natural resource located on the delimitation line between two countries, then, new negotiations will be conducted involving the two countries. In addition to these, an extra maritime zone of ten n.m. has been designated for fishing, whereas the rest of the sea has remained shared, i.e., the soviet-era principle of condominium has been preserved.[4]

Next to the demarcation provisions, there were also others of particular strategic significance. First, the presence of military forces not belonging to the littoral states has been forbidden (Prezident Rossii, 2018, Article 3, par. 6). Second, the construction of a trans-caspian energy network, following the agreement of the interested parties and the adherence to particular environmental standards, has been sanctioned. It is noteworthy that the environmental standards have been stipulated quite exhaustively, with reference to be made to all international environmental conventions the pipeline-interested parties are members, as well as to the "Framework Convention for the Protection of the Marine Environment of the Caspian Sea," signed in Tehran in 2003 (Prezident Rossii, 2018, Article 14, pars. 1, 2).[5]

CONFLICTING INTERESTS AROUND THE CASPIAN SEA LEGAL REGIME

Russia

Since the collapse of the USSR, Russia had developed a swerving position as far as developments in the Caspian Sea region are concerned. To begin with, the issue of the Caspian Sea's demarcation is well epitomized by the antagonism that existed in the early 1990s between two main state institutions, the Ministry of Foreign Affairs and the Ministry of Fuel and Energy (Lee, 2004, p. 103). The former opposed any division of the sea and insisted on the legal validity of the Soviet-Iranian Treaties of 1921 and 1940. Furthermore, it claimed that all ex-Soviet littoral states, being successor states of the USSR and having signed the declaration of "Alma-Ata," which referred to treaties signed by the latter, were bound by the abovementioned treaties (Mehdiyoun, 2000, p. 186). On the contrary, the Ministry of Fuel and Energy kept a more

flexible position, trying to reap as much as possible from potential cooperation with the natural resources-rich littoral states, emphasis placed on Azerbaijan and Kazakhstan. Thus, it assessed any division of the sea within the
framework of "doing business" (Kubicek, 2013, p. 174).

Azerbaijan and Kazakhstan account for a high percentage of crude oil and
natural gas production in the wider Caspian Sea region. As early as in 1991,
Kazakhstan started the exploitation of the "Tengiz" oil and gas field, where a
joint venture by the Russian "LUKoil" and the British "BP," "LukArco," has
been participating along with other energy companies (EIA, 2017). In the
same vein, in September 1994, Azerbaijan signed the "contract of the century" with numerous Western companies, aiming at the exploitation of the vast
"Azerbaijani-Chirag-Guneshli (ACG)" oil and gas field. In this major and
lucrative project, "LUKoil" was offered a 10% stake, in an Azerbaijani effort
to soften the fierce opposition by the Russian Ministry of Foreign Affairs as
far as the division of the Caspian is concerned (Lee, 2004). This effort,
however, came to no avail, with the latter denouncing the contract on
grounds of legitimacy (Lee, 2004).

The regional energy developments, nevertheless, took their own course,
with new offers by the "State Oil Company of Azerbaijan (SOCAR)" to
"LUKoil" to keep being made, skirmishes among the littoral states over
ownership of specific offshore fields to keep taking place, and all these, in
turn, to stress the necessity for the Russian administration to strike a new
balance—that between its national interest as the biggest energy (natural gas)
power in Eurasia and the restoration of order in the Caspian Sea region.

In light of these, Russia presented, in 1995, a draft convention on the
Caspian Sea's legal regime, which stipulated for the establishment of a forty-
five-mile band of national sectors (subdivided into territorial waters and
exclusive economic zones), beyond which, the middle part of the Sea would
lay under common ownership and join management, i.e., condominium
(Raczka, 2000, p. 209). Russia's intention to approach as much as possible
the generally desired balance in the Caspian Sea region, without, however,
sacrificing its national (energy) interests, is obvious; employing concepts
defined in the United Nations Convention on the Law of the Sea (UNCLOS),
Russia tried to appease to an extent the growing ownership skirmishes
among the littoral states. Concurrently, being aware of the fact that a complete division of the sea into national sectors would undermine its position as
the major energy supplier of the EU, given the possibility for (a Kazakh-
Azerbaijani oil pipeline or) a Turkmen-Azerbaijani gas pipeline to multiply
the available quantities for the European/EU market through a Southern Corridor, it proposed the maintenance of the Soviet-era condominium principle,
this time limited only to the middle part of the sea. Thus, any underwater
energy project would require the consent of all littoral states. This proposal
did not meet the support of the other littoral states, with Kazakhstan and

Azerbaijan favoring the complete division of the sea into national sectors according to the UNCLOS.

Later, in 1997, Russia ratified the UNCLOS, a fact that led to new maneuvers in its diplomacy as far as the latter's full application is concerned. Making use of the provisions which called for agreements on the basis of international law in cases of states with opposite or adjacent coasts, and of Caspian's recognition by it as "unique inland body of water," it approached Kazakhstan and Azerbaijan in an effort to demarcated the northern part of the Sea (UNCLOS, 1982, Articles 83, 74, par. 1; Raczka, 2000). Inadequate bilateral agreements were signed, that retained their legal validity until the 5th Caspian Summit on August 12, 2018, when the five-party, not that different from Russia's 1995 draft convention, agreement was signed.[6]

Although the possibility for the construction of a trans-caspian network has been provided for, a fact that certainly serves as a "decompression valve" for the long-lasting demands of the other littoral states, Russia has maintained the loophole of the "environmental criteria." In fact, it would not be much of an exaggeration to argue that Russia proceeded to the (safe) concession of a possible trans-caspian energy network as a *quid pro quo* for the other littoral states to endorse the agreement. Furthermore, extra benefits have been accrued to Russia in the critical sphere of security, since it has managed to establish its naval (military) superiority in the region, and thus control terrorism-suspicious flows from hardly stable regions, such as the Middle East and Afghanistan. All things considered, Russia has increased its overall relative gains, handling with discretion the lucrative energy sphere, and institutionalizing its military superiority, if not monopoly, in the strategic region in point.

Kazakhstan

Kazakhstan, just like Azerbaijan, was clear on its position towards dividing the Caspian Sea into national sectors. In its draft convention (1995) on Caspian's legal regime, Kazakhstan suggested the UNCLOS be taken into prime consideration (Mamedov, 2001, p. 227). Thus, the establishment of special maritime zones, such as territorial waters and an exclusive economic zone, became standard priorities (UN A/52/424, p. 3).

In establishing these zones, the internationally dominant method of the median / equidistant line figured as a constant. As early as in March 1997, the presidents of Kazakhstan and Turkmenistan, Nursultan Nazarbaev and Saparmurat Niyazov respectively, signed a joint statement declaring that "until the Caspian states reach an agreement on the status of the Caspian Sea, the parties will adhere to the delimitation of administrative and territorial borders along a line running through the middle of the Sea" (UN A/52/93, p. 2). Similarly, Kazakhstan signed an agreement also with the like-minded

Azerbaijan on December 5, 2001, consenting to the application of the median/equidistant line method, but only to the delineation of the seabed, excluding the superjacent waters (CIS Legislation, 2003). Undoubtedly, such a consensus narrows the normative power of the agreement, raising the following question: how should this development be explained?

Kazakhstan, Azerbaijan, and—to a lesser and less stable manner—Turkmenistan consented to the complete (underground, seabed, and superjacent waters) division of the sea. This would result to the formation of full national sectors where the littoral states could employ their sovereignty rights with full security, i.e., oil and natural gas drilling and across-the-sea pipelines, so as to carry their resources to cash-generating markets such as Europe/the EU. In the case in point, Kazakhstan has the second largest reservoirs of crude oil in Eurasia, right after Russia, and the twelfth largest on global scale, right after the US (EIA, 2017). The same picture holds for the natural gas sector too, with the two largest oil fields, "Karachaganak" and "Tengiz," containing the two largest natural gas fields as well (EIA, 2017).

So, Kazakhstan (as well as the other natural resources-rich littoral states), in order to be able to reap the benefits of such an economically promising situation, it should also come to an understanding with the largest, in terms of energy reserves, state and north Caspian neighbor, Russia. The latter had been a staunch opponent of any trans-caspian network prospect (Pannier, 2018a). Consequently, a "balanced" agreement should be coined, which, on the one hand, would uphold the division of sea according to the median/equidistant line method, but, on the other hand, would not lead to an utter formation of national sectors. On July 6, 1998, Russia and Kazakhstan agreed on the following:

> The seabed of the northern part of the Caspian Sea and the subsoil thereof, without prejudice to the continued common use of the water's surface, including protection of the freedom of navigation, agreed fishing quotas and environmental protection, shall be delimited between the Parties along a median line adjusted on the basis of the principle of justice and the agreement of the parties. (UN A/52/983, Article 1)

The Article above stipulated for the division of the seabed as well as the subsoil according the median/equidistant line method, maintaining, however, the superjacent water volume under the regime of condominium, i.e., common use. In this manner, Kazakhstan, was halfway its goals; on the bright side, a legal framework for its natural resources had been achieved, but the way towards their safer development and export through a trans-caspian network was laying ahead, when wider consensus would be feasible. The 2018 five-party agreement, although it met the wider consensus, it has not simplified things for Kazakhstan. By linking the possibility of a trans-caspian network with particular environmental standards, the long-discussed Kazakh-

Azerbaijani initiative to construct the oil pipeline "Kazakhstan Caspian
Transportation System (KCTS)" from Kirik to Baku is encountered with
many difficulties (Pannier, 2018a); aside from the objections that traditionally averse to such projects states, like Russia, may raise, Kazakhstan is also
burdened by a tainted environmental record, when in 2013, two pipelines
(one of oil and another of natural gas) leaked into the Caspian, causing
serious damage to the ecosystem of the Sea (Pannier, 2018).

Reading between the lines, Russia has succeeded in "compartmentaliz-
ing" the region. In particular, Kazakhstan has two major gas export networks:

* the Russia (Gazprom) controlled Central Asia Center (CAC) network,
  which transports supplies to the western (Europe/EU) markets through
  Russia
* the recently constructed Turkmenistan-China (Central Asia-China) network, which Kazakhstani supplies feed into *en route* to the Chinese market (EIA, 2017; Sotiriou, 2015, pp. 193–196).[7]

Considering, now, that most supplies are heading to the west (Europe/EU),
Russia's controlling position plausibly emerges.

As illustrated in figure 6.1., Kazakhstan's natural gas production in 2017
reached 27.1 bcm, out of which 13.9 bcm (or 51%) were reserved for domestic consumption, 1.1. bcm (or 4%) were exported to China, and 12.1 bcm (or
45%), the lion's share of the exported quantities, were exported to the lucrative western (European/EU) market *via* the Russia-controlled CAC network.

Azerbaijan

From the outset of its existence as a newly independent state, Azerbaijan had
been adamant in dividing the Caspian Sea into full national sectors. In fact,
this determination is epitomized by the state's constitution, which states that

> Internal waters of the Azerbaijan Republic, sector of the Caspian Sea (lake)
> belonging to the Azerbaijan Republic, air space over the Azerbaijan Republic
> are integral parts of the territory of the Azerbaijan Republic. (The Constitution
> of the Azerbaijan Republic, 1995, Article 11, par. 2)

This Article refers to the Caspian as a Sea, while, concurrently, mentions the
term "Lake" in parentheses, showing the convergence, if not tautology, between the two terms, when it comes to issues of demarcating a body of water
which is shared by states with opposite or adjacent coasts. This fact becomes
even better understood by comparing Baku's and Almaty's nominally different positions with regard to the demarcation of the Sea; in particular, while
Baku, preparing its own draft convention in early 1990s on the legal status of
the Sea referred to the latter as a "border lake," and Almaty, endorsing the

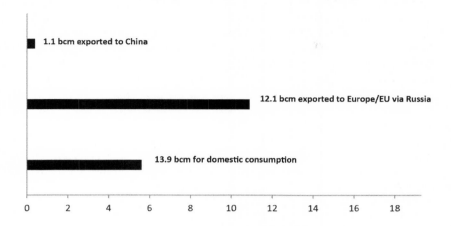

Figure 6.1. Kazakhstan natural gas production in bcm, 2017. Source: BP, 2018.

UNCLOS, referred to its own draft convention as an "enclosed sea," both states arrived at "basically analogous conclusions stressing the need to establish national sectors" (Raczka, 2000, p. 207; Mamedov, 2001, p. 226).

Azerbaijan's argumentation over the "national sectors" solution drew back to the early 1950s; then, the manner according to which the economic activities were being conducted between the Soviet government and the main Caspian ports, implied the subdivision of the soviet sector of the Caspian Sea into republic sectors, following which Republic each of the main ports belonged to (Croissant and Croissant, 1998; UN A/52/424, p. 2). In the same line of reasoning, Azerbaijan, along with Kazakhstan, presented a 1970s document of the USSR Ministry of Oil Industry that "divided the soviet part of the Caspian among Azerbaijan, Kazakhstan, Russia, and Turkmenistan 'on the center line basis accepted in international practice'" (Mehdiyoun, 2000, p. 183).

This method of the "center line basis" or median/equidistant line was at the heart of the Azerbaijani argumentation when calling for the demarcation of both the superjacent waters as well as the seabed of the Caspian. In fact, the Azerbaijani position met also the US support, with Glen Rase, the State Department's director of international energy policy, stating, "to my knowledge, no body of water like the Caspian is treated as condominium as the Russians prefer . . . the more normal course . . . would be to have lines of divisions for economic purposes on the seabed to create exclusive economic zones . . . that seems to be what the Kazakhs, Azerbaijanis . . . desire" (Mehdiyoun, 2000, 184).

For Azerbaijan, establishing sovereignty over its Caspian Sea sector was of utmost importance, primarily, due to economic considerations. Major oil and gas fields are located at its sector, namely "ACG," "Shah Deniz," and "Araz-Alov-Shag" (EIA, 2013). The "ACG" field holds over 70% of Azerbaijan's total reserves, and in 2013 produced almost 75% of Azerbaijan's total oil output. Equally important, the "Shah Deniz" field is considered one of the largest gas development projects on a global scale, and is considered the main source of non-Russian natural gas supplies to European markets, provided that the necessary infrastructure is in place (EIA, 2014).

Azerbaijan signed two landmark bilateral agreements in 2001 and 2002, with Kazakhstan and Russia respectively, over the demarcation of the Caspian Sea, following in the footsteps of the first, "pacesetter," agreement ever to be signed since the collapse of the USSR, that between Russia and Kazakhstan in 1998.

As far as the agreement with Kazakhstan is concerned, both parties agreed to divide only the seabed according to the median/equidistant line, excluding the superjacent waters. Likewise, on September 24, 2002, the Azerbaijani President Heidar Aliyev proceeded to another landmark bilateral agreement, this time with his Russian counterpart Vladimir Putin (Feifer, 2002). The agreement stipulated for the delimitation of the seabed and the subsoil on the basis of a modified median/equidistant line, recognizing, concurrently, the principles of the international law and the dominant practice in the sea (Prezident Rossii 2002, Article 1, par. 1). It also provided for the sovereignty rights of each party regarding the use of the mineral resources in the respective national sectors (Prezident Rossii 2002, Article 2, par. 2).

Both aforementioned landmark agreements highlight the fact that the "national sectors" solution, endorsed by and fervently promoted by Azerbaijan, was partly accomplished; while the seabed as well as the subsoil were indeed divided into national sectors, thus ownership issues over the mineral resources were clearly resolved, the legal regime of the superjacent waters remained unaddressed, this meaning joint ownership, i.e., condominium. Such a development, while falling short of Azerbaijan's position, which would provide for the unconditional exploitation of its natural resources, including laying a trans-Caspian energy network, it was "a very important step, which observes the principles of international law" (Feifer, 2002).

These arrangements retained their legal validity up to the 2018 five-party agreement. The latter, although it did modify many of the abovementioned provisions, it would be highly unlikely to bring about any major policy *volte-face*, especially in the direction of laying a trans-caspian pipeline, either this is an oil one (KCTS) and stems from Kazakhstan, or is a natural gas one (Trans-Caspian Pipeline/TCP) and provides Turkmenistan's natural resources wealth with a European outlet through Azerbaijan (Pannier, 2018a). Consequently, the "compartmentalization" of the region further expanded.

Currently, Azerbaijan is counting on the BTE network to ship its gas supplies westwards, a network that has become operational since December 15, 2006, when the first gas deliveries from "Shah Deniz" field were transferred to Turkey (*OilVoice*, 2006). It is considered the first out of the three "backbone networks" of the EU-planned SGC, and, in theory, has the potential to expand its capacity to 60 bcm/y, if connected to the Turkmen production *via* a TCP (Socor, 2012). Nevertheless, the Azerbaijani natural gas flows as of 2017 presented a rather moderate picture, as shown in figure 6.2. As illustrated, Azerbaijan produced 17.7 bcm of natural gas in 2017, out of which 8.7 bcm (or 49%) were reserved for domestic consumption, 6.3 bcm (or 35%) were shipped to Turkey, 2.1 bcm (or 12%) were exported to Europe, and 0.6 bcm (or 3%) were dispatched to Iran.

On the whole, the best-case scenario for Azerbaijan as a supply-source, and for the SGC as a non-Russian network, is the latter to reach 25 bcm/y transfer capacity when the "Shah Deniz" field becomes fully developed, with exports to Turkey to increase at 11 bcm/y, and those to Europe/EU at 14 bcm/y (BP, 2016). On the contrary, prospects for the SGC reaching a 60 bcm/y capacity as a result of a TCP are highly doubtful, given Russia's steadfast opposition to such projects, and the widespread high sensitivity when it comes to environmental issues.[8] The latter case is further illuminated later on, with the case-study of Iran.

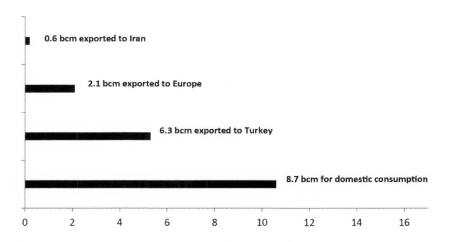

Figure 6.2.   Azerbaijani natural gas production in bcm, 2017. Source: BP, 2018a.

Turkmenistan

Turkmenistan followed a swerving course as far as the issue of the demarcation is concerned. As early as in 1993, it adopted the "Law on the State
Border," stipulating for internal waters, a 12 n.m. territorial sea and an exclusive economic zone (Roach and Smith, 2005, p. 3542). This law, although it
did not make any reference to the seabed, clearly, showed the state's early
inclination towards the adoption of the UNCLOS, i.e., the "national sectors"
solution, in resolving the legal regime of the sea. This position, however, did
not last for long, with the Turkmen side to align with the then position of the
Russian Ministry of Foreign Affairs, and the two Presidents, Boris Yeltsin
and Saparmurat Niyazov respectively, to sign, in May 1995, an agreement
against the full implementation of the UNCLOS (Lee, 2004, p. 106). Turkmenistan, would also find itself being an ally with Iran in support of Russia's
1995 draft convention on the Caspian Sea's legal regime, which is reminded
that it was a combination of the "national sectors" solution with the principle
of condominium in the middle part of the sea. Nevertheless, this "trilateral
understanding" would prove moribund, lasting only for two years, until
1997, when Turkmenistan would change its position again.

That time, Turkmenistan became embroiled in a dispute with Azerbaijan
over the ownership of major Caspian offshore oilfields which have been
developed by the Azerbaijan International Operating Company (AIOC). In
particular, Turkmenistan claimed that the "flagship oilfields" of "Azerbaijani" and "Chirag" were located in the "Turkmen sector" of the sea, either
completely (Azerbaijani) or partially (Chirag) (Raczka, 2000, p. 210). Although these claims were outright rejected by Azerbaijan, the latter could not
help noticing Turkmenistan's relapse to the "national sectors" solution, a
position which had been fervently and unswervingly upheld by it. Such a
relapse, however, was of very limited impact, given the disagreement between the two parties over the exact points (coordinates) from which the
median line should pass in designating the respective national sectors.

In view of such a "challenging" for the Turkmen interests situation, Turkmenistan anew approached Iran. On July 8, 1998, the two parties issued a
joint statement, declaring the legal validity of the USSR-Iranian treaties
(1921, 1940). In parallel, they declared that in case of division, "the principle
of equal share for all littoral states and equitable exploitation of the resources
of the Caspian Sea" should apply (UN A/53/453, Article 5). Evidently, these
points secured Turkmenistan from disputes such as those previously mentioned, while they also satisfied Iran's firm opposition to any division of the
sea into national sectors, which would leave the latter with the smallest
share.[9]

The 2018 five-party agreement ended Turkmenistan's vacillating course,
without, however, being able to reverse certain *fait accomplis* regarding the

country's energy profile. Being the third largest natural gas producer in the region behind Russia (first) and Iran (second), it dispatches almost all export quantities to the more secure destination of China (51.1%) *via* the "Turkmenistan-China" network, with the Europe/E.U. destination to receive none (BP, 2018b, p. 34).[10] As illustrated in figure 6.3, Turkmenistan produced 62.1 bcm of natural gas in 2017, out of which 28.4 bcm (or 45.7%) were reserved for domestic consumption, 31.7 bcm (51%) were exported to China, 0.8 bcm (or 1.2%) were exported to Kazakhstan, and 7.2 bcm (or 2.7%) were exported to Iran.

This flows-allocation demonstrates how the Caspian Sea "compartmentalization" affected Turkmen exports. The western (Europe/EU) markets have ended up receiving no Turkmen supplies, while China absorbs almost all of Turkmenistan's gas exports. Moreover, Turkmenistan and China signed several natural gas contracts in September 2013, stipulating for the supply of 65.3 bcm by 2020 *via* the incumbent network (EIA, 2016). By the end of 2015, the "Turkmenistan-China" network had satisfied almost 20% of China's natural gas consumption, whereas its current expansion (line D) to Kyrgyzstan and Tajikistan stands to make China the dominant, if not the sole, outlet for every single Central Asian state (Cooley, 2015). In this regard, a reverse analogy emerges: the greater China's role in the Turkmen (Central Asian) natural gas production, the lower the available quantities for the western (Europe/EU) markets, which, in any case, have been terminated as of 2017.

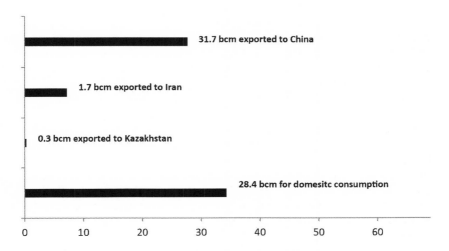

Figure 6.3.   Turkmenistan natural gas production in bcm, 2017. Source: BP, 2018.

Iran

Iran viewed the Caspian as "a body of water with a unique character" and staunchly qualified the Soviet-Iranian treaties (1921, 1940) to govern a sea considered *res communis* (UN A/52/324, p. 2; Mehdiyoun, 2000, p. 182). Moreover, it was against the "national sectors" solution and the use of the median/equidistant line as the demarcation method, since it would leave it with the smallest share (13%) in the Caspian, given the morphology of its shore (Pannier, 2010).

On this basis, Iran initially supported Russia's 1995 draft convention on the Caspian Sea's legal regime, since it avoided the delineation of full national sectors and maintained, to certain degree, the condominium principle of the Soviet era. Consequently, Iran's share of the sea would be just as much as that of all the other littoral states. When Russia, however, would redefine its diplomacy by singing "pacesetter" bilateral agreements, Iran would find itself in the plight of a *de facto* demarcation. In light of this, it reiterated its abstention from recognizing any bilateral agreements on the Caspian Sea issue (Blagov, 2011).

Moreover, on July 8, 1998, two days after the "pacesetter" agreement between Russia and Kazakhstan was signed, Iran, along with Turkmenistan, issued a joint statement, declaring the legal validity of the USSR-Iranian treaties, and calling for the principle of equal share and equitable exploitation of the resources by all littoral states in case of division (UN A/53/453, Article 6). In this manner, Iran would be in control of 20% of the sea, a serious increase compared with the 13% share, which would be awarded if the division was realized according to the median/equidistant line method.

By and large, the issue of the "share" was of prime importance in the negotiating line of Iran, a fact which would not be toned down even by the 2018 five-party agreement. Then, the Iranian President, Hassan Rouhani, made no secret of the fact that the issue of the delimitation of the Sea, most probably referring to the "share," remained open, despite the endorsement of the agreement (Pannier, 2018b). In parallel, however, Iran viewed also the bright side of the agreement, being the producer of the most expensive caviar on the world, the so-called Almas caviar, whose market price is $30,000/kg (Pannier, 2018a). Thus, the environmental provisions of the agreement are critical for Iran, and, from this perspective, it also becomes a pious ally of Russia in the steady opposition against the construction of any trans-caspian energy network.

In this manner, Iran contributed to the "compartmentalization" of the Caspian Sea region. Notwithstanding the third largest natural gas producer, on a global scale, behind the US and Russia, its usefulness to the energy needs of Europe/EU is marginal. Its impact is confined almost solely to Turkey (EIA, 2018, p. 17). Turkey absorbs more than 73% of Iran's exports, with the remainder earmarked either for Armenia or Azerbaijan (EIA, 2018, p. 18). [11] Moreover, the further increase of Iran's exports is hampered by:

- the growth in the domestic demand for natural gas
- the re-injection of gas into oil wells in order to augment oil recovery
- the international sanctions (Gardiner and Ewing, 2018; EIA, 2018, pp. 14–18)

As illustrated in figure 6.4, Iran's natural gas production reached 223.9 bcm in 2017. From this quantity, 214.4 bcm (or 95.5%) were reserved for domestic consumption, 8.9 bcm (or 4%) were exported to Turkey, and 2 bcm (or 0.8%) were exported to Armenia and Azerbaijan.

In light of these, Iran's regional energy profile remains very limited. To make things worse, this situation does not only pertain to the trade via gas networks, but expands also to the field of Liquefied Natural Gas (LNG); while on the agenda since the 1970s, the lack of technology and foreign investments as a result of international sanctions has deprived Iran of the necessary infrastructure for LNG exports (EIA, 2018, p. 17). "South Pars," Iran's largest natural gas field, which holds almost 40% of the country's total proved natural gas reserves and is located at the Persian Gulf near the maritime borders with Qatar, is left without export potential, either inland or seagoing (EIA, 2018, pp. 16–17).

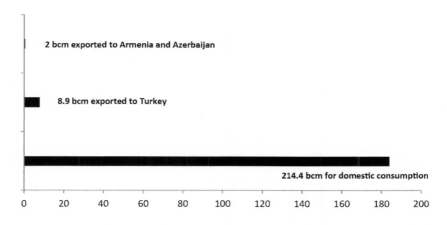

Figure 6.4.   Iran's natural gas production in bcm, 2017. Source: BP, 2018a.

CONCLUSION

With the international trade of natural gas to require the supplier and the consumer to be connected directly through pipelines, a fact, which frequently, gives rise to the phenomenon of "dependence" between the two sides, the EU and Russia have found themselves in an interdependent relationship, which, from the mid-2000s, is challenged as far as its reliability is concerned. After cut-offs in the supply of natural gas in critical times, the EU has started to ponder whether Russia hides political motives behind its economic transactions with European consumers. Insecurity and lack of trust, dominant elements of an anarchical international environment, have instigated Brussels to conceive of policies that could diversify its energy imports. The opening to new supplies from new regions has been highly prioritized. One of these openings has been to the rich in natural resources Caspian Sea region.

Azerbaijan, Kazakhstan, and Turkmenistan rank high as possible suppliers of the EU, and the construction of new networks has been expedited. Nevertheless, in order to counterbalance the dominance of Russia in the European/EU market in terms of both supplies and pipelines, the Caspian suppliers should get connected through trans-caspian energy networks, multiplying, in this manner, the available supplies for export. That is exactly the point, or the vulnerability, that Russia has taken advantage of, in order to maximize its relative gains, not only in the Caspian Sea region but in the whole Eurasian context as well.

Making use of the nature of the Caspian Sea, which combines features of a lake (landlocked) and a sea (saltwater), Russia identified the sea as a "unique inland body of water." Then, it addressed a call for its *ad hoc* division, deviating from the full application both of the UNCLOS and of a legal regime fitting to a lake. It is noteworthy, however, that in any case, the extent of the adjacent coasts does not leave any room for any other method but that of the median line, which would result in the same outcome. Regardless of these, Russia, in the end of 1990s early 2000s, managed to seal bilateral agreements with Kazakhstan and Azerbaijan, that settled, somehow, the northern part of the sea and made the possibility of constructing a transcaspian pipeline highly insecure. In essence, the ownership of the offshore energy fields was resolved, making, in this manner, any (foreign) investments safer, but any possibility of developing these fields, much more export the produced quantities through routes not controlled by Russia, remained highly vulnerable. These developments were not recognized by the remaining two Caspian states, Iran and Turkmenistan, which for some time had forged an alliance.

Finally, in 2018, a watershed seemed to have been reached as far as the adoption of a legal regime for the Caspian Sea is concerned, with all littoral States signing the respective agreement in Aktau. Azerbaijan, Kazakhstan, and Turkmenistan have, indeed, been given the right to a trans-caspian pipe-line, but Russia is the actor that has succeeded in institutionalizing its long-standing powerful position in the region, and thus increase its relative gains in the long-term. The provision of exhaustive environmental standards neces-sary for any trans-caspian pipeline, allows Russia to have the final say and "block" the project in every stage of its construction. Moreover, they have brought Iran next to its side, forging a stable alliance, considering the large economic profits that the latter has been relishing from the fishery of stur-geon in the Caspian.

Even though the 2018 agreement has given the impression of converting the thus far anarchical (international) environment into a structured one (de-spite Iran's inhibitions), the fact is that Russia, being the most power actor in the region, has managed to filter its diachronic interests through this institu-tional structure. In essence, for the years that followed the collapse of the USSR up to 2018, Russia has succeeded in:

- creating difficult-to-reverse export patterns in the Caspian states, erecting, somehow, an "iron curtain" between west-oriented and east-oriented countries
- maintaining the institutional power to intercept transcaspian energy net-works
- *de facto* tightening the existent and already powerful energy bond with the lucrative market of Europe/EU

It is a hard-to-deny fact that Russia has managed to keep regions such as the Caspian in check. But it is also a hard-to-deny fact that, as Russia has been trying as powerfully as possible to establish its position in the region and increase its relative gains, the same thing have been trying to do also the Central Asian states; in their attempt to maximize their power and gain relatively more from Russia, they have not only sought foreign direct invest-ments in their energy sector, but also have "opened the door" to new (energy) alliances with major Asian actors, emphasis placed on China. Interesting is the fact, that China, too, has been in search of new ways to cover its constant-ly and rapidly growing energy needs, which, more often than not, have been acquiring strategic connotations, being associated with its national security.

NOTES

1. These policies, aimed at energy security, refer to the imports of both oil and natural gas. Nevertheless, at present, emphasis is placed on natural gas. Natural gas, in contrast to oil, is a non-fungible (i.e., not many suppliers and consumers in the same market concurrently) com-modity, given constraints in its transport—the main way of transportation thus far, is through pipelines. Consequently, suppliers and consumers are directly connected, forming, in this man-ner, separate markets, i.e., North America, Europe. This fact allows for the emergence of the

phenomenon of "dependence," and most probably, for the encroachment of political considerations (i.e., give and take on the basis of each actor's power) in an otherwise economic transaction. In the separate market of Europe, Russia is the biggest, if not dominant, supplier, and the EU the most lucrative consumer, experiencing an interdependent relationship, which, more often than not, is challenged by mistrust and fears of one actor taking advantage of the other. For more on these issues, see European Commission, 2008; Sotiriou, 2015, pp. 57–60 and 83–88.

2. See also Raptopoulos and Sotiriou, 2015.

3. For a map on these developments, see http://www.europeaninstitute.org/index.php/component/content/article/181-blog/august-2013/1771-azerbaijan-chooses-tap-over-nabucco-to-provide-gas-pipeline-to-europe-88.

4. For a map of the Caspian legal regime according to the 2018 five-party agreement, see https://www.rferl.org/a/iran-official-spin-challenges-perceived-caspian-setback/29439866.html.

5. For the "Framework Convention for the Protection of the Marine Environment of the Caspian Sea," see https://www.ecolex.org/details/treaty/framework-convention-for-the-protection-of-the-marine-environment-of-the-caspian-sea-tre-001396.

6. In fact, from 2000 onwards, four Caspian Summits had been carried out (2002—Ashgabat, 2007—Teheran, 2010—Baku, and 2014—Astrakhan), with no developments as far the demarcation of the sea is concerned (Levchenko, 2015). Progress had only been achieved in issues that trace their roots back to the 1940 USSR-Iran treaty, such as confining any militarization of the sea to the littoral states, and awarding exclusive fishing zones of 15–25 n.m. to each riparian state (RFE/RL, 2014).

7. For a map of this gas network, see https://www.eia.gov/todayinenergy/detail.php?id=12931.

8. To give but an example, Turkmenistan hosts the Caspian Environmental Service (CaspEcoControl), which, according to the State Committee for Environmental Protection and Land Resources, is monitoring the activities of foreign and domestic energy companies across the chain of production (i.e., geophysical and geological surveys, production, sea and land transportation). For more on the issue, see https://menafn.com/1097267835/Turkmenistan-holding-environmental-monitoring-of-oil-companies-in-Caspian-Sea.

9. In 2000, Niyazov would again revise his country's position, stating that Turkmenistan is in support of both the sectoral solution for the division of the Caspian as well as of the "earlier concept of a 'common sea'" (UN A/55/309, p. 6).

10. For reasons of inclusiveness, it is mentioned that when some quantities were exported to the European/ EU market (e.g., in 2015, 2.5 bcm were exported), these were taking place through the Russia-controlled "CAC" network.

11. Iran and Armenia have a twenty-year swap contract, according to which Iran exports natural gas to Armenia in return for electric power. Moreover, Iran has a gas swap contract with Azerbaijan, according to which Iran delivers natural gas to Nakhichevan, an Azerbaijani enclave between Armenia, Turkey and Iran, in exchange for Azerbaijani volumes *via* the Baku-Astara pipeline connection (EIA, 2018, p. 18).

Chapter Seven

China's Policies and Politics

AT THE OTHER END OF EURASIA'S UNDERBELLY

China covers a geographic expanse of 9,600,000 square kilometers, with its population reaching 1.3 billion, or 1/5 of the global population (World Bank, 2018b). The primary occupation for the majority of the population is agriculture.

After Mao Tse-tung's death and Deng Xiaoping's rise to power in 1977–1978, a moderate opening was attempted; capitalist market reforms were initiated, while China, in total, was redirected to the road of the "Four Modernizations" in the respective policy spheres of agriculture, industry, national defense, and science and technology (Bessière, 2007, p. 21). As a result, the first mass flows of population towards the urban centers were reported.[1]

The 1978-initiated market reforms laid the foundations of prosperous and energy-intensive economy, which saw its GDP to grow by 10% on annual basis from 1980 until 2012, "the fastest sustained expansion by a major economy in history," lifting out of poverty more than 800 million people (World Bank, 2018b).[2] China accomplished all the Millennium Development Goals (MDGs) by 2015, contributing considerably to the attainment also of the MDGs on a global scale (World Bank, 2018b). Holding the second position in the world, behind Germany, concerning the trade volume, and third, behind the US and the United Kingdom, as far as inflows of Foreign Direct Investments (FDIs) are concerned, China is the world's largest producer and consumer of many commodities, emphasis placed on coal, iron ore, aluminum, lead, tin, zinc, nickel, gold, copper (UNCTAD, 2017, pp. 50, 55; World Bank, 2018c, pp. 37–66). These energy-intensive industries hold a primary role in the maintenance of economic and political stability in the country.

Located at urban centers, they absorb thousands of incoming labor from the rural areas, contributing further to the urbanization and the wider possible diffuse of the produced wealth.[3] Consequently, industrialization and urbanization constitute the pillars of the Chinese economic miracle.

China is a rich in natural resources country; coal, oil, and natural gas exist in considerable amounts, with coal and oil to lay at the heart of the country's development model. Coal, in particular, is found in such large quantities, that its share in the total consumption has risen to 51% (BP, 2018a, p. 39). Moreover, strong presence in China's energy mix holds the oil, since from mid 1960s, when production begun, the country has been maintaining a leading position in the Asia-Pacific region, having produced, as of 2017, 3846 thousand barrels per day (Mbbl/d) (BP, 2018a, p. 14).[4] From 1990s, China figures among the countries with the highest oil consumption, whereas from 2010 onward, it has established itself in the second position, only behind the US (World Bank, 2018b). Nevertheless, the rapid economic development has skyrocketed the demand for oil, surpassing the domestically produced quantities (Downs, 2004, p. 23). Thus, the Chinese leadership has been forced to start oil imports from 1993, compromising the doctrine of "self-sufficiency" as the founding stone of its energy security; ever since, it has been searching for new policies, that would mitigate an alarming (over)dependence on external actors, i.e., foreign energy suppliers (IEA, 2007, p. 261).[5]

Having attempted this initial acquaintance with the country, China's energy identity is characterized by the dominance of coal, which is far cheaper but more polluting, and oil, whose role is constantly gaining ground (EIA, 2015, p. 3).

An alarming problem of this energy model is its environmental repercussions (Sutter, 2000, pp. 34–35).[6] In 1998, the Energy Conservation Law was enacted, providing for the rational use of energy resources and the prioritization of energy-saving technology (IEA, 2007, p. 275). Nevertheless, it proved of limited efficiency, not managing to control the energy consumption; emissions of carbon dioxide (CO_2) as well as of the smallest polluting particles "PM 2.5," which pose the greatest health risks, spiraled in 2002–2004 and in 2013, the year of the notorious "airpocalypse" (*Economist*, 2018; IEA, 2007, p. 261).[7]

Since 2013, draconian anti-pollution measures have been introduced in the context of a national action plan on air pollution (*Economist*, 2018). A nationwide cap on coal use has been imposed, particularized according to provinces. To provide but an example, Beijing had to constrain its coal consumption by 50% from 2013 to 2018 (*Economist*, 2018). Moreover, new coal-burning capacity has been prohibited, while the use of filters and scrubbers has been highly prioritized. From mid-October 2017 until March 2018, further command-and-control measures were introduced, aiming at the occasional air pollution spikes, especially in northern China (Beijing, Tianjin and the province of Hebei), and especially in the wintertime. Emphasis was placed on the coal-fired domestic heating, steel and aluminum smelters, and on the cement production and diesel trucks, all of which produce smog, thus heavily contributing to the air pollution (*Economist*, 2018).[8]

The command-and-control measures have shown some efficiency, given that the biggest polluters are state-owned and thus directly controlled.[9] Furthermore, from 2013 until 2016, a shift from heavy industry and infrastructure towards services was observed in the composition of the country's GDP (*Economist*, 2018). But these improvements were fragile and spatial; in 2016–2017, when infrastructure spending rose again, this went hand in hand with the rise in emissions. In parallel, in 2017, the PM 2.5 levels were only 4.5% lower than in 2016, indicating that pollution rose in the less strictly controlled Southern China (*Economist*, 2018). Moreover, the cost of the command-and-control measures, only for northern territories, was quite high ($38bln), let alone the opportunity cost of putting whole industries and constructions projects on hold for protracted periods (*Economist*, 2018).

China's environmental challenges have also met the sincere concerns of the international community, propelling its authorities to commit, during the 2009 UN Climate Change Conference, known as the Copenhagen Summit, to achieve a 40% to 45% reduction of the CO_2 emissions below 2005 levels by 2020 (IEA, 2011, p. 78).

The analysis so far has revealed the multifaceted energy reality of China. As a country with a huge rural population, it sees the coal-intensive industrialization as a vehicle of urbanization, distribution of wealth, and overall social cohesion. Nevertheless, the excessive exposure to the polluting coal and the steady increase of the imported oil, have caused across-the-board unease, concerning the sustainability of the country's energy model. Its security, in the mid-term, as well as its composition, in the long-term, are associated with the country's socio-political security.

Consequently, energy constitutes a discrete policy sphere, which is analyzed below in two levels: first, China's decision making political apparatus is presented. Second, the ways with which the country's energy security is guaranteed come to the forefront, with particular focus on the geopolitics of energy in the wider area of Asia.

CHINA'S ENERGY POLICY: THE DECISION-MAKING APPARATUS

China's energy decision-making is allocated within a complex, and at times, overlapping apparatus. While under the leadership of Mao Tse-tung and Deng Xiaoping very few actors played a role in the formation of the energy policy, a result of over-centralization of authority, the ensuing third and fourth generation of leaders made the administration model more open, allowing for the participation of interest groups, special consultants, and research institutes (Meidan et al., 2009, p. 52). Soon, this opening got out of hand, resulting, from 1993 to 2003, to an immense compartmentalization and to a hardly efficient leadership.

That highly disorganized institutional reality would be challenged by a series of critical events; initially, the terrorist attacks in the US on September 11, 2001, expedited the deployment of American military bases in Central Asia and the Middle East (Karagiannis, 2010a, pp. 70–71; Kreft, 2006, p. 112). Moreover, at the domestic level, the surge in the consumption of electricity increased the pressure on the leadership, which was found in a plight in 2004, when power failures affected twenty-one provinces, with the problem to become rather intense in periods of high demand (Cheng, 2008, p. 301). These two events came to add up to an already distressed Chinese leadership, which, in the meantime, was struggling with Taiwan's unsettled regime, and concurrently, tried to guarantee the oil imports from Persian Gulf states (Bessière, 2007, p. 109; Lee, 2005, pp. 279–283; Levin, 2008, pp. 50–59; Tucker, 2005, pp. 1–15).

In view of these, Beijing was propelled to take some decisive steps, aimed at forming a concrete and coherent energy policy that would reverse the aforementioned situation and set a new course in the new millennium; reforms were conducted across the board, starting from the level of political institutions, and reaching as far as the state energy companies and their international policies (Sotiriou and Karagiannis, 2013, p. 306). In particular, in 2002, the once-in-a-decade "changing of the guard" in the Chinese political system brought to power the newly elected Hu Jintao (President) and Wen Jiabao (Prime Minister). Then, the foundations of a new institutional "big-bang" were set. In March 2003, the "Energy Bureau" was established.[10] That verticalization attempt was an early, if not the first, internal effort on behalf of the Chinese administration to instigate the course towards the maximization of its (energy) power. Nevertheless, it stumbled upon fierce objections by the also recently established "National Development and Reform Commission (NDRC)" and the state energy companies, which being in a power struggle with the Energy Bureau, called for and succeeded in having the latter's jurisdictions gravely trimmed, thus affecting its overall prospects (Downs, 2006, p. 18). Yet, the severity of the geopolitical reconfigurations would anew urge towards fresh political initiatives, this time more successful.

In June 2005, PM Wen Jiabao institutionalized the "National Energy Leading Group (NELG)" in an effort to fill the power gap that the "impaired" Energy Bureau was leaving behind. Composed of thirteen civil servants coming from the NDRC and other critical ministries, the NELG was headed by the PM himself and served as the leading institution in the energy policy sector, submitting draft legislation and suggestions to the supreme state institution, the State Council (Meidan et al., 2009, p. 595).[11] In parallel, the "Office of the National Energy Leading Group (ONELG)" was also institutionalized, assuming the responsibilities for administratively supporting and submitting draft legislation to the NELG (IEA, 2007, p. 268). The "Energy Bureau" reserved the jurisdiction of formulating suggestions on energy supplies and implementing the every-time qualified policies (Downs, 2006, pp. 18–19; IEA, 2007, p. 268). Finally, the NDRC remained a state institution of prime importance in the sectors of environment, pricing, energy efficiency, and issuing project approvals (IEA, 2007, p. 268). This situation would purposefully change in the years that followed, seeking the further verticalization of power; in particular, as of 2017, the NELG and the ONELG have been included in the "National Energy Administration (NEA)," with the NDRC to have been upgraded to where formerly the NELG had been standing, controlling all issues related to the energy policy sector (e.g., energy mix, supplies, environmental aspects), and directly feeding into the State Council (IEA, 2017).

Next to these state institutions of strategic significance, there are also other state institutions that are equally involved in the devising and implementation of the country's energy policy (see figure 7.1). Of particular reference are the following: the Ministry of Environmental Protection, which is first in the row directly under the State Council indicating the urgency of its subject, the Ministry of Land and Resources, the Ministry of Transport, the Ministry of Commerce, the Ministry of Water Resources, the Ministry of Science and Technology, the Ministry of Industry and Information technology, and the state-owned Assets Supervision and Administration Commission (IEA, 2017).[12]

Of course, strong influence in the energy policy-making exert also the state energy companies (Wilson, 2017). This influence traces its roots back in the post-war period; then, today's energy companies were ministries with extensive involvement in the decision-making (Sotiriou and Karagiannis, 2013, p. 310). In 1953, when the economic bureaucracy was still in its offing, the leadership decided to create an industry-centered administrative structure, which would recognize the role of heavy industry in the national development. As a result, the heavy industry acquired its own ministry (Downs, 2006, p. 22).

Later, in the 1980s, those ministries would be restructured according to the corporate standards (Sotiriou and Karagiannis, 2013, p. 310). In particular, three big energy companies (National Oil Companies—NOCs) were created (Lewis 2007; Xu, 2007). The "China National Petroleum Corporation (CNPC)" emerged in 1988 out of the thus far Ministry of Oil Industry, the "China Petroleum & Chemical Corporation (Sinopec)" was put together out

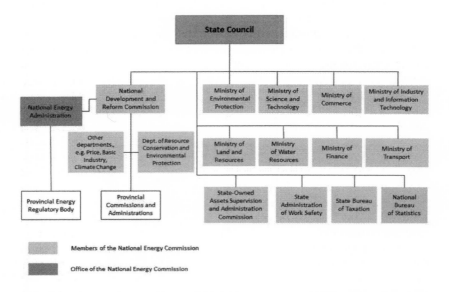

Figure 7.1.   Energy policy-making and administration in China. Copyright OECD/IEA 2017 World Energy Outlook, IEA Publishing. Licence: www.iea.org/ t&c.

of the merger of the assets of the Ministry of Oil Industry and the Ministry of Chemical Industry, and, finally, the "China National Offshore Oil Corporation (CNOOC)" was formed in 1982 as a company of the Ministry of Oil Industry (Lieberthal and Oksenberg, 1988, p. 122; Downs, 2006, p. 22). From these companies, the first two relish the status of a ministry, whereas the latter is in a hybrid situation, swaying between ministry and directorate general (Lieberthal and Oksenberg, 1988, p. 124). In this manner, an environment of advanced osmosis has been forged, within which state energy companies with ministerial "identity" interact with powerful state institutions as such (e.g., the State Council).

Finally, the process of the energy policy-making complete numerous other agencies and bodies, such as the "Development Research Center of the State Council (DRC)" and the "Energy Research Institute of the National Development and Reform Commission," academic institutions, interest groups, NGOs, and local communities (Downs, 2004, pp. 27–28; Meidan et al., 2009, p. 597).[13]

CHINA'S ENERGY POLICY: THE GEOPOLITICAL DIMENSION

Theoretically, a country's energy security can be guaranteed with policies that focus either on the side of demand, or on the side of supply, or on both concurrently. On the side of demand, emphasis is placed on policies of mainly economic content, like the liberalization of the energy market, the fuel tax, the implementation of energy-saving standards, as well as the tax regime for purchasing new vehicles. On the side of supply, which exhibits greater importance given that it exceeds the absolute control of the national leadership and the internal efforts towards the maximization, or securitization, of (energy) power, priority is given to policies such as the diversification of supplie(r)s and transport routes, acquisition of equity stakes in exploration and development projects abroad ("going abroad" policy), and the construction of Strategic Petroleum Reserves (SPRs) (Downs, 2006, pp. 26–27). China systematically advances policies on both sides (internal and external efforts), focusing on the supply side. So, the analysis below is adjusted accordingly.

China's major oil suppliers comprise many states from various regions of the world. South and Central America, North Africa, Middle East (emphasis placed on Saudi Arabia, Iran, and Iraq), Russia, all constitute a diversified amalgam, and indicate the multiple alliances that Beijing has forged towards shielding itself against any alarming dependence and securitizing its supplies. African states such as Soudan, Angola, Chad, Libya, Nigeria, and Gabon account for almost one third of the country's energy needs in imported oil (BP, 2018; Downs, 2006, p. 31; Eisenman, 2007, p. 38). Moreover, Beijing has strived towards further strengthening its profile by upgrading its cooperation with the remainder members of the "Gulf Cooperation Council (GCC)" (Zhao, 2008, p. 211).[14]

These imports follow long and easily jam-packed sea routes. Indicatively, in 2005, 15 mlm barrels of oil per day (roughly 40% of the international oil trade) had to cross the Straits of Hormuz in the Persian Gulf, out of which 10mln (i.e., 26% of the international oil trade), had to cross also the Straits of Malacca in Malaysia, *en route* to the Asian markets (Kreft, 2006, p. 112; Dadwal, 2007, p. 897).[15] The Straits of Malacca is a diode of 2.41km width and 1,013.9km length, which connect the Indian Ocean with the South China Sea, and quite frequently exhibits outbreaks of piracy. Through this sea routes passes almost 80% of China's oil imports (Fengying and Jiejun, 2008, p. 52).[16]

After the beginning of the US "War on Terror," the strategic significance of the aforementioned sea routes acquired special weight, since the US could take advantage of the dominance of its navy in the Indian Ocean in order to obstruct the passage of oil tankers to China (Fishelson, 2007, p. 28; Hansen, 2008, pp. 218–219). In November 2003, the Chinese leadership, in the words of President Jintao, highlighted the special weight of the Straits of Malacca, and claimed that "certain major powers" were determined to place this crossing under their control (Dadwal, 2007, p. 895). In fact, part of the media argued that "it is no exaggeration to say that whoever controls the Strait of Malacca will also have a stranglehold on the energy route of China" (Storey, 2006).

In view of such an all the more precarious situation, the Chinese leadership started to seek ways to further guarantee its energy security. The "going abroad" policy by the Chinese energy companies constitutes the cornerstone of a strategy, according to which numerous African, Asian, and Latin American states have been (re)approached in pursuit of not only deepening the (energy) ties and controlling the sea routes, but also further diversifying the existent supplie(r)s and supply routes (Lewis, 2007, p. 55; Dadwal, 2007, p. 900; Wilson, 2017).

Thinking and acting holistically, the Chinese energy companies are offering to countries-producers economic cooperation deals in the scheme of "loan-for-oil/gas" deals (Jiang and Sinton, 2011, p. 23; Eisenman, 2007, pp. 46–48).[17] In this manner, the Chinese side appears to be far more competitive than the western states, which offer much smaller deals of economic support and with far stricter conditions. Moreover, China focuses solely on the economic aspect of every deal, trying to avoid any involvement in the internal affairs of the countries-producers in point, which, in the end, may result in not getting the much-needed oil.

The Chinese energy companies have seriously expanded their presence to countries-producers such as Sudan, Algeria, Libya, Nigeria, Angola, Guinea-Bissau, Venezuela, Iran, Oman, Myanmar, Yemen, Kazakhstan, Uzbekistan, and Turkmenistan (Dadwal, 2007; Lee, 2005, p. 270; Eisenman, 2007, pp. 38–40). What is more, in particular cases, like in Sudan and Venezuela, the massive Chinese investment in the energy sector led to the reinforcement of local regimes; in the first cases, the forces of Khartoum found the necessary resources to expand their military presence in Darfur, while in the second case, former President Hugo Chavez, managed to limit his country's almost total dependence on oil exports to the US (Dadwal, 2007; Zhao, 2008). Supplementary to these, China has multiple times opposed UN Security Council resolutions calling for condemnation of breaches in human rights in states like Myanmar, Iran, and Sudan, with which, as has already been mentioned, it shares deep and extensive energy ties (Pen, 2007; BBC, 2012b).

Parallel to these, China has concluded a series of bilateral agreements with states across the wider area of South Asia, which is referred to by American analysts as "String of Pearls" (Pehrson, 2006). Each "pearl" is a symbol of the Chinese military presence and geopolitical influence.[18] So, the Hainan Island, south of China and northeast of Vietnam, which hosts upgraded military bases, is considered a "pearl." Likewise, the Woody Island in the Paracel archipelago, 300 n.m. east of Vietnam, is considered a "pearl." A commercial naval base in Sittwe (Myanmar) is also considered a "pearl" (Pehrson, 2006, p. 3). The same reasoning accounts for the construction of a Chittagong (Bangladesh) port facility, for the naval base in Gwadar (Pakistan), and for the access of the Chinese navy in ports in Sri Lanka, Maldives, Seychelles, Mauritius, and Madagascar (Pehrson, 2006, p. 3; Dadwal, 2007, p. 897; Walsh, 2013). All these, in combination with other construction projects, diplomatic ties, and broader forms of cooperation, constitute the "String of Pearls," which China has painstakingly build up, in order to guarantee its constant naval presence from the South China sea and the Straits of Malacca up to the Arabic sea and the Persian Gulf (Pehrson, 2006, p. 3; Walsh, 2013).[19] Consequently, it has seriously increased its capacity to keep a close look on the transport of its oil supplies.

Of course, except for its maritime presence, China has periodically processed a series of plans to circumvent the vulnerabilities of sea-born supplies by investing in land projects. Remaining in the region of South Asia, the most costly and complex-to-accomplish idea, was the construction of an 100km-long canal ("Thai Canal" or "Kra Canal") that would connect the Andaman Sea (Indian Ocean) with the Gulf of Thailand (Pacific Ocean) across southern Thailand, in the footsteps of an "Asian Panama Canal" (Storey, 2006). Such a project would help bypass Singapore, and shorten the sea journey between the Middle East and East Asia by at least 1,000km (*The Straits Times*, 2018). Nevertheless, its soaring, if not prohibitive, cost ($20–25 bln) has clouded its realization prospects. In 2003, Thailand made a counter-proposal, suggesting the construction of much cheaper Strategic Energy Land Bridge (SELB), a 241km-long underground oil pipeline, again across the southern part of the country (Storey, 2006). As of 2018, neither project has advanced, with the Thai PM, Prayut Chan-o-cha, to declare, in February 2018, the government's opposition to such projects (The Straits Times, 2018). Furthermore, security observers in Thailand have also cited security concerns, given that for two decades the south has been home to a simmering conflict between the government forces and Muslim insurgents (*The Straits Times*, 2018).

After Thailand, China approached Myanmar. Having established diplomatic ties with this state since 1954, China participates in the development of twenty-one natural gas fields (onshore and offshore) through its three main state energy companies (Burma Project, 2008, p. 7). In 2004, Beijing and Rangoon discussed the possibility of a 1207km-long and $2 bln cost oil pipeline from the coastal city Sittwe, in the bay of Bengal, to the Yunnan province, in China (Storey, 2006). In addition to this, the two governments agreed for the supply of 6.5 trillion cubic meters of natural gas from Myanmar to China in a time-span of thirty years (Storey, 2006). In 2017, following street demonstrations in China's Yunnan province and amid accusation of land grabs in Myanmar, the cross-border pipeline into south-east China was finally opened, being able to cover 6% of China's crude oil imports (Hornby, 2017). Operated by CNPC, the standard-bearer for China's "going abroad" policy, this pipeline allows China to avoid the chokepoint of the Strait of Malacca, and to diversify oil supply routes not only away from the American navy-dominated Indian Ocean but also from the contentious South China sea (Hornby, 2017).[20] Next to this oil pipeline, there is a natural gas one, which is also operational (Hornby, 2017).

In the same logic, China made an opening to Pakistan, discussing the transport of oil and natural gas supplies through an "energy corridor" that would start from the port of Gwadar in Pakistan and end up, after 2,665km, to Kashgar (Kashi), in the Chinese province Xinjiang (XUAR) (Storey, 2006). In particular, oil tankers would off-load their cargoes at Gwadar. Then the supplies would be transported by road, rail or pipeline, to Islamabad, 1448km north, before dispatched another 1207km to Kashgar in XUAR, along the Karakoram Highway that links Pakistan with China (Storey, 2006). Initially, the two governments supported the project, agreeing, in 2006, that the Karakoram highway needed upgrade. It is a fact that such a project would help China to circumvent all maritime choke points except for the Straits of Hormuz, plus that Pakistan has been a close ally of China. But inhibitions have been there from the very beginning; on the one hand, the long distances and the rocky terrain, and on the other hand, Gwadar's Baluchistan province, which is home to separatist insurgents striving to overthrow the Pakistani state, gravely limited any prospects (Kugelman, 2018). This situation has remained stagnant, even though China's Belt and Road Initiative (BRI), part of which is the $62 bln transport corridor project "China-Pakistan Economic Corridor (CPEC)," has been enacted since 2014 (Kugelman, 2018).

Moving from South Asia towards the middle and north Asia, China has made an opening, at first, to the Central Asian states. The latter were stranded by the protracted nebulousness around the Caspian Sea legal regime, especially up to 2018, which had limited their prospects to maximize their (energy) power status by making a legally safe opening to FDIs, as well as to counterbalance the dominant player in the region, Russia, by forging an alternate and equally, if not more, profitable alliance. Thus, China's interest in diversifying supplie(r)s and transport routes dovetailed the Central Asian states' interests towards risk-taking investors and the formation of a new alliance with a lucrative market.

In 1997, CNPC made its presence in Kazakhstan's energy sector with a series of major acquisitions that allowed it access to a handful of oil and natural gas fields (Sotiriou, 2015, p. 190).[21] Of course, connecting these resources to the Chinese reality would not take long to happen, with an agreement to be clinched also in 1997, stipulating for the construction of a 2227km-long oil pipeline, from Atyrau port in northwestern Kazakhstan to Alashankou, in China's XUAR province (EIA, 2017).[22] With "Aktobe" and

"Kumkol" to have been identified as the resource bases, the project was carried out in three stages: in Phase (1) the Kenkiyak-Atyrau line was completed in 2003, in Phase (2) the Atasu-Alashankou line was completed in 2005, and in Phase (3) the Kenkiyak-Kumkol line was completed in 2009 (EIA, 2017). It is worth mentioning that the Kenkiyak-Atyrau line was the first oil network ever to be constructed in post-soviet Kazakhstan and, initially, it was flowing westwards (EIA, 2017). Later, when China would have seriously expanded its energy presence in the country and the other lines would have also been completed, its flow would be reversed, so as from October 6, 2009, the "Kazakhstan-China" oil pipeline to be established (Sotiriou, 2015, p. 191).

On July 17, 2007, CNPC signed with the State Agency for Management and Use of Hydrocarbon Resources and Turkmengaz, the national gas company of the country, which is also the largest in Central Asia, a Production Sharing Agreement (PSA) on Amu Darya River right shore's "Bagtiyarlik" natural gas field (CNCP, 2007). That was a turning-point agreement, since, for the first time, Turkmenistan allowed a third country to have direct access to the upstream sector. Of course, China would also try to ensure the transport of this wealth to its own territory. Thus, it contacted also Uzbekistan (April 2007) and Kazakhstan (October 2008), laying the groundwork for the construction of what it would become known as the "Central Asia Gas Pipeline (GAGP or Turkmenistan-China)" (Sotiriou, 2015, p. 194).[23] On December 14, 2009, the line A of the CAGP was opened, transporting in its maiden year 6–7bcm, all originating from CNPC's production at "Bagtiyarlik" (Sotiriou, 2015, p. 195). This dynamic would be continued, with CNPC to initiate a new round of negotiations, in 2010, with all three Central Asian states agreeing in increasing the dispatched quantities as well as the lines of the CAGP. By the end of 2015, Line C became operational, with China to have received in 2017 38.7 bcm, an amount expected to surge into 51.37 bcm in 2018, maxing out the CAGP overall capacity of 55bcm per year (Lelyveld, 2018). To take the point one step further, there has also been a Line D in negotiations, with Presidents of China, Xi Jinping, and Kyrgyzstan, Sooronbai Jeenbekov, to place particular emphasis on the project, when they met on June 6, 2018, ahead of the SCO summit in Qingdao, China (Lelyveld, 2018).[24]

Finally, Russia, constitutes another important component in China's energy security. Russia is among the leading, if not the dominant, actors in the region, holding the third position in the world in the oil production (554.4 mln tones), behind the US (571 mln tones) and Saudi Arabia (561.7 mln tones), and the second position in the natural gas production (635.6 bcm), only behind the US (734.5 bcm) (BP, 2018a, pp. 16, 28). Given these, China and Russia agreed on February 17, 2009, to extend the "East Siberia–Pacific Ocean (ESPO)" oil pipeline towards China; the new extension from the

Russian city of Skovorodino to the Chinese city of Daqing was completed in December 2010 (Xinhua News Agency, 2010, 2011; Interfax, 2010).[25] Just like in every other previously examined case, China employed its substantial hard currency reserves to ensure a package deal; not only the diversion of the ESPO pipeline to Daqing was funded, but also CNPC secured the right to buy 300 kb/d of crude oil at market price for twenty years (Jiang and Sinton, 2011, p. 23).[26]

In parallel, China, being environmentally hard-pressed, tapped also into Russia's natural gas reserves. On October 14, 2004, Gazprom and CNPC endorsed a Strategic Cooperation agreement, according to which the foundations were set towards ironing out all the issues pertaining to the supply of gas from the former to the latter (Gazprom, 2012). After decade-long negotiations, during which China exhibited a rather hard line profile exploiting the fact that it would be Russia's only major customer of gas—the routing of the pipeline would be too far east for Gazprom to balance against China with western customers—in May 2014, a $400bn deal was struck, stipulating for the delivery of 38bcm/y of gas to China, through the "eastern" route, i.e., the "Power of Siberia" pipeline (RT, 2014; Foy, 2018).[27] This 3,000km-long and $55bn-cost pipeline, which is expected to have been completed by December 2019, runs from the eastern Siberia gas fields to the Chinese border in the south-east, and it will connect for the first Russia with its largest energy importer (Foy, 2018).[28]

China's gas consumption in 2017 reached 240bcm, whereas in 2018, this figure is expected to reach 258.7bcm, making the domestic production to account for a mere 4.3% of this figure, thus further accentuating the strategic importance of China's overall northwestern pivot, in the case in point towards Russia (BP, 2018a, p. 29; Lelyveld, 2018).

Reaching the end of China's holistic approach towards energy security, the SPRs should not be omitted. Initiated in the tenth five-year plan (2001–2005) of the country, a government-administered SPR project would be constructed in three phases, aiming at a total capacity of around 500 million barrels of oil (mmbbl) by 2020 or a bit later (EIA, 2015, p. 14).[29] In the end of 2008, Phase I was completed, exhibiting a capacity of 103 mmbbl and 15 days of autonomy. Phase II is under construction, having, thus far, contributed 77 mmbbl and 11 days autonomy, whereas, when completed by the end of 2019, another 99 mmbbl and 15 days autonomy will be added. Finally, Phase III, which is scheduled to be accomplished by the end of 2020, will supplement an extra amount of 232 mmbbl and 35 days of autonomy, totaling China's reserve to 511 mmbbl and 77 days of autonomy (EIA, 2015, p. 14; Upadhyay, 2017).

Taking all these policies together, it is noteworthy that China has multiple times been subject to widespread criticism, especially from the US, charged with undermining the principles of good governance and assisting numerous pariah-states of further deviating from standards of the international community (Zhao, 2008, p. 213; Sutter, 2000).

CONCLUSION

The year 1978 saw the foundations of today's China being set. Then, capitalist reforms were carried out, and a densely populated agricultural country was initiated to the road of "four modernizations." Soon, a new model of development arose, according to which "industrialization" and "urbanization" were the main pillars. The quicker the industrialization, the more people were heading towards the major urban centers, and more labor was available for the quick industrialization. A staggering diachronic economic development brought China's GDP to grow by a two digit figure on an annual basis from 1980 until 2012. This rapid economic growth turned the attention to the very fundamentals of the economic miracle, i.e., the energy mix. Coal and oil have been the decades-long dominant fuels, causing quite frequently major environmental crises in major urban centers, such as in Beijing in 2013. These crises have mobilized the domestic leadership, and quickly acquired an international dimension too, with pressure to be exerted on the containment, if not total reversal, of the whole situation. The country's energy mix has been the key out of this plight.

With the country's once-in-a-decade change in the political leadership to occur in 2002, President Hu Jintao and Wen Jiabao prioritized the country's energy security. It was not only the safeguarding in the short term of the energy mix as such, given the all the more increasing oil imports, but also its sustainability in the long-term, with the diversification of fuels towards cleaner ones, such as the natural gas.

Addressing the issue as thoroughly as possible, the new leadership engaged, first and foremost, in a series of internal reforms towards the more efficient restructuring in the energy policy sector. New political institutions were established in a hierarchy and connected directly with the highest political body in the country, the State Council. Consequently, all draft legislation and any other immediate reforms may be required in the energy sector have been given a kind of an institutional self-standing of preferential status. Furthermore, with their status to appear to be of supra-ministerial level, the new political institutions not only inform on the needs that the energy sector may require, but also get informed, if not having a say, on every policy under consideration by the State Council could pertain to the country's economic miracle and resonate in the energy sector. Next to these, China's three main energy companies relish ministerial status and preferential access into the administrative structure. As a result, they are powerful enough to support the leadership's foreign policies towards energy security.

Once the political leadership's internal efforts managed to strengthen the standing of the energy sector and set the foundations for the maximization of the country's energy power, it was time for the international dimension or the external efforts towards toward energy security. Without compromising the security of the mounting oil imports, it has been concurrently attempted the diversification of supplie(r)s, transport routes, and reap as much as possible from the international oil trade through SPRs. Although China has numerous oil suppliers, most of these supplies cross the specific and complex sea routes that make their security rather precarious. In fact, these fears have been intensified after the 09/11 events and the very often, if not, constant presence of the American navy in the Indian Ocean and the Pacific Ocean. In view of this, China has sought to tighten its energy bond with numerous suppliers, initiating the "going abroad" strategy, part of which is, first, the "loan-for-oil/gas" deals, second, the acquisition of facilities in pivotal posts across the supply sea routes, and third, the construction of land projects in order to further diversify the supplie(r)s and the transport routes. Part of these outward FDIs has also to do with the natural gas sphere, a fact that takes the Chinese energy security one step further, from that of the ensuring the incumbent energy mix to that of diversifying towards cleaner sources and thus guaranteeing its sustainability. Particular emphasis deserve the dovetailing energy interests between China, the Central Asian states, and Russia, given that traditionally have been experiencing a fickle relationship. China has managed to tap into the Central Asian resources the same moment that the latter were seeking for an outlet that would allow them to poor money into their coffers. Furthermore, this has happened with Russia's silent consent, or at least not fierce opposition. Russia has succeeded in keeping the Central Asian region in check as far as its prospects as an EU energy supplier are concerned, and, although such a situation has opened the Central Asian door to China, this does not go against the wider picture of Russia's dominance in the Eurasian energyland. It could even be argued that Russia chose to "risk" a small or controllable Chinese energy "intrusion" in a region heavily exposed to its energy influence, in a exchange for controlling the commanding (energy) heights across Eurasia, a prospect seriously pushed forward by the construction of the "Power of Siberia" and Russia's direct access to China.

Viewing the aforementioned from a different perspective, it could be argued that China's preference also for states which have been repeatedly criticized for their human rights record or have experienced protracted, if not permanent, embargoes, indicates the relative gains logic in its international energy trade; it seeks to guarantee the maximum possible quantities paying little attention to rules (or resolutions), regulations, or (informal) norms may occasionally have been set or attempted to be set either by major organizations, such as the UN, the International Energy Administration (IEA), the Organization for Petroleum Exporting Countries (OPEC), or the international community *per se*. To the same direction point also the country's SPRs, whose rather big storage capacity—second in the world only behind that of the US—aside from the fluctuations it could cause to the international oil trade due to supply and demand considerations, it primarily indicates China's focus on relative gains.[30]

NOTES

1. The population flows in China are controlled by the government through the "Hukou" system. Having been introduced in the 1950s, it covers both the rural and the urban areas, aiming at controlling the flows towards the major urban centers (IEA, 2007, p. 258). The largest urbanization has occurred in the coastal areas, which are the most developed, gathering close to 800 million inhabitants (*Statista*, 2018). Nevertheless, in today's China, a mere 57% of the population lives in urban areas (*Statista*, 2018).

2. Special reference deserves the success of the Special Economic Zones (SEZs). Aiming at the boost of export-oriented commodities in the international market, these zones were created for the first time in 1978 in the areas around Canton and Hong Kong (Bessière, 2007, p. 38). Later, in 1985, open economic zones would form an open coastal belt, seeking to attract foreign fund to propel exports (Bessière, 2007, p. 38). In this manner, the foundations for the inflow of FDIs and upgrading of the incumbent industry had been set (Bessière, 2007, p. 38). For more on the Chinese economy, see Sutter, 2000, pp. 4–6 and 19–31.

3. As of 2017, the GDP per person employed (constant 2011 PPP $) was 27,152. Moreover, the poverty headcount ratio at national poverty lines was 3.1% of the population (roughly 41 mln). For these data, see: http://databank.worldbank.org/data/source/world-development-indicators

4. In 1970, China produced a mere 616 (Mbbl/d), in 1980, this quantity more than tripled (2,122 Mbbl/d), reaching, in 2015, 4,309 (Mbbl/d) (World Bank 2018c, p. 45).

5. "Energy Security" is a state's capacity "to assure adequate, reliable supplies of energy at reasonable prices and in ways that do not jeopardize major national values and objectives" (Downs, 2004, pp. 22–23). In simpler words, is a state's capacity to diversify its fuels, supply sources, and routes of transportation, so as no supplier to be more powerful and take advantage of the state's dependence on it.

6. Among the most polluting industries have been those of leather, color printing, coking, and paper (Sutter, 2000, p. 34).

7. The problem of air pollution has been rather critical in China, exhibiting rather sharp spikes. Such a case was in January 2013, when the PM 2.5 flooded the air in Beijing (Wong, 2013; *Xinhua News Agency*, 2013). Furthermore, the fact that local media, most of which are state-owned or under regime of strict censorship, were allowed to cover the event indicates that the Chinese leadership, too, recognized the necessity for urgent measures to be adopted. To this direction, *People's Daily*, the official party mouthpiece, published a front-page editorial entitled "Beautiful China starts with healthy breathing," in which it was mentioned that "the seemingly never-ending haze and fog may blur our vision," but make "us see extra clearly the urgency of pollution control and the urgency of the theory of building a socialist ecological civilization, revealed at the 18th Party Congress" (Wong, 2013).

8. Pressure on the authorities in many cities was so hard that, aside from promises towards converting almost 4 mln households from coal-burning to electricity or gas in 2017, there were cases of houses, hospitals and schools that were totally coal-deprived before a replacement system was in place (*The Economist*, 2018).

9. More than half of the country's pollution stems from coal-burning power stations.

10. The Energy Bureau would be responsible for coordinating and regulating the affairs of the energy industry. At the beginning, its staff was thirty civil servants, a number which was, later, increased to fifty-seven (Meidan et al., 2009, p. 595; Downs, 2006).

11. The Leading Groups are *ad hoc* coordinating and consulting bodies that relish supraministerial status and aim at building consensus in matters that concern the government, the party, and the military, and the incumbent bureaucracy falls short of attaining this target. Furthermore, in order to simplify their mission, no concrete policies (*zhengce*) are formulated, but instead, is indicated the direction the bureaucratic activities should move towards (*fangzhen*) (Downs, 2006, p. 20).

12. According to IEA, the allocation of jurisdictions is as follows: Ministry of Land and Resources (exploitation of fossil fuel resources and reserves); Ministry of Water Resources (management and development of hydropower resources); Ministry of Transportation (development of transport infrastructure and devising of energy-saving measures in the transport sector); and Ministry of Commerce (energy trade); Ministry of Finance and State Bureau of Taxation (taxes, fees, and reforms that involve financial incentives).

13. For the agencies and bodies, see http://en.drc.gov.cn/ and http://www.chinacsrmap. org/ Org_Show_EN.asp?ID=573.

14. The member-states of the GCC are Bahrain, Kuwait, Oman, Qatar, Saudi Arabia, United Arab Emirates. For more on the issue, see http://www.gcc-sg.org/en-us/Pages/default.aspx.

15. The reference to the volumes of 2005 was chosen on purpose, because, then, the global economy had been showing a continuously expansive (or upward) trend. For more on the issue, see http://databank.worldbank.org/data/source/world-development-indicators.

16. In 2003–2004, there was an upsurge of pirate attacks, a fact that led many analysts to underscore the possibility of pirate groups conspiring with international terrorist networks in an attempt to intercept international trade. Under this pressure, and the spin-off international outcry, Indonesia, Singapore, and Malaysia intensified their maritime and air patrols, seriously limiting such a scenario (Storey, 2006).

17. For the structure of a "loan-for-oil/gas" deal, see Jiang and Sinton, 2011, p. 22.

18. For a map on this, see https://www.google.gr/search?q=String+of+pearls+China& source=lnms&tbm=isch&sa=X&ved=0ahUKEwjY47ydspjfAhUFjiwKHUusAPQQ_AUI DigB&biw=1536&bih=754#imgrc=ZR9JWqJXRYrKmM.

19. Discussing the militarization prospects of the "String of Pearls," of particular significance is the analysis by the former commander of the Indian navy, the Four-Star Admiral Arun Prakash, in which is, *inter alia*, mentioned that India "is in the middle of the Indian Ocean, and that is where China has implemented its 'string of pearls' strategy by creating around [India] what are best described as 'weapon-client states': Bangladesh, Myanmar, Sri Lanka, Saudi Arabia, Iran, and Pakistan" (Prakash, 2007).

20. In fact, in this manner China has fulfilled its "two-oceans" strategy. For more on this, see Hornby, 2017.

21. For a detailed account on these acquisitions as well as for the "loan-for-oil/gas" deals in Kazakhstan, as well as in the other Central Asian states, see Sotiriou, 2015, p. 190.

22. For a map on this, see https://www.kmgep. kz/eng/the_company/our_business/transportation_and_sales/.

23. Seeing the converging interests around this project, it is noteworthy that Turkmenistan had started to negotiate the price of the dispatched quantities at $80/tcm as early as 2005, Uzbekistan was for years pressed by Gazprom's suppressive pricing policy, a fact that, in turn, created serious shortages in the country's hard currency reserves, whereas Kazakhstan very positively saw the whole prospect, desiring not only to host it, but also to expand its length and transport capacity (EIA, 2017; Sotiriou, 2015, p. 195). For a map of this network, see https:// www.eia.gov/todayinenergy/detail.php?id=12931.

24. Truth be told, the SCO has proved a great host of the regional energy sector initiatives. In the case of the CAGP, a lot of developments (i.e., the framework agreement between the Chinese and the Kazakh authorities on expanding the natural gas production as well as the CAGP on October 31, 2008) had taken place within the context of the SCO meetings. For a detailed account, see CNPC, 2008, and Sotiriou, 2015, p. 194.

25. For this network, see https://www.eia.gov/beta/international/analysis.php?iso=RUS.

26. For a schematic presentation of the Sino-Russian "loan-for-oil" deal structure, see Jiang and Sinton, 2011, p. 22.

27. In November 2014, Vladimir Putin and Xi Jinping signed also a Memorandum of Understanding (MoU) on what it became known as the "western" gas supplies route to China (RT, 2014). This agreement opens up the prospects for China to become Russia's biggest consumer of natural gas, since the "western" or "Altay" route would dispatch to China an extra 30bcm/y (RT, 2014). So, taken together, China secured an aggregate 68bcm/y of Russian as soon as both gas networks were in place.

28. At the time of writing, 83% of the pipeline has been constructed (Lelyveld, 2018). For this network, see https://www.eia.gov/beta/international/analysis.php?iso=RUS.

29. In essence, the administration of the SPRs has been assigned to the country's three major NOCs (EIA, 2015).

30. Back in 1973–1974, the fuel embargo coupled with a dwindling US production, deeply shook the US, which, in 1975, launched the SPRs as an attempt to shield their economy against unexpected supply disruptions (Upadhyay, 2017). In 2017, the US SPRs contained 693.4 million barrels of oil, not far from the all-time record of 727 million barrels of oil held in 2009 (Upadhyay, 2017). Nevertheless, in March 2017, China bought, for the first time in history, crude oil from the US SPR, taking up 550,000 barrels, benefiting from the US decision to sell quantities from its reserve due to maintenance costs as well as of not considering them, at the time, that critical for its energy security (Upadhyay, 2017).

Chapter Eight

Conclusion

Eurasian Politics as a Two-Level Game

THE CONTEXT OF THE BOOK IN A NUTSHELL

The purpose of this book is to focus on critical issues that are met across Eurasia, with this term to refer to the post-soviet space, plus China. It is a fact that following the collapse of the USSR, the wider region of Eurasia has reemerged, presenting a new reality, the two main features of which are "frozen conflicts" and "energy politics." In fact, these two features are currently portrayed as two distinct analytical levels, with the first to give prime emphasis on the domestic politics and the second on the international politics. Moreover, the fact that politics in both two levels take place in comparable socio-political conditions, allows the analysis to develop as a two-level game.

LEVEL I, DOMESTIC: "FROZEN CONFLICTS" IN EURASIA

Searching for the main takeaways in the first level of analysis, everything revolves around the question "What are the causes lying behind the 'frozen conflicts' across Eurasia?" and by extension "What are the useful policy implications to be drawn?" Keeping this in mind, the late years of the USSR serve as critical point of departure. That time, the long-standing institutional framework of the USSR, including both the state institutions as well as much of the unofficial institutions of the civil society, entered a protracted period of fluidity and reconfiguration. What for years was perceived as fixed and unchallengeable was subject to a rapid and fundamental change. This period is called a "critical juncture" and is characterized by the prevalence of a

177

condition that pretty much resembles that of anarchy. Within this context, conflicts broke out in the post-soviet states of Moldova, Ukraine, Georgia and Azerbaijan.

In particular, the whole region sunk in a condition of anarchy, insecurity, and lack of trust, where former soviet citizens resorted to the very fundamentals attributes of the human nature such as language, ethnicity, in order to form alliances that could better their prospects towards survival and security. In more measurable terms, atomized rational actors, using the fundamental attributes of human nature as connective strands, allied themselves seeking to guarantee their existence by having their political standing ensured within the emerging, new, statehoods. The institutionalization of regional political preferences mattered the most to the citizens of Transdniestria, Crimea, Abkhazia, South Ossetia, and Nagorno-Karabakh, and, in fact, it became an enduring, if not institutionalized, demand, as they were witnessing the condition of anarchy of the early independence period to continue unabated for the years that followed. Typically, when new Constitutions were adopted by the newly independent states (more or less in mid-1990s), crystallizing a new reconfiguration of power or, in other words, a new institutional equilibrium, the critical juncture period of late 1980s, early 1990s was terminated. But in reality, the atomized-turned-ethnicized reality, or mode of administration, was kept being reproduced, deepening the survival and insecurity fears, and paving the way for the period of the second major eruption or critical juncture in the course of the states in point. No efficient institutional framework had been established so as to shape and shove the rational actors' interests towards the gradual formation of a civic type of national identity, which, in it turn, would propel the society, as a balanced total of different interests, towards Pareto's optimal outcome.

The book in hand adopts a flexible approach that allows it to move across the agent (interests)-structure axis and highlight the interconnectedness that exists between the two, with the former to inform the latter and *vice-versa*, in an endless course of mutual constitutiveness. Moreover, by examining the "frozen conflicts" within a comparative historical continuum that places emphasis on the major eruption periods in the respective states throughout the post-soviet period, it manages to detect probable root causes, to show the preservation of anarchy-resembling conditions within the respective states, and most importantly to consider possible solutions to a hard-to-reverse reality of *de facto* statehoods within *de jure* statehoods.

As the analysis reveals, a federation-leaning restructuring within the states that host "frozen conflicts" would alleviate survival and security concerns, leading, finally to the gradual accumulation of social trust, seriously expedited by the efficient functioning of the tate institutions as well as by the everyday interaction between the citizens. Taking the point one step further, the federation-leaning restructuring, should have at its core an ethnofederal institutional setup, where despite the existence of a dominant group in terms of population, this would be "divided up into a number of distinct federal regions rather than united in one core ethnic region" as means of seriously lessening any survival and security threats perceived by the minority (ethnic) groups, and of intercepting any efforts by the political entrepreneurs to capitalize on fomenting the creation of "an independent core nation-state" (Hale, 2004, p. 167). In this way, the foundations would be set towards constructing an environment where the civic type of national identity would characterize the overwhelming majority of citizens, and the society as a total would be striving towards Pareto's optimal outcome. It is exactly the situation where otherwise uncontained rational actors that seek to maximize their power and guarantee their relative gains just to survive and be secure in conditions of anarchy, have their interests filtered through the regulative power of institutions.

LEVEL II, INTERNATIONAL: ENERGY POLITICS IN EURASIA

If "frozen conflicts" constitute one of the critical issues across Eurasia, "energy politics" is certainly the other. With the cross-national energy networks to give the impression that energy builds upon and unites what the "frozen conflicts" leave as compartmentalized and segregated, the energy politics across Eurasia's underbelly come to the forefront.

Today's interdependence between the EU and Russia is traced back in late 1940s, when the western Europe and the USSR initiated their energy relationship, and started gradually to build transport networks between them (Sotiriou, 2015, pp. 123–177). Things, however, would take the downturn, when in critical points throughout the 2000s (2006, 2009), the European (EU) energy security would be seriously jeopardized due to Russia's energy (natural gas) standoffs with post-soviet neighbors that held the role of a transit state in the Russia-EU energy trade, emphasis placed on Ukraine. Geopolitical competition immediately found its way to the front scene, with the actors-states to pursue their power maximization and accumulation of relative gains in anarchy-resembling/or interests-driven conditions.

The EU, ever since, has been seeking to diversify its suppliers and transport networks away from Russia, constraining as much as possible the dominant (energy) status of the latter. Among the options that have been prioritized by Brussels is that of the Caspian Sea, with the regional subsystems surrounding it (including the Caucasus and Central Asia). The ideal scenario would be to tap in the Central Asian resources and connect them through a trans-Caspian network to Azerbaijan, onwards to the EU through the transit state of Turkey.

But, all this area is of high sensitivity to Russia, let alone that Russia is one of the five littoral states of the Caspian Sea. Throughout the post-soviet period the legal regime of the Caspian Sea had remained unsettled, and when a breakthrough finally seemed to have been reached (the 2018 five-party agreement), this happened only after Russia had succeeded in safeguarding its interests. It is not only the environmental provisions that allow Russia to have the final say in every trans-caspian network project and bring Iran, the second major actor and caviar producer in the region, to its side, but also the fact that by the time the 2018 agreement was reached, the Central Asian states had already made an opening to, or a commitment with, the vast Chinese market. The resource-wealth of the Central Asian states matched the widely pressured pressed energy mix of China, with both sides to establish firm energy ties, leaving very narrow prospects, if any, for the Central Asian states to address the EU demand.

Moreover, China has also been a critical element for Russia's effort to further curb, if not eliminate, the EU ambitions to turn the interdependent relationship to its favor by diversifying its suppliers and supply routes to-wards the Caspian Sea region. The turn towards an energy "thirsty" and environmentally "cornered" China, provides, for the first time, Russia with a powerful lever. As stated by Alexander Medvedev, Gazprom's deputy chair-man, "having concluded a single contract, China equaled our largest Euro-pean consumer" (Foy, 2018). Thus, Russia acquires the strategic advantage to be able to convert its relationship with the EU from interdependent, to a unilaterally dependent one, in which, while both actors still sensitive, vulner-able remains only the actor with fewer, if any, alternatives. Overall, Russia has managed to strengthen its position across Eurasia, being able to push for its relative gains, and find way outs of "difficult turns."[1]

With these facts on the ground, at this level too, the book addresses the energy diplomacy within a flexible agent-structure axis, highlighting the interconnectedness that exists between the two, with the former to inform the latter and *vice-versa*, in an endless course of mutual constitutiveness. In essence, it is observed how states, acting as rational actors, have been seek-ing to maximize their power by internal and external efforts, paying, concur-rently, attention to the relative gains as a necessary means of survival and security. Moreover, it is aptly shown how the interests of powerful actors (e.g., Russia) have been codified, if not dominated, within the provisions of institution-leaning arrangements (e.g., the 2018 five-party agreement on the Caspian Sea legal regime).

Assessing the prospects of the fermentations at the eastern end of Eurasia, the truth is that Russia, the Central Asian states, and China have not been experiencing a free-of-challenges confluence of interests. It is well known fact that traditionally they have had a fickle relationship.[2] But in 1996, for first time since the collapse of the USSR, commonly shared security interests, brought all regional actors in point under the umbrella of the "Shanghai Five." China's Xinjiang region (XUAR) has been inhabited by separatism-inclined Turkic-speaking Muslim Uyghurs, which, affected by the rise of the belligerent form of Islam in the neighboring Central Asian states, created, more often than not, destabilization tendencies in the county. Russia, itself, has also been challenged by the rise of Islamist groups. That initial international cooperation was upgraded in 2003, when it was renamed Shanghai Cooperation Organization (SCO), and its 2001-signed charter entered into force. Ever since, numerous cooperation projects have been undertaken in various policy areas, emphasis placed also on the energy sector. In fact, in October 2005, during the Moscow Summit of the SCO, it was announced that SCO would prioritize joint energy projects that pertain to the oil and gas sector, and to the exploration for new hydrocarbon reverses, whereas in November 2006 the Russian Ministry of Foreign Affairs circulated the idea for a SCO "Energy Club." Since then, the oil and gas projects in the region have skyrocketed, with Russia's, Central Asian states', and China's interests to all the more overlap and form a powerful pole, able to counterbalance, if not overpower, in energy terms, the European end of Eurasia. Much more, this alliance constantly expands, with major regional players like India and Pakistan to have gained membership in June, 2017, and others, like Iran, to hold observer status.[3]

LEVELS I AND II: ARE THEY CONNECTED?

Drawing parallels between the two levels and seeing how useful one level may be to the other as a policy paradigm, Russia, China, and the Central Asian states, at the international level, just like the residents of Transdniestria with the remainder citizens of Moldova, the residents of Crimea and Eastern Ukraine with the remainder citizens of Ukraine, the residents of South Ossetia and Abkhazia with the remainder citizens of Georgia, and residents of Nagorno-Karabakh with the remainder citizens of the Azerbaijan, at the national level, had their coexistence gravely challenged in multiple occasions and persistently.

Back in the Soviet times, the USSR and China had been on opposite, if not collision, tracks as far as the role of the two countries as development and ideological flagships in the world communist movement and their approach to the international relations (especially with regards to the US) are concerned. In fact, this deepening standoff would not take long to express itself in more measurable terms, when in March 1969, the Chinese forces would unleash an attack against the Soviet ones over controlling a small, uninhabited, border island in the Ussuri river (Shlapentokh, 2007, p. 4). This military action, which caused the death of thirty-two soldiers, was repeated again later that year, without the same death toll, at the Lake Zhalanashkol, in the eastern part of the Soviet Kazakhstan (Shlapentokh, 2007, p. 4). This overall hostile environment put down deep roots in the collective conscience, which would remain intact for the years to come, albeit the U-turn by the political elites following the death of Mao Tse-tung.[4]

This atmosphere of insecurity, mutual distrust and relative gains consider-ations continued also after the collapse of the USSR. Russia's Far Eastern Region (RFE) encountered very harsh economic conditions with no govern-ment aid, a fact that resulted into a steady outmigration from the region, and Sino-phobia among the remainder Russian population in view of the massive Chinese population on the other side of the border; in fact, the Russians of the region perceived the Chinese of the northeastern borders as the "yellow peril" (Garnett, 1998). But China, too, had issues with the Central Asian states as far as its energy resources-rich XUAR region is concerned; the latter, being home to considerable oil and gas reserves (the Tarim Basin) and energy projects (e.g., networks) has attracted numerous Han Chinese, which outnumbered the local population in almost every aspect of the socio-politi-cal life, causing widespread distress and outbursts of violence (Lelyveld, 2009; Karagiannis, 2010).[5] There are no little cases, where China has ac-cused Central Asian states, and particularly Kazakhstan, for an inefficient state apparatus providing shelter to violent events in XUAR, with this kind of accusation to go both ways, with Kazakhstan to also blame China for detain-ing its citizens to "reeducation camps" in XUAR (RFE/RL, 2018b). Thus, the institution-leaning reboot of the regional cooperation within the SCO offered Beijing the chance "to normalize relations with Russia and neighbors in Central Asia . . . and win their support . . . to impose full control over the XUAR" (Hansen, 2008, p. 218). As earlier mentioned, the first thing that brought Russia, the Central Asia states and China together within the SCO was the securitization of their border and the guarantee of their sovereign standing. Once these issues were settled, cooperation in the energy sphere started to soar up.

When, in 2018, the "Power of Siberia" energy network was approaching its completion, in Blagoveshchensk, a small city on the Russian side of the Sino-Russian border which at times had had a fraught relationship with its eastern neighbor, Aleksandr Kozlvov, the governor, built an ice hockey pitch, whose center line is along the international border, calling for matches between the two sides in an indication of a new era in the relations between the two countries.[6] Furthermore, in the city's main street, a statue was erected illustrating a young man carrying huge bags, in memory of the one-man traders of early 1990s that carried goods across the borders, and most probably had been associated with the once "yellow peril" (Foy, 2018). As stated by Kozlov, the statue "reminds us of turbulent times, but now we're witnessing new projects that elevate our relations and enhance economic cooperation" (Foy, 2018). In the same direction, as the Chinese engineers were tunneling under the Amur river to place pipes to transport the gas into China and concrete pillars were gradually standing out from the thick river ice in realization of a bridge that almost got lost in limbo, Evgeniy Pisotskiy, the person in charge of the company constructing Russia's half of the bridge, stated: "For 25 years we have been attempting to do this, so the decision to go ahead is definitely historic moment . . . it is a sign that we have buried differences and found ways to work together. It is bringing nations and people together" (Foy, 2018).

This is exactly the point that the two levels of analysis of this book are connected; just like the anarchy dominated environment of East Asia found its way towards enhanced and tight cooperation once sovereignty, security, and political standing issues were substantially resolved or at least addressed via the SCO, in the same manner, the "frozen conflicts," notwithstanding the flood of bitter memories which have given rise to, could meet a better tomorrow once survival, security, and political standing considerations are essentially and functionally institutionalized in the Constitutions of the respective states. Then, the road towards gradually intensifying cooperation and accumulation of social capital will be wide open. Just like the energy sector could not have flourished without the political issues to have been resolved first, in the same manner, the confidence-building measures initiated by the OSCE in many of the "frozen conflicts" have a long and strenuous way to cover should not be associated with, if not start from, concrete measures (e.g., ethnofederal restructuring of the states with no core ethnic group), focusing on guaranteeing the political standing of the *de facto* states within the borders of the respective *de jure* states.

NOTES

1. As of 2018, US sanctions against Russia have locked on new pipelines, such as the Nord Stream 2, which would double direct supplies to Germany (Foy, 2018).
2. See the bibliography.
3. For an exact account, see http://eng.sectsco.org/.
4. For reasons of inclusiveness, it is mentioned that the USSR and China followed different courses during military developments in South East Asia (Vietnam's invasion to Cambodia) and during the Soviet invasion of Afghanistan. For more on the issue, see Sutter, 2008, p. 328.
5. From XUAR pass both the Turkmenistan-China gas pipeline and the Kazakhstan-China oil pipeline.
6. The pipeline created numerous jobs in RFE. Indicatively, it is mentioned that for a construction of a new gas plant outside Svobodny, 25,000 jobs were created in the construction sector, and another 3,000 were permanent, having to do with running the plant (Foy, 2018).

Bibliography

Agamalova, Anastasya, and Raibman, Natalya (2014), "Rada otpravila Ianukovicha v otstavku [The parliament declared the President deposed]," *Vedomosti.ru.*, February 22, in https://www.vedomosti.ru/politics/articles/2014/02/22/rada-otpravila-yanukovicha-v-otstavku-i-naznachila-novye (date of retrieval 01-08-2018).

Akiner, Shirin (2000), "Emerging political order in the new Caspian States," Gary K. Bertsch, Cassady Craft, Scott A. Jones, and Michael Beck (eds.), *Crossroads and Conflict: Security and Foreign Policy in the Caucasus and Central Asia*, New York: Routledge.

Altstadt, Audrey L. (1997), "Azerbaijan's struggle toward democracy," Karen Dawisha and Bruce Parrot (eds.), *Conflict cleavage, and change in Central Asia and the Caucasus*, Glasgow: Cambridge University Press, pp. 110–155.

Ambrosio, Thomas, and Lange, William A. (2016), "The architecture of annexation? Russia's bilateral agreements with South Ossetia and Abkhazia," *Nationalities Papers*, Vol. 44(16): 673–693.

Ambrosio, Thomas (2011), "Unfreezing the Nagorno-Karabakh conflict? Evaluating peace-making efforts under the Obama administration," *Ethnopolitics*, Vol. 10(1): 93–114.

Amnesty International (2008), *Civilians in the line of fire: The Georgia-Russia conflict*, London: Amnesty International Publications.

Antidze, Margarita (2007), "Russia closes last military base in Georgia," *Reuters*, November 13, in https://www.reuters.com/article/us-georgia-russia-bases/russia-closes-last-military-base-in-georgia-idUSL1387605220071113 (date of retrieval 13-08-2018).

Antonenko, Oksana (2005), "Frozen Uncertainty: Russia and the conflict over Abkhazia," Bruno Coppieters and Robert Legvold (eds.), *Statehood and security: Georgia after the Rose Revolution*. Cambridge MA: The MIT Press, pp. 205–269.

Artman, Vincent A. (2013), "Documenting territory: Passportisation, Territory, and Exception in Abkhazia and South Ossetia," *Geopolitics*, Vol. 18(3): 682–704.

Athanasiadis, Titos (1988), *I epanastasi apo ton Lenin ston Gorbachev [The revolution from Lenin to Gorbachev]*, Athens: I.Sideris.

Avaliani, Dmitry, Bukia, Sopho, Tskhurbayev, Alan, and De Waal, Thomas (2008), *How the Georgian War began*, London: IWPR (Institute for War and Peace Reporting).

Axelord, Robert, and Keohane, Robert O. (1985), "Achieving cooperation under anarchy: Strategies and institutions," *World Politics*, Vol. 38(1): 226–254.

Bakke, Kristin M., O'Loughlin, John, Toal, Gerard and Ward, Michael D. (2014), "Convincing State-Builders? Disaggregating Internal Legitimacy in Abkhazia," *International Studies Quarterly*, Vol. 58: 591–607.

Batt, Judy (1997), "Federalism versus nationalism in post-communist state-building: The case of Moldova," *Regional & Federal Studies*, Vol. 7(3): 25–48.

Baumgartner, Pete (2018), "Moscow watches anxiously as Pashinian realigns Armenia's Foreign Policy," RFE/FL, September 8, in https://www.rferl.org/a/moscow-watches-anxiously-as-pashinian-realigns-armenia-s-foreign-policy/29477633.html (date of retrieval 08-09-2018).

BBC (British Broadcasting Corporation) (2017), "Abkhazia profile," August 10, in http://www.bbc.com/news/world-europe-18175030 (date of retrieval 01-09-2017).

BBC (2016a), "Xinjiang territory profile," November 16 in http://www.bbc.com/news/world-asia-pacific-16860974 (date of retrieval 05-07-2017).

BBC (2016b), "South Ossetia profile," April 21 in http://www.bbc.com/news/world-europe-18269210 (date of retrieval 01-09-2017).

BBC (2016c), "Nagorno-Karabakh violence: Worst clashes in decades kill dozens," April 3 in https://www.bbc.com/news/world-europe-35949991 (date of retrieval 06-09-2018).

BBC (2016d), "Nagorno-Karabakh fighting: Azerbaijan 'calls truce,'" April 3 in https://www.bbc.com/news/world-europe-35953916 (date of retrieval 06-09-2018).

BBC (2015a), "Nagorno-Karabakh: 'Frozen' conflict threatens to reignite," April 7 in https://www.bbc.co.uk/news/world-europe-32202426 (date of retrieval 06-09-2018).

BBC (2015b), "Nagorno-Karabakh conflict: Azerbaijanis dream of return," January 8 in https://www.bbc.co.uk/news/world-europe-30718551 (date of retrieval 06-09-2018).

BBC (2012a), "Timeline: Georgia," January 31 in http://news.bbc.co.uk/2/hi/europe/country_profiles/1102575.stm (date of retrieval 13-08-2018).

BBC (2012b), "Q&A: Iran sanctions," October 16 in http://www.bbc.co.uk/news/world-middle-east-15983302 (date of retrieval 20-01-2013).

BBC (2001a), "Eyewitness: A republic loses faith," August 15 in http://news.bbc.co.uk/2/hi/europe/1477933.stm (date of retrieval 16-11-2017).

BBC (2001b), "Abkhazia 'on the verge of war,'" October 12 in http://news.bbc.co.uk/2/hi/europe/1595847.stm (date of retrieval 13-08-2018).

BBC (1990), "1990: Gorbachev explains crackdown in Azerbaijan," January 22 in http://news.bbc.co.uk/onthisday/hi/dates/stories/january/22/newsid_4099000/4099647.stm (date of retrieval 06-09-2018).

BBC Russian.com (2005), "Advekatnomu ponimaniyu armyano-azerbaidzhanskovo konflikta meshaet pasprostranenie I povtorenie lozhnoi statistiki," July 15 in http://newsvote.bbc.co.uk/mpapps/pagetools/print/news.bbc.co.uk/hi/russian/in_depth/newsid_4685000/4685287.stm (date of retrieval 06-09-2018).

Beissinger, Mark R. (2002), *Nationalist mobilization and the collapse of the Soviet state*, New York: Cambridge University Press.

Belitser, Natalya (2000), "The Constitutional process in the Autonomous Republic of Crimea in the context of interethnic relations and conflict settlement," *Fuzzy Statehood and European Integration in Eastern Europe conference*, University of Birmingham, England in http://www.iccrimea.org/scholarly/nbelitser.html (date of retrieval 31-07-2018).

Berg, Eiki (2012), "Parent states versus secessionist entities: Measuring political legitimacy in Cyprus, Moldova and Bosnia & Hercegovina," *Europe-Asia Studies*, Vol. 64(7): 1271–1296.

Bessière, Stephanie (2007), *I Kina stin augi tou 21ou aiona (in greek) [China at the outset of 21 century]*, Athens: Ekdoseis "Kedros."

Birch, Julian (1995), "Ossetia: A Caucasian Bosnia in microcosm," *Central Asian Survey* Vol. 14(1): 43–74.

Bilgin, Mert (2009), "Geopolitics of European natural gas demand: Supplies from Russia, Caspian and the Middle East," *Energy Policy*, Vol. 37: 4482–4492.

Bilgin, Mert (2007), "New prospects in the political economy of inner-Caspian hydrocarbons and western energy corridor through Turkey," *Energy Policy*, Vol. 35: 6383–6394.

Blagov, Sergei (2011), "Littoral states struggle to agree on the Caspian settlement," *Eurasia Daily Monitor*, Vol. 8(88).

Blank, Stephen (2008), "Threats to and from Russia: An assessment," *The Journal of Slavic Military Studies*, Vol. 21(3): 491–526.

BP (British Petroleum) (2018a), "The southern gas corridor," in http://www.bp.com/en_az/caspian/operationsprojects/Shahdeniz/SouthernCorridor.html (date of retrieval 26-02-2018).

BP (2018b), *BP statistical review of world energy June 2018*, London: BP p.l.c.

BP (2017), *BP statistical review of world energy June 2017*, London: BP p.l.c.

BP (2016), *BP statistical review of world energy June 2016*, London: BP p.l.c.

BP (2015), "The southern gas corridor," in http://www.bp.com/en_az/caspian/operationsprojects/Shahdeniz/SouthernCorridor.html (date of retrieval 09-10-2015).

BP (2014), *BP statistical review of world energy June 2014*, London: BP p.l.c.

Broers, Laurence (2016), "The Nagorny Karabakh conflict defaulting to war," *Chatham House*, July, in https://www.chathamhouse.org/publication/nagorny-karabakh-conflict-defaulting-war (date of retrieval 06-09-2018).

Broers, Laurence (2015), "From 'frozen conflict' to enduring rivalry: Reassessing the Nagorno Karabakh conflict," *Nationalities Papers*, Vol. 43(4): 556–576.

Brzezinski, Zbigniew (1997), *The Grand Chessboard: American primacy and its geostrategic imperatives*, New York: Basic Books.

Bugriy, Maksym (2014), "Southeastern Ukraine unrest and domestic politics," *Eurasia Daily Monitor*, Vol. 11(68).

Bull, Hedley (1977), *The anarchical society: A study of order in world politics*, London: Macmillan.

Burma Project (2008), *China in Burma: The increasing investment of Chinese multinational corporations in Burma's hydropower, oil and natural gas, and mining sectors*, Chiang Mai: Chiang Mai University, Canadian Institute of Ukrainian Studies (2001), "New Russia," in http://www.encyclopediaofukraine.com/display.asp?linkpath=pages%5CN%5CE%5CNew Russia.html (date of retrieval 31-07-2018).

Capoccia, Giovanni, and Kelemen, Daniel R. (2007), "The study of critical junctures: Theory, narrative, and counterfactuals in historical institutionalism," *World Politics*, Vol. 59(3): 341–369.

Cash, Jennifer R. (2013), "Performing hospitality in Moldova: Ambiguous, alternative, and undeveloped models of national identity," *History and Anthropology*, Vol. 24(1): 56–77.

CCPA (1925), http://abkhazia.narod.ru/constitution1.htm (date of retrieval 26-07-2017).

Charter of the Collective Security Treaty Organization—CSTO (2002), 2235 UNTS 79, entered into force 18 September 2003.

Cheng, Joseph Y. S. (2008), "A Chinese view of China's energy security," *Journal of Contemporary China*, Vol. 17(55): 297–317.

Chinn, Jeff, and Roper, Steven D. (1995), "Ethnic mobilization and reactive nationalism: The case of Moldova," *Nationalities Papers*, Vol. 23(2): 291–325.

Chivers, Christopher J. (2004), "Threat of civil war is turning the Abkhaz into Russians," *New York Times*, August 15, in http://www.nytimes.com/2004/08/15/world/threat-of-civil-war-is-turning-the-abkhaz-into-russians.html (date of retrieval 06-09-2017).

Chivers, Christopher J., and Herszenhorn, David (2014), "Separatists defy Kiev and Putin on referendum," *New York Times*, May 8, in http://www.nytimes.com/2014/05/09/world/europe/ukraine.html?hp&_r=0 (date of retrieval 01-08-2018).

Chrysogonos, Kōstas Ch., and Vlachopoulos, Spyros B. (2017), *Civil and social rights*, Fourth Edition, Athens: Nomikē Bibliothēkē S.A.

Chrysogonos, Kōstas Ch. (2003), *Syntagmatiko dikaio* [Constitutional law], Thessaloniki: Ekdoseis Sakkoula.

CIS (Commonwealth of Independent States) Legislation (2003), "The protocol to the Agreement between the Republic of Kazakhstan and the Azerbaijan Republic about differentiation of the bottom of the Caspian Sea between the Republic of Kazakhstan and the Azerbaijani Republic," February 27 in http://cis-legislation.com/document.fwx?rgn=3984 (date of retrieval 10-02-2016).

CISR (Center for Strategic Studies and Reforms) (2010), *The economy of Transnistria: View from the outside*. Chisinau. http://www.cisr-md.org/pdf/viewfromoutside.pdf (date of retrieval 29-01-2018).

Civil Georgia (2008), "Georgia decided to restore constitutional order in South Ossetia—MoD Official," August 8 in http://www.civil.ge/eng/article.php?id=18941&search (date of retrieval 13-08-2018).

Cleary, Laura (2016), "Half measures and incomplete reforms: the breeding ground for a hybrid civil society in Ukraine," *Southeast European and Black Sea Studies*, Vol. 16(1): 7–23.

CNPC (2008), "CNPC and KazMunayGas sign framework agreement on expanding natural gas and gas pipeline cooperation," November 1 in https://www.cnpc.com.cn/en/Kazakhstan/country_index.shtml (date of retrieval 06-09-2012).

CNPC (2007), "CNPC and Turkmenistan sign new gas cooperation agreement," July 17 in http://www.cnpc.com.cn/en/press/newsreleases/2007/7-17.htm (date of retrieval 03-09-2012).

Cojocaru, Natalia (2006), "Nationalism and identity in Transnistria," *Innovation: The European Journal of Social Science Research*, Vol. 19(3–4): 261–272.

Comfort, Nicholas, and Bierman, Stephen (2010), "EU Seeks Caspian Gas Accord to Cut Russian Dependence," *Bloomberg*, August 4, in http://www.bloomberg.com/news/articles/2010-08-03/eu-seeks-turkmen-Azerbaijani-gas-pipeline-accord-to-reduce-russian-dependence (date of retrieval 28-02-2018).

Constitution of Crimea (1998), in http://www.rada.crimea.ua/en/bases-of-activity/konstituciya-ARK (date of retrieval 31-07-2018).

Constitution of Ukraine (1996), in http://www.justice.gov/sites/default/files/eoir/legacy/2013/11/08/constitution_14.pdf (date of retrieval 31-07-2018).

Constitution of the USSR (1977), in http://www.constitution.org/cons/ussr77.txt (date of retrieval 06-09-2018).

Contessi, Nicola P. (2016), "Central Asia *in* Asia: Charting growing trans-regional linkages," *Journal of Eurasian Studies*, Vol. 7: 3–13.

Cooley, Alexander (2015), "China's changing role in Central Asia and implications for U.S. policy: From trading partner to collective goods provider," *U.S.-China Economic and Security Review Commission*, March 18,

Cooper, Helen, and Shanker, Thom (2008), "After mixed U.S. messages, a war erupted in Georgia," *New York Times*, August 12, in http://www.nytimes.com/2008/08/13/washington/13diplo.html (date of retrieval 13-08-2018).

Corden, Max, and Neary, Peter (1982), "Booming sector and de-industrialization in a small open economy," *The Economic Journal*, Vol. 92: 825–848.

Cornell, Svante E. (1998), "Turkey and the conflict in Nagorno Karabakh: A delicate balance," *Middle Eastern Studies*, Vol. 34(1): 51–72.

Croissant, Michael P. (1998), *The Armenia-Azerbaijan conflict: Causes and implications*, Connecticut: Praeger Publishers.

Croissant, Michael P., and Croissant, Cynthia M. (1998), "The Caspian Sea status dispute: Azerbaijani perspectives," *Caucasian Regional Studies*, Vol. 3(1).

Crowther, William (1998), "Ethnic politics and the post-communist transition in Moldova," *Nationalities Papers*, Vol. 26(1): 147–164.

CSCE (Commission on Security and Cooperation in Europe) (2017), "In brief: The Nagorno-Karabakh conflict," June 15, in https://www.csce.gov/international-impact/publications/nagorno-karabakh-conflict?page=1 (date of retrieval 06-09-2018).

Cvetkovski, Nikola (1999), "The Georgian–South Ossetia conflict," PhD diss., University of Aalborg.

Dadwal, Shebonti Ray (2007), "China's search for energy security: Emerging dilemmas," *Strategic Analysis*, Vol. 31(6): 889–914.

Daily Sabah (2016), "Turkey to chair 2017 Energy Club of Shanghai Cooperation Organization," November 26, in:https://www.dailysabah.com/energy/2016/11/23/turkey-to-chair-2017-energy-club-of-shanghai-cooperation-organization (date of retrieval 23-06-2017).

De Lima, Vigo Iara, and Guizzo, Danielle (2015), "An archeology of Adam Smith's epistemic context," *Review of Political Economy*, Vol. 27(4): 585–605.

De Waal, Thomas (2015), "Losing control in the Caucasus," *Politico*, November 10 in https://www.politico.eu/article/losing-control-in-the-caucasus-armenia-azerbaijan-russia-nagorno-karabakh/ (date of retrieval 28-08-2018).

De Waal, Thomas (2014), "Nagorno-Karabakh: Helicopter downing threatens shaky truce," *BBC*, November 14 in https://www.bbc.com/news/world-europe-30044414 (date of retrieval 28-08-2018).

De Waal, Thomas (2013), *Black Garden: Armenia and Azerbaijan through peace and war*, 10-Year Anniversary Edition, revised and updated, New York: New York University Press.

De Waal, Thomas (2010), "Remaking the Nagorno-Karabakh peace process," *Survival*, Vol. 52(4): 159–176.

Dempsey, Judy (2008), "EU natural gas pipeline project gets first order," *New York Times*, June 11, in http://www.nytimes.com/2008/06/11/business/worldbusiness/11iht-pipe.4.13640390.html?_r=3& (date of retrieval 10-09-2018).

Dias, Vanda A. (2013), "The EU's post-liberal approach to peace: framing EUBAM's contribution to the Moldovan-Transnistria conflict transformation," *European Security*, Vol. 22(3): 338–354.

Downs, Erica S. (2010), "Sino-Russian energy relations: An uncertain courtship," in James Bellacqua (ed.), *The future of China-Russia relations*, Lexington: University Press of Kentucky, pp. 146–175.

Downs, Erica S. (2009), "Who's afraid of China's oil companies?" in Carlos Pascual and Jonathan Elkind (eds.), *Energy security: Economics, politics, strategies and implications*, Washington, DC: Brookings Institution Press, pp. 73–102.

Downs, Erica S. (2006), *Energy security series: China*, Washington, DC: The Brookings Institution Press.

Downs, Erica S. (2004), "The Chinese energy security debate," *The China Quarterly*, Vol. 177: 21–41.

Eckel, Mike (2016), "Nagorno-Karabakh witnesses debut of 'Kamikaze' drone," *RFE/RL*, April 6 in https://www.rferl.org/a/nagorno-karabakh-kamikaze-drone-debut/27658645.html (date of retrieval 06-09-2018).

Economist (2018), "How China cut its air pollution," January 25 in https://www.economist.com/the-economist-explains/2018/01/25/how-china-cut-its-air-pollution (date of retrieval 13-09-2018).

EEC (Eurasian Economic Commission) (2016), *Eurasian economic integration: Facts and figures*, Report number: 1H 2016.

EIA (Energy Information Administration) (2018), "Country analysis brief: Iran," April 9, in https://www.eia.gov/beta/international/analysis_includes/countries_long/Iran/iran.pdf, (date of retrieval 11-09-2018).

EIA (2017), "Kazakhstan," January 14, in http://www.eia.gov/beta/international/analysis_includes/countries_long/Kazakhstan/kazakhstan.pdf (date of retrieval 11-09-2018).

EIA (2016), "Turkmenistan," July, in https://www.eia.gov/beta/international/analysis.php?iso=TKM (date of retrieval 11-09-2018).

EIA (2015), "China," May 14, in https://www.eia.gov/beta/international/analysis_includes/countries_long/China/china.pdf (date of retrieval 12-09-2018).

EIA (2014), "Azerbaijan," August 1, in http://www.eia.gov/countries/cab.cfm?fips=AJ (date of retrieval 10-02-2016).

EIA (2013), "Caspian Sea region," August 26, in https://www.eia.gov/beta/international/analysis_includes/regions_of_interest/Caspian_Sea/caspian_sea.pdf (date of retrieval 27-02-2018).

Eisenman, Joshua (2007), "China's post-Cold War strategy in Africa: Examining Beijing's methods and objectives," in Eisenman J., Heginbotham E., and Derek M. (eds.), *China and the Developing World: Beijing's strategy for the twenty-first century*, New York: M.E. Sharpe, Inc., pp. 29–59.

Euractiv (2013), "EU-backed Nabucco project 'over' after rival pipeline wins Azerbaijani gas bid," June 28, in http://www.euractiv.com/section/energy/news/eu-backed-nabucco-project-over-after-rival-pipeline-wins-Azerbaijani-gas-bid/ (date of retrieval 05-07-2107).

European Commission (2008), "An EU energy security and solidarity action plan," COM (2008) 781, May 13, 2018, in http://eur-lex.europa.eu/legal-content/EN/TXT/HTML/?uri=LEGISSUM:en0003&from=EN (date of retrieval 26-07-2017).

Eurostat (2014), *Energy, transport and environment indicators*, Luxembourg: Publications Office of the European Union.

Eyal, Jonathan (1990), "Moldavians," in Graham Smith (ed.), *The nationalities question in the Soviet Union*, London: Longman, pp. 123–141.

Eyal, Jonathan, and Smith, Graham (1996), "Moldova and the Moldovans," in Graham Smith (ed.), *The nationalities question in the post-Soviet states*, New York: Longman, pp. 223–244.

Fabry, Mikulas (2012), "The contemporary practice of state recognition: Kosovo, South Ossetia, Abkhazia, and their aftermath," *Nationalities Papers*, Vol. 40(5): 661–676.

Fawkes, Helen (2008), "Despair among Georgia's displaced," *BBC News*, August 20, in http://news.bbc.co.uk/2/hi/europe/7572736.stm (date of retrieval 13-08-2018).

Fedyakina, Anna (2014), "DNR i LNR gotovy vypolnyam' minskie soglasheniya" [The DPR and the LPR ready to comply with the Minsk agreement], *Rossiĭskaia Gazeta*, November 5, in http://www.rg.ru/2014/11/05/soglasheniya-site.html (date of retrieval 01-08-2018).

Feifer, Gregory (2002), "Caspian: Russia, Azerbaijan sign agreement on sea boundaries," *RFE/RL*, September 24, in http://www.rferl.org/content/article/1100881.html (date of retrieval 23-03-2015).

Felgenhauer, Pavel (2014), "The self-styled separatist referendum in Eastern Ukraine is on despite Putin's request," *Eurasia Daily Monitor*, Vol. 11(86).

Fengying, Chen, and Jiejun, Ni (2008), "Asian energy security: The role of China and India," *Strategic Analysis*, Vol. 32(1): 41–55.

Figes, Orlando (2002), *Natasha's dance: A cultural history of Russia*, New York: Metropolitan Books.

Financial Times (2008), "Countdown in the Caucasus: Seven days that brought Russia and Georgia to war," August 26, in https://www.ft.com/content/af25400a-739d-11dd-8a66-0000779fd18c (date of retrieval 13-08-2018).

Fishelson, James (2007), "From the silk road to Chevron: The geopolitics of oil pipelines in Central Asia," *Vestnik, The Journal of Russian and Asian Studies*, Vol. 1(7): 22–53.

Foy, Henry (2018), "Russia's $55bn pipeline gamble on China's demand for gas," *Financial Times*, April 3, in https://ig.ft.com/gazprom-pipeline-power-of-siberia/ (date of retrieval 17-09-2108).

Franke, Anja, Gawrich, Andrea, and Alakbarov, Gurban (2009), "Kazakhstan and Azerbaijan as post-Soviet rentier states: Resource incomes and autocracy as a double 'curse' in post-Soviet regimes," *Europe-Asia Studies*, Vol. 61(1): 109–140.

Freeman, Carla P. (2017), "New strategies for an old rivalry? China-Russia relations in Central Asia after the energy boom," *The Pacific Review*, DOI: 10.1080/09512748.2017.1398775.

Freizer, Sabine (2014), "Twenty years after the Nagorno Karabakh ceasefire: An opportunity to move towards more inclusive conflict resolution," *Caucasus Survey*, Vol. 1(2): 109–122.

Fukuyama, Francis (1999), "Social capital and civil society," *Paper presented at IMF Conference on Second Generation Reforms* in https://www.imf.org/external/pubs/ft/seminar/1999/reforms/fukuyama.htm#1 (date of retrieval 17-11-2017).

Fuller, Liz (2006), "Georgia: South Ossetia seeks to contain opposition challenge," *Radio Free Europe / Radio Liberty (RFE/RL)*, November 10 in http://www.rferl.org/a/1072652.html (date of retrieval 13-08-2018).

Fuller, Liz (2004a), ". . . But fails to reassure local authorities," *Radio Free Europe/ Radio Liberty (RFE/RL)*, May 18, in http://www.rferl.org/a/1143161.html (date of retrieval 13-08-1982).

Fuller, Liz (2004b), ". . . As Georgian officials continue to send mixed signals," *Radio Free Europe / Radio Liberty (RFE/RL)*, May 21, in http://www.rferl.org/a/1143164.html (date of retrieval 13-08-2018).

Gahramanova, Aytan (2009), "Internal and external factors in the democratization of Azerbaijan," *Democratization*, Vol. 16(4): 777–803.

Gardiner, Harris and Ewing, Jack (2018), "U.S. to restore sanctions on Iran, Deepening divide with Europe," *New York Times*, August 6, in https://www.nytimes.com/2018/08/06/us/politics/iran-sanctions-trump.html (date of retrieval 11-09-2018).

Garnett, Sherman (1998), *Limited partnership: Russia-China relations in a changing Asia*, Washington, DC: Carnegie Endowment for International Peace.

Gazprom (2018a), "Голубой поток" [Blue Stream] in http://www.gazprom.ru/about/production/projects/pipelines/active/blue-stream/ (date of retrieval 23-02-2018).

Gazprom (2018b), "Turetskiy поток" [TurkStream] in http://www.gazprom.ru/about/production/projects/pipelines/built/turk-stream/,(date of retrieval 26-02-2018).

Gazprom (2018c), "China—Gazprom's strategic partner," September 17, in http://www.gazprom.com/press/news/2018/september/article460569/ (date of retrieval 20-09-2018).

Gazprom (2015), "Yuzhnyi potok [South Stream pipeline]," February 10, in http://www.gazprom.ru/about/production/projects/pipelines/south-stream/ (date of retrieval 11-02-2015).

Gazprom (2014), "Novy gazoprovod v Turtsyu [New gas pipeline to Turkey]," December 2, in http://www.gazprom.ru/press/news/2014/december/article208495/ (date of retrieval 10-07-2016).

Georgakopoulos, Theodoros, Lianos, Theodoros, Mpenos, Theofanis, Tsekouras, Ioannis, Chatziprokopiou, Mikhail, and Christou, Georgios (2002), *Eisagogē stēn Politikē Oikonomia* [Introduction to Political Economy], Athens: Ekdoseis Mpenou.

George, Julie A. (2009), "The dangers of reform: State building and national minorities in Georgia," *Central Asian Survey*, Vol. 28(2): 135–154.

Georgiatimes (2012), "South Ossetia in charge for nothing," May 3, in http://www.georgiatimes.info/en/analysis/75509.html (date of retrieval 13-08-2018).

Geostat.ge (2002), "Ethnic groups by major administrative-territorial units," in http://www.geostat.ge/cms/site_images/_files/english/census/2002/03%20Ethnic%20Composition.pdf (date of retrieval 13-08-2018).

German, Tracey (2016), "Russia and South Ossetia: Conferring statehood or creeping annexation?" *Southeast European and Black Sea Studies*, Vol. 16(1): 155–167.

German, Tracey (2012), "The Nagorno-Karabakh Conflict between Azerbaijan and Armenia: Security Issues in the Caucasus," *Journal of Muslim Minority Affairs*, Vol. 32(2): 216–229.

German, Tracey (2009), "Pipeline politics: Georgia and energy security," *Small Wars & Insurgencies*, Vol. 20(2): 344–362.

Gerring, John (2001), *Social science methodology: A criterial framework*, New York: Cambridge University Press.

GfK (2014), "Public opinion survey in Crimea," March 12–14, in https://avaaz-press.s3.amazonaws.com/558_Crimea.Referendum.Poll.GfK.pdf (date of retrieval 01-08-2018).

Gilpin, Robert G. (1984), "The richness of the tradition of political realism," *International Organization*, Vol. 38(2): 287–304.

Gorenburg, Dmitry (2011), "Ukraine after Yushchenko," *Russian Politics & Law*, Vol. 49(5): 3–7.

Grieco, Joseph M. (1993), "Understanding the problem of international cooperation: The limits of neo-liberal institutionalism and the future of realist theory," in David Baldwin (ed.), *Neorealism and neoliberalism: The contemporary debate*, New York: Columbia University Press, pp. 301–338.

Gulbrandsen, Lars H., and Moe, Arild (2007), "bp in Azerbaijan: a test case of the potential and limits of the CSR agenda?" *Third World Quarterly*, Vol. 28(4): 813–830.

Hale, Henry E. (2004), "Divided we stand: Institutional sources of ethnofederal state survival and collapse," *World Politics*, Vol. 56: 165–193.

Hall, Peter A., and Taylor, Rosemary C.R. (1996), "Political science and the three new institutionalisms," *Political Studies*, Vol. 44(5): 936–957.

Hansen, Holley E., and Hesli, Vicki L. (2009), "National identity: Civic, ethnic, hybrid, and atomised individuals," *Europe-Asia Studies*, Vol. 61(1): 1–28.

Hansen Splidsboel, Flemming (2008), "The Shanghai Co-operation organization," *Asian Affairs*, Vol. XXXIX (II): 217–232.

Haqqin.az (2016), "Minoborony: Azerbaydzhan v odnostoronnem poryadke priostabovil boe-vye deystviya [MoD: Azerbaijan stop unilaterally the hostilities]," in https://haqqin.az/news/67220 (date of retrieval 29-08-2018).

Harutyunyan, Sargis (2016), "Senior Armenian military officials sacked," *RFE/RL*, April 26, in https://www.azatutyun.am/a/27699843.html (date of retrieval 06-09-2018).

He, Kai (2008), "Institutional balancing and international relations theory: Economic interdependence and balance of power strategies in Southeast Asia," *European Journal of International Relations,* Vol. 14(3): 489–518.

Herb, Michael (2005), "No representation without taxation? Rents, development, and democracy," *Comparative Politics*, Vol. 37(3): 297–316.

Herszenhorn, David M., and Roth, Andrew (2014a), "Protesters in Ukraine's east call on Putin to send troops," *New York Times*, April 7, in https://www.nytimes.com/2014/04/08/world/europe/russia-crimea-ukraine-unrest.html?hp&_r=0 (date of retrieval 01-08-2017).

Herszenhorn, David M., and Roth, Andrew (2014b), "Conflict fatigue deepens in east Ukraine, just days before vote," *New York Times*, May 20, in https://www.nytimes.com/2014/05/21/world/europe/conflict-fatigue-deepens-in-east-ukraine-just-days-before-vote.html?hp&_r=0 (date of retrieval 31-01-2018).

Herszenhorn, David M. (2013), "Thousands demand resignation of Ukraine leader," *New York Times*, December 1, in:http://www.nytimes.com/2013/12/02/world/europe/thousands-of-protesters-in-ukraine-demand-leaders-resignation.html?ref=international-home (date of retrieval 01-12-2014).

Herzig, Edmund M. (1996), "Armenia and the Armenians," in Graham Smith (ed.), *The nationalities question in the post-Soviet states*, New York: Longman, pp. 248–268.

Hesli, Vicki L., Reisinger, William M., and Miller, Arthur H. (1998), "Political party development in divided societies: The case of Ukraine," *Electoral Studies*, Vol. 17(2): 235–256.

hetq (2016), "Azerbaijani soldiers execute elderly Armenian couple in Artsakh, then cut off their ears," April 3, in http://hetq.am/eng/news/66976/Azerbaijani-soldiers-execute-elderly-armenian-couple-in-artsakh-then-cut-off-their-ears.html (date of retrieval 29-08-2018).

Heywood, Andrew (2002), *Politics (Second Edition)*, Hampshire: Palgrave MacMillan.

Hiden, Johan and Salmon, Patrick (1994), *The Baltic Nations and Europe*, Harlow: Longman.

Hincks, Joseph (2017), "Uighur militants reportedly threaten China in ISIS video," *Time*, March 1, in http://time.com/4686836/isis-video-china-uighur/ (date of retrieval 19-06-2017).

Hirschman, Albert O. (1969), *National power and the structure of foreign trade*, Berkeley: University of California Press.

Hobbes, Thomas (1651), *Leviathan or the matter, forme, & power of a common-wealth ecclesiastical and civill.*, London: Andrew Crooke.

Hornby, Lucy (2017), "China and Myanmar open long-delayed oil pipeline," *Financial Times*, April 11, in https://www.ft.com/content/21d5f650-1e6a-11e7-a454-ab04428977f9 (date of retrieval 15-09-2018).

HRW (Human Rights Watch) (1995a), *Georgia/Abkhazia: Violations of the laws of war and Russia's role in the conflict*, New York: Human Rights Watch.

HRW (1995b), *Playing the "communal card": Communal violence and human rights*, New York: Human Rights Watch.

HRW (1994), *Azerbaijan: Seven years of conflict in Nagorno-Karabakh*, New York: Human Rights Watch.

HRW (1992), *Bloodshed in the Caucasus: Violations of humanitarian law and human rights in the Georgian–South Ossetian conflict*, New York: Human Rights Watch.

Huntington, Samuel (1968), *Political order in changing societies*, New Haven, CT: Yale University Press.

Hutchings, Graham (2001), *Modern China: A guide to a century of change*, Cambridge, MA: Harvard University Press.

Huttenback, Henry R. (1990), "In support of Nagorno-Karabakh: Social components of the Armenian nationalist movement," *Nationalities Papers*, Vol. 18(2): 5–14.

ICG (International Crisis Group) (2016), *Nagorno-Karabakh: New opening, or more peril?* Report number 239.

ICG (2008a), *Russia vs Georgia: The fallout*, Report number 195.

ICG (2008b), *Georgia and Russia: Clashing over Abkhazia*, Report number 193.

IDMC (Internal Displacement Monitoring Centre) (2018), "Georgia," in: http://www.internal-displacement.org/countries/georgia (date of retrieval 13-08-2018).

IEA (2011), *World energy outlook 2011*, Paris: OECD/IEA.

IEA (2007), *World energy outlook 2007: China and India insights*, Paris: OECD/IEA.

Iglesias, Julien D. (2015), "Eurovision song contest and identity crisis in Moldova," *Nationalities Papers*, Vol. 43(2): 233–247.

IMF (International Monetary Fund) News (2016), "Azerbaijan's opportunity to reboot, diversify economy," September 15, in http://www.imf.org/en/News/Articles/2016/09/15/NA091516-Azerbaijan-Opportunity-to-Reboot-Diversify-Economy (date of retrieval 16-11-2017).

Infoshos.ru (2015), "SCO energy club: Structure ready for international interaction, not Shanghai Six's elite club," March 26, in http://infoshos.ru/en/?idn=13913 (date of retrieval 23-06-2017).

Interfax.ru. (2014), "Iugo-vostok Ukraini vzial na sebia obespetsenie konstitutsionnovo poriadka" [Southeastern Ukraine took over the responsibility for maintaining the constitutional order], February 22, in http://www.interfax.ru/world/txt/360367 (date of retrieval 31-07-2018).

Interfax.ru. (2014a), "Krym voshel v sostav Rossiĭskoĭ Federatsii" [Crimea became part of the Russian Federation], March 18, in http://www.interfax.ru/russia/365492 (date of retrieval 01-08-2018).

Interfax.ru. (2014b), "Slavyansk stal tsentrom napryazhennosti na yugo-vostoke Ukrainy" [Slovyansk became the center of tension in Southeastern Ukraine], April 13, in http://www.interfax.ru/world/371315 (date of retrieval 01-08-2018).

Interfax.ru. (2010), "Transneft, China to finish underwater transfer in Amur River for ESPO branch in April–May," March 24, in http://business.highbeam.com/407705/article-1G1-231255441/transneft-and-china-finish-underwater-transfer-amur (date of retrieval 05-06-2010).

IRI (2013), "Public opinion survey residents of the Autonomous Republic of Crimea," May 16–30, in http://www.iri.org/sites/default/files/2013%20October%207%20Survey%20of%20Crimean%20Public%20Opinion%2C%20May%2016-30%2C%202013.pdf (date of retrieval 01-08-2018).

Istomin, Igor, and Bolgova, Irina (2016), "Transnistrian strategy in the context of Russian-Ukrainian relations: The rise and failure of 'dual alignment,'" *Southeast European and Black Sea Studies*, Vol. 16(1): 169–194.

Izvestya.ru. (2008), "Pochemu nasha armiya voshla v Yuzhniyu Osetiyu" [Why did our army entered South Ossetia], August 11, in http://izvestia.ru/news/339570 (date of retrieval 13-08-2018).

James, Toby S. (2016), "Neo-statecraft theory, historical institutionalism and institutional change," *Government and Opposition*, Vol. 51(1): 84–110.

Janusz, Barbara (2005), "The Caspian Sea: Legal status and regime problems," *Chatham House*, August, in http://www.chathamhouse.org/sites/files/chathamhouse/public/Research/Russia%20and%20Eurasia/bp0805caspian.pdf (date of retrieval 05-07-2017).

Jarosiewicz, Aleksandra, and Falkowski, Maciej (2016), "The four-day war in Nagorno-Karabakh," *Ośrodek Studiów Wschodnich—OSW*, April 6, in https://www.osw.waw.pl/en/publikacje/analyses/2016-04-06/four-day-war-nagorno-karabakh (date of retrieval 06-09-2018).

Jervis, Robert (1978), "Cooperation under the security dilemma," *World Politics*, Vol. 30(2): 167–214.

Jiang, Julie, and Sinton, Jonathan (2011), *Overseas investments by Chinese national oil companies: Assessing the drivers and impacts*, Paris: OECD/IEA.

Johansson, Andreas (2006), "The Transnistrian conflict after the 2005 Moldovan parliamentary elections," *Journal of Communist Studies and Transition Politics*, Vol. 22(4): 507–516.

Karagiannis, Emmanuel (2016), "Ukrainian volunteer fighters in the eastern front: Ideas, political-social norms and emotions as mobilization mechanisms," *Southeast European and Black Sea Studies*, Vol. 16(1): 139–153.

Karagiannis, Emmanuel (2014), "The Russian interventions in South Ossetia and Crimea compared: Military performance, legitimacy and goals," *Contemporary Security Policy*, Vol. 35(3): 400–420.

Karagiannis, Emmanuel (2010a), *Political Islam in Central Asia: The challenge of Hizb ut-Tahrir*, New York: Routledge.

Karagiannis, Emmanuel (2010b), "China's energy security and pipeline diplomacy: Assessing the threat of low-intensity conflicts," *Harvard Asia Quarterly*, Vol. XII(3–4): 54–60.

Karagiannis, Emmanuel (2002), *Energy and security in the Caucasus*, Oxon: RoutledgeCurzon.

Kaufman, Stuart J. (1998), *Ethnic fears and ethnic war in Karabakh*, Program on New Approaches to Russian Security, Davis Center for Russian Studies, Harvard University, in https://csis-prod.s3.amazonaws.com/s3fs-public/legacy_files/files/media/csis/pubs/ruseur_wp_008.pdf (date of retrieval 06-09-2018).

Kaufmann, Daniel, Kraay, Aart, and Mastruzzi, Massimo (2010), "The worldwide governance indicators: Methodology and analytical issues," *World Bank Policy Research Working Paper*, No. 5430: 1–28.

Kauppi, Mark V. (1995), "Thucydides: Character and capabilities," *Security Studies*, Vol. 5(2): 142–168.

Kazantsev, Andrei (2008), "Russian policy in Central Asian and the Caspian Sea region," *Europe-Asia Studies* 60(6): 1073–1088.

Kechichian, Joseph A., and Karasik, Theodore W. (1995), "The crisis in Azerbaijan: How clans influence the politics of an emerging republic," *Middle East Policy*, Vol. 4(1–2): 57–71.

Kegley, Charles W., Jr. (1995), *Controversies in international relations theory: Realism and the neoliberal challenge*, Belmont: Wadsworth Group.

Keller, Bill (1988), "Riot's legacy of distrust quietly stalks a Soviet city," *New York Times*, in https://www.nytimes.com/1988/08/31/world/riot-s-legacy-of-distrust-quietly-stalks-a-soviet-city.html (date of retrieval 06-09-2018).

Kendall-Taylor, Andrea (2012), "Purchasing power: Oil, elections and regime durability in Azerbaijan and Kazakhstan," *Europe-Asia Studies*, Vol. 64(4): 737–760.

Kennedy, Ryan (2016), "The limits of soft balancing: The frozen conflict in Transnistria and the challenge to EUA and NATO strategy," *Small Wars & Insurgencies*, Vol. 27(3): 512–537.

Keohane, Robert O. (1986), *Neorealism and its critics*, New York: Columbia University Press.

Keohane, Robert O., and Nye, Joseph S. Jr. (2011), *Power and interdependence*, Fourth Edition, Boston: Longman.

Khamdokhov, Stanislav (2017), "Predpolagaemovo ubiytsu pilota Su-24 prigovorili k 5 godam" [The alleged killer of the Su-24 pilot was sentenced to five years], *Rossiyskaya gazeta*, May 22, in https://rg.ru/2017/05/22/predpolagaemogo-ubijcu-pilota-su-24-prigovorili-k-5-godam.html (date of retrieval 05-07-2017).

King, Charles (2001), "The benefits of ethnic war: Understanding Eurasia's unrecognized states," *World Politics*, Vol. 53(4): 524–552.

King, Charles (1998), "Ethnicity and institutional reform: The dynamics of 'indigenization' in the Moldavian ASSR," *Nationalities Papers*, Vol. 26(1): 57–72.

Kissinger, Henry (1994), *Diplomacy*, New York: Simon & Schuster.

Kissinger, Henry (1975), "A new national partnership," *The Department of State Bulletin*, Vol. 72(1860): 197–204.

Kolossov, Vladimir, and O'Loughlin, John (1998), "Pseudo-states as harbingers of a new geopolitics: The example of the transdniester Moldovan republic (TMR)," *Geopolitics*, Vol. 3(1): 151–176.

Kolstø, Pal, Edemsky, Andrei, and Kalashnikova, Natalya (1993), "The Dniester conflict: Between irredentism and separatism," *Europe-Asia Studies*, Vol. 45(6): 973–1000.

Kommersant.ru. (2014), "Sergey Glazev: federalizatsiya—uzhe ne ideya, a ochevidnaya neobxodimost" [Federalization—no longer an idea, but a clear need], February 6, in http://www.kommersant.ru/doc/2400532 (date of retrieval 01-08-2018).

Konstitutsiya soyuza [Constitution of the Union] (1924), http://constitution.garant.ru/history/ussr-rsfsr/1924/red_1924/5508661/chapter/1/#block_1000 (date of retrieval 22-07-2017).

Korosteleva, Elena (2010), "Moldova's European Choice: 'Between Two Stools'?" *Europe-Asia Studies*, Vol. 62(8): 1267–1289.

Kosienkowski, Marcin (2017), "The Gagauz Republic: Internal dynamics of de facto statehood," *Annales Universitatis Mariae Curie—Sklodowska Sectio K Politologia*, Vol. 24(1): 115–133.

Kramer, Andrew E. (2008), "Peace plan offers Russia a rationale to advance," *New York Times*, August 13, in http://www.nytimes.com/2008/08/14/world/europe/14document.html (date of retrieval 13-08-2018).

Kramer, Mark (2014), "The transfer of Crimea from Soviet Russia to Soviet Ukraine, 1954," *Wilson Center: Cold War international history project*, March 19, in https://www.wilsoncenter.org/publication/why-did-russia-give-away-crimea-sixty-years-ago?gclid=CLHnyZC7ndACFSLicgod-UEIXw#_ftn3 (date of retrieval 26-07-2017).

Kreft, Heinrich (2006), "China's energy security conundrum," *The Korean Journal of Defense Analysis*, Vol. XVIII(3): 107–120.

Kubicek, Paul (2013), "Energy politics and geopolitical competition in the Caspian Basin," *Journal of Eurasian Studies*, Vol. 4: 171–180.

Kubicek, Paul (2005), "The European Union and democratization in Ukraine," *Communist and Post-Communist Studies*, Vol. 38: 269–292.

Kucera, Joshua (2016), "Karabakh fighting highlights Azerbaijan's new Israeli weapons," *eurasianet*, April 6, in https://www.eurasianet.org/karabakh-fighting-highlights-azerbaijans-new-israeli-weapons (date of retrieval 06-09-2018).

Kudenko, Alexey (2015), "TurkStream falls under Russia's restrictive measures against Turkey," *Sputniknews*, November 26, in https://sputniknews.com/world/201511261030796887-turkish-stream-russia/ (date of retrieval 05-07-2017).

Kugelman, Michael (2018), "The China-Pakistan economic corridor and energy geopolitics in Asia," *Wilson Center*, January 9, in https://www.wilsoncenter.org/blog-post/the-china-pakistan-economic-corridor-and-energy-geopolitics-asia (date of retrieval 15-09-2018).

Kusznir, Julia, and Smith Stegen, Karen (2015), "Outcomes and strategies in the 'New Great Game': China and the Caspian states emerge as winners," *Journal of Eurasian Studies*, Vol. 6: 91–106.

Kuzio, Taras, and D'Anieri, Paul (2018), *The sources of Russia's great power politics: Ukraine and the challenge to the European order*, Bristol: E-International Relations Publishing.

Kuzio, Taras (2007), "Oligarchs, tapes and oranges: 'Kuchmagate' to the Orange Revolution," *Journal of Communist Studies and Transition Politics*, Vol. 23(1): 30–56.

Kylymar, Victor (2014), "Nastroyi Ukrayini" [Ukraine is ready], in https://www.slideshare.net/victorkylymar/prezent-socis-kiispress (date of retrieval 01-08-2018).

Kyrkilis, Dimitrios (2010), "Einai i Rosia mia oikonomia physikon poron? Oikonomiki metavasi, oikonomiki anaptyxi kai o rolos toy petrelaioy" [Is Russia a natural resources economy? Economic transition, economic development, and the role of oil], in Emmanuel Karagiannis (ed.), *I Rosia Simera: Politiki, Oikonomia kai Exoterikes sxeseis [Russia today: Politics, Economics and Foreign Relations]*, Athens: Ekdoseis Papazisi: 83–113.

Lally, Kathy (2014), "Putin's remarks raise fears of future moves against Ukraine," *Washington Post*, April 17, in https://www.washingtonpost.com/world/putin-changes-course-admits-russian-troops-were-in-crimea-before-vote/2014/04/17/b3300a54-c617-11e3-bf7a-be01a9b69cf1_story.html (date of retrieval 12-07-2015).

Lamont, Neil V. (1993), "Territorial dimensions of ethnic conflict: The Moldovan case, 1991–March 1993," *The Journal of Slavic Military Studies*, Vol. 6(4): 576–612.

Lamy, Steven L. (2001), "Contemporary mainstream approaches: Neo-realism and neo-liberalism," in John Baylis and Steve Smith (eds.), *The globalization of world politics*, Second Edition, New York: Oxford University Press, pp. 182–199.

Landru, Nicolas (2006), "Two referendums and two 'presidents' in South Ossetia," *Caucaz europenews*, November 20, in https://web.archive.org/web/20061128064202/http://www.caucaz.com/home_eng/breve_contenu.php?id=279 (date of retrieval 13-08-2018).

Lang, David Marshall (1966), *The Georgians*, New York: Preager.

Lazzerini, Edward J. (1996), "Crimean Tatars," in Graham Smith (ed.), *The nationalities question in the post-Soviet states*, Second Edition, London: Longman, pp. 412–435.

Le Monde (2018), "La mer Caspienne au cœur d'un accord historique," August 12, in https://www.lemonde.fr/international/article/2018/08/12/la-mer-caspienne-au-c-ur-d-un-accord-historique_5341696_3210.html (date of retrieval 11-09-2018).

Lecours, André (2000), "Theorizing cultural identities: Historical institutionalism as a challenge to the culturalists," *Canadian Journal of Political Science*, Vol. 33(3): 499–522.

Lee, Pak K. (2005), "China's quest for oil security: Oil (wars) in the pipeline?" *The Pacific Review*, Vol. 18(2): 265–301.

Lee, Yusin (2004), "Policies of five Caspian coastal States: Do concerns about relative gains play any role?" *Global Economic Review: Perspectives on East Asian Economies and Industries* 33(3): 97–111.

Lelyveld, Michael (2018), "China nears limit on Central Asian Gas," *RFA (Radio Free Asia)*, June 25, in https://www.rfa.org/english/commentaries/energy_watch/china-nears-limit-on-central-asian-gas-06252018100827.html (date of retrieval 16-09-2018).

Levin, Michael L. (2008), *The next great clash: China and Russia vs. the United States*, Westport: Praeger Security International.

Lewis, Steven W. (2007), *Chinese NOCs and world energy markets: CNPC, Sinopec and CNOOC*, Houston: James A. Baker III Institute for Public Policy.

Lieberthal, Kenneth, and Oksenberg, Michel (1988), *Policy making in China: Leaders, structures, and processes*, New Jersey: Princeton University Press.

Lieven, Dominic (2001), *Empire: The Russian empire and its rivals*, New Haven: Yale University Press.

Lipson, Charles (1984), "International cooperation in economic and security affairs," *World Politics*, Vol. 37(1): 1–23.

LNTS (1921), Persia and the Russian Socialist Federal Soviet Republic Treaty of Friendship, 26 February (League of Nations, Treaty Series, no. 268) in http://www.worldlii.org/cgibin/download.cgi/download/int/other/LNTSer/1922/69.pdf (date of retrieval 10-07-2016).

Loshkariov, Ivan D., and Sushentsov, Andrey A. (2016), "Radicalization of Russians in Ukraine: From 'accidental' diaspora to rebel movement," *Southeast European and Black Sea Studies*, Vol. 16(1): 71–90.

Lragir.am (2016), "Draft resolution on secession of Armenia from Eurasian Union has been introduced," April 14, in https://www.lragir.am/en/2016/04/14/35616 (date of retrieval 06-09-2018).

MacFarquhar, Neil (2016), "Warming relations in person, Putin and Erdogan revive pipeline deal," *New York Times*, October 10, in https://www.nytimes.com/2016/10/11/world/europe/turkey-russia-vladimir-putin-recep-tayyip-erdogan.html?hp&action=click&pgtype=Homepage&clickSource=story-heading&module=first-column-region&region=top-news&WT.nav=top-news&_r=0 (date of retrieval 05-07-2017).

Mackinder, Halford J. (2006), "Dēmokratika ideodi kai pragmatikotēta" [Democratic Ideals and Reality], Ioannis Th. Mazis (Epimeleia), *Dēmokratika ideodi kai pragmatikotēta kai alles treis eisēgēseis* [Democratic Ideals and Reality and three other essays], Athens: Ekdoseis Papazēsē.

Mackinder, Halford J. (1943), "The round world and the winning of peace," *Foreign Affairs,* Vol. 21(4): 595–605.

Mackinder, Halford J. (1942), *Democratic ideals and reality*, Washington DC: National Defense University Press.

Mackinder, Halford J. (1904), "The geographical pivot of history," *The Geographical Journal*, Vol. 23(4): 421–437.

Mahoney, James (2000), "Path dependence in historical sociology," *Theory and Society*, Vol. 29(4): 507–548.

Makhorkina, Anna (2005), "Ukrainian political parties and foreign policy in election campaigns: Parliamentary elections of 1998 and 2002," *Communist and Post-Communist Studies*, Vol. 38: 251–267.

Malyarenko, Tetyana and Galbreath, David J. (2016), "Paramilitary motivation in Ukraine: Beyond integration and abolition," *Southeast European and Black Sea Studies*, Vol. 16(1): 113–138.

Mamedov, Rustam (2001), "International legal status of the Caspian Sea: Issues of theory and practice," *The Turkish Yearbook* (32): 217–259.

Mamedov, Rustam (2000), "International-legal status of the Caspian Sea in its historical development" *The Turkish Yearbook* (30): 107–137.

Matveeva, Anna (2016), "No Moscow stooges: Identity polarization and guerilla movements in Donbass," *Southeast European and Black Sea Studies*, Vol. 16(1): 25–50.

McDevitt, Andrew (2015), *The state of corruption: Armenia, Azerbaijan, Georgia, Moldova and Ukraine*, Berlin: Transparency International.

Mehdiyoun, Kamyar (2000), "Ownership of oil and gas resources in the Caspian Sea," *The American Journal of International Law*, Vol. 94(1): 179–189.

Meidan, Michal, Andrews-Speed, Philip and Xin, Ma (2009), "Shaping China's energy policy: Actors and processes," *Journal of Contemporary China*, Vol. 18(61): 591–616.

Melintei, Mihai (2017), "Ekonomika Pridnestrov'ya—Potentsial I tsifry za yanvar'—Sentyabri 2017 goda [The economy of Transdniestria—Potential and numbers for the period January–September 2017]," *ANUARUL: Yearbook of the Laboratory for the Transnistrian Conflict Analysis*, Vol. 1(1): 46–53.

Meyers, Steven Lee (2014), "Ousted leader seeks Russian aid as tensions rise in Crimea," *The New York Times*, February 27, in http://www.nytimes.com/2014/02/28/world/europe/ukraine.html?hp (date of retrieval 31-07-2018).

MFA (Ministry of Foreign Affairs) AZ (2016), "Statement on the use of white phosphorous bomb by the armed forces of Armenia against civilians and civilian objects of Azerbaijan," May 17, in http://www.mfa.gov.az/en/news/909/4104 (date of retrieval 29-08-2018).

MFA NK (1994), "Soglashenie o prekrashchenie ognya [Ceasefire agreement]," May 11, in http://www.nkr.am/ru/ceasefire-agreement/147/ (date of retrieval 25-08-2018).

MFA NK (1991), "Akt o rezul'tatakh referenduma o nezavisimosti Nagorno-Karabakhskoy Respubliki" [Report on the results of the NK independence referendum], December 10, in http://www.nkr.am/ru/referendum/42/ (date of retrieval 25-08-2018).

Mihalka, Michael (1996), "Nagorno-Karabakh and Russian peacekeeping: Prospects for a second Dayton," *International Peacekeeping*, Vol. 3(3): 16–32.

Mill, John S. (1950), *Philosophy of scientific method*, New York: Hafner Publishing Company.

Minasyan, Sergey (2017), "The Nagorno-Karabakh conflict in the context of South Caucasus regional security issues: An Armenian perspective," *Nationalities Papers*, Vol. 45(1): 131–139.

Minority Rights Group International (2018), "World directory of minorities and indigenous peoples—Moldova: Russians and Russian-speakers," January, in http://minorityrights.org/minorities/russians-and-russian-speakers/ (date of retrieval 05-06-2018).

Minsk soglasheniya (2015), "Kompleks mer po vipolneniyu Minskikh soglasheniy" [Complexities in the implementation of the Minsk agreements], *OSCE*, February 12, in http://www.osce.org/cio/140156 (date of retrieval 01-08-2018).

Morgenthau, Hans (1973), *Politics among nations: The struggle for power and peace*, New York: Knopf.

Müller (2005), "South Ossetia (Georgia), 19 January 1992: Independence," in http://www.sudd.ch/event.php?lang=de&id=ge011992 (date of retrieval 13-08-2018).

Nagorno Karabakh Republic (2016), *Atrocities committed by Azerbaijani military forces against the civilian population of the Nagorno Karabakh republic and servicemen of the Nagorno Karabakh defense army on 2–5 April 2016*, Shushi: Human Rights Defender (ombudsman).

NATO (2006), "Statement by the NATO secretary general on 'referendum' and 'presidential elections' in South Ossetia/Tskhinvali region of Georgia," November 11, in http://www.nato.int/docu/pr/2006/p06-142e.htm, (date of retrieval 13-08-2018).

Newsru.com (2017), "Minoboroni Azerbaydzhana: novaya voyna za Karabakh neizbezhna" [Ministry of Defense of Azerbaijan: A new war for Karabakh is inevitable], December 7, in https://www.newsru.com/world/04jun2011/karabah.html (date of retrieval 15-08-2018).

Nielsen, Christian Axboe (2009), "The Kosovo precedent and the rhetorical deployment of former Yugoslav analogies in the cases of Abkhazia and South Ossetia," *Southeast European and Black Sea Studies*, Vol. 9(1–2): 171–189.

O'Hara, Sarah (2004), "Great game or grubby game? The struggle for control of the Caspian," *Geopolitics*, Vol. 9(1): 138–160.

O'Lear, Shannon (2004), "Resources and conflict in the Caspian Sea," *Geopolitics*, Vol. 9(1): 161–186.

OilVoice (2006), "Azerbaijan's Shah Deniz Field on Stream," December 15, in http://web.archive.org/web/20070114195148/www.oilvoice.com/Azerbaijans_Shah_Deniz_Field _On_Stream/8238.htm (date of retrieval 11-09-2018).

Olearchyk, Roman (2008), "Six killed in Georgian fighting," *Financial Times*, August 4, in http://www.ft.com/cms/s/0/7f5e9170-61bc-11dd-af94-000077b07658.html?ft_site=falcon& desktop=true#axzz4UL3J7nkA (date of retrieval December 27, 2016).

OSCE (Organization for Security and Cooperation in Europe) (2017a), "Who we are," in http://www.osce.org/minsk-group/108306 (date of retrieval 16-11-2017).

OSCE (2017b), "Progress on 'package of eight' will advance Transdniestrian settlement process and improve people's lives, says OSCE Special Representative," March 24, in https://www.osce.org/chairmanship/307386 (date of retrieval 04-07-2018).

OSCE (2017c), "Protocol of the official meeting of the permanent conference for political questions in the framework of the negotiating process on the Transdniestrian settlement," November 27–28, in https://www.osce.org/chairmanship/359196?download=true (date of retrieval 04-07-2018).

OSCE (2016a), "Ministerial statement on the negotiations on the Transdniestrian settlement process in the '5+2' format," MC.DOC/2/16, December 9, in https://www.osce.org/cio/ 288181 (date of retrieval 04-07-2018).

OSCE (2016b), "Protocol of the official meeting of the permanent conference for political questions in the framework of the negotiating process on the Transdniestrian settlement," June 2–3, in https://www.osce.org/moldova/244656?download=true (date of retrieval 04-07-2018).

OSCE (2016c), "Self-Determination of the people of Nagorno-Karabakh," September 20, in https://www.osce.org/odihr/268826?download=true (date of retrieval 06-09-2018).

OSCE (2014), "Protokol po itogam konsultatsiy trekhstoronney kontaktnoy gruppy otnositelno sovmestnikh shagov, napravlennikh na implementatsiyu mirnovo plana" [Protocol on the results of the three-party contact group consultations on joint steps aimed at the implementation of peace plan], September 1, in http://www.osce.org/ru/home/123258?download=true (date of retrieval 01-08-2018).

OSCE (2009), "Statement by the OSCE Minsk group co-chair countries," July 10, in http://www.osce.org/mg/51152 (date of retrieval 17-11-2017).

OSCE (2006), *OSCE: Annual Report 2006*, Vienna: OSCE Secretariat.

OSCE (2005), "On the meeting of mediators from Ukraine, the Russian Federation, and the OSCE with the representatives of the Republic of Moldova and Transdniestria," CIO.GAL/ 142/05, 26–27, in https://www.osce.org/cio/16558?download=true (date of retrieval 04-07-2018).

OSCE (1997), "Memorandum: On the Bases for Normalization of Relations Between the Republic of Moldova and Transdniestria," May 8, in https://www.osce.org/moldova/42309 (date of retrieval 04-07-2018).

PanArmenian.net (2016), "Karabakh lost 800 ha that played no strategic role: Armenia," May 17, in http://www.panarmenian.net/eng/news/212454/ (date of retrieval 15-08-2018).

Pannier, Bruce (2018a), "A landmark Caspian agreement—and what it resolves," *RFE/RL*, August 9, in https://www.rferl.org/a/qishloq-ovozi-landmark-caspian-agreement--and-what-it-resolves/29424824.html (date of retrieval 02-09-2018).

Pannier, Bruce (2018b), "Caspian Summit delivers less than expected," *RFE/RL*, August 12, in https://www.rferl.org/a/qishloq-ovozi-caspian-summit-delivers-less-than-expected/ 29428866.html (date of retrieval 02-09-2018).

Pannier, Bruce (2010), "Caspian Summit fails to clarify status, resource issues," *RFE/RL*, November 19, in http://www.rferl.org/content/Caspian_Summit_Fails_To_Clarify _Status_Resource_Issues/2225159.html (date of retrieval 10-07-2016).

Panossian, Razmik (2001), "The irony of Nagorno-Karabakh: Formal institutions versus informal politics," *Regional & Federal Studies*, Vol. 11(3): 143–164.

Paraskevopoulos, Christos J. (2001), "Social capital, learning and EU regional policy networks: Evidence from Greece," *Government and Opposition*, Vol. 36(2): 253–278.

Pehrson, Christofer J. (2006), *String of pearls: Meeting the challenge of China's rising power across the Asian Littoral*, Carlisle: Strategic Studies Institute.

Pen, Qiang (2007), "China opposed more Sudan sanctions," *China Daily*, May 30, in http://www.chinadaily.com.cn/china/2007-05/30/content_882954.htm (date of retrieval 01-02-2013).

Peters, Guy B., Pierre, Jon, and King, Desmond J. (2005), "The politics of path dependency: Political conflict in historical institutionalism," *The Journal of Politics*, Vol. 67(4): 1275–1300.

Platias, Athanasios G. (2002), *Diethneis sxeseis kai stratēgikē ston Thoukydidē* [International Relations and Strategy in Thucydides], Athens: Ekdoseis Estia.

Postanovlenie Soveta Ministrov RSFSR [Decree of the RSFR Council of Ministers] (1954), "O peredache Krimskoi oblasti iz sostava RSFSR v sostav U(kr)SSR [Concerning the Transfer of the Crimean Oblast' from the RSFSR to the UkSSR]," No. 156, February 5, in http://digitalarchive.wilsoncenter.org/document/119634 (date of retrieval 26-07-2017).

Potier, Tim (2012), "Referendum to determine Nagorno Karabakh's final status: A critical appraisal," *Journal of Muslim Minority Affairs*, Vol. 32(2): 269–276.

Powell, Robert (1991), "Absolute and relative gains in international relations theory," *The American Political Science Review*, Vol. 85(4): 1303–1320.

Prakash, Arun (2007), "China's naval gazers," *The Indian Express*, September 4, in http://www.indianexpress.com/news/china-s-naval-gazers/214471/4 (date of retrieval 07-02-2012).

Prezident Rossii (2018), "Konventsiya o pravom statuse Kaspiyskovo Morya" [Convention on the legal status of the Caspian Sea], August 12, in http://kremlin.ru/supplement/5328 (date of retrieval 01-09-2018).

Prezident Rossii (2008), "Zayavlenie Prezidenta Rossiiskoi Federatsii Dmitriya Medvedeva" [Statement by the president of the Russian Federation, Dmitry Medvedev], August 26, in https://web.archive.org/web/20080902083633/http://kremlin.ru/appears/2008/08/26/1445_type63374type82634type205158_205744.shtml (date of retrieval 13-08-2018).

Prezident Rossii (2002), "Soglashenie mezhdu Rossiiskoi Federatsieĭ I Azerbaidzhanskoi respublikoi o razgranichenii sopredel'nykh uchastkov dna kaspiiskogo moray" [Agreement between the Russian Federation and the Republic of Azerbaijan on the delimitation of neighboring sections in the Caspian Sea], September 23 in http://archive.kremlin.ru/text/docs/2002/09/30520.shtml (date of retrieval 10-02-2015).

Prezidium Berkhovnovo Soveta SSSR [Presidium of the Supreme Soviet of the USSR] (1954), "Zasedanie" [Meeting], February 19, in http://digitalarchive.wilsoncenter.org/document/119638 (date of retrieval 28-07-2017).

Prina, Federica (2015), "Linguistic Justice, Soviet Legacies and Post-Soviet Realpolitik: The Ethnoliguistic Cleavage in Moldova," *Ethnopolitics*, Vol. 14(1): 52–71.

Proedrou, Filippos (2010), "Ukraine's foreign policy: Accounting for Ukraine's indeterminate stance between Russia and the West," *Southeast European and Black Sea Studies*, Vol. 10(4): 443–456.

Putin, Vladimir (2014), "Vladimir Putin omvetil na voprosy zhurnalistov o situattsii na Ukraine" [Vladimir Putin answered journalists' questions on the situation in Ukraine], *Press Conference*, March 4, in http://kremlin.ru/events/President/news/20366 (date of retrieval 01-08-2017).

Putnam, Robert D., Leonardi, Robert, and Nanetti, Raffaella Y. (1993), *Making democracy work: Civic traditions in modern Italy*, Princeton, NJ: Princeton University Press.

Rabinowitz, Philip D., Yusifov, Mehdi Z., Arnoldi, Jessica, and Hakim, Eyal (2004), "Geology, oil and gas potential, pipelines, and the geopolitics of the Caspian Sea region," *Ocean Development & International Law*, Vol. 35(1): 19–40.

Raczka, Will (2000), "A sea or a lake? The Caspian's long odyssey," *Central Asian Survey* Vol. 19(2): 189–221.

Radnitz, Scott (2012), "Oil in the family: Managing presidential succession in Azerbaijan," *Democratization*, Vol. 19(1): 60–77.

Raibman, Natalya (2014), "Delegaty sezda v Kharkove vziali na sebia vlast na svoey territorii" [The congress delegates in Kharkiv reinstated their authority over the territory], *Vedomosti.ru.*, February 22, in https://www.vedomosti.ru/politics/articles/2014/02/22/delegaty-sezda-v-harkove-vzyali-na-sebya-vlast-na-svoej (date of retrieval 01-08-2018).

Raptopoulos, Nikolaos, and Sotiriou, Stylianos A. (2015), "Between cooperation & competition in energy issues with the major client/partner: A comparative study of Russian and Turkish foreign policies towards EU in the port-Crimean crisis era," *Paper presented to the 9 Pan-European Conference of the European International Studies Association*, Sicily, 23–26 September.

Rasizade, Alec (2011), "Azerbaijan's prospects in Nagorno-Karabakh," *Journal of Balkan and Near Eastern Studies*, Vol. 13(2): 215–231.

Rauta, Vladimir (2016), "Proxy agents, auxiliary forces, and sovereign defection: Assessing the outcomes of using non-state actors in civil conflicts," *Southeast European and Black Sea Studies*, Vol. 16(1): 91–111.

Razumkov Center (2014), "Is Ukraine threatened by . . . ? (list, recurrent, 2006–2012)," in http://www.razumkov.org.ua/eng/poll.php?poll_id=607 (date of retrieval 20-07-2015).

Razumkov Center (2008), "Prospects of Crimea: Regional status," http://old.razumkov.org.ua/eng/files/category_journal/NSD104_eng_2.pdf (date of retrieval 01-08-2018).

Regnum (2005), "Memorandum Kozaka: Rossiyskiy plan obedineniya Moldovy i Pridnestrov'ya," May 23, in https://regnum.ru/news/458547.html (date of retrieval 04-07-2018).

Reuters (2014), "Bodies of Armenian pilots removed from helicopter crash site," November 22, in https://uk.reuters.com/article/uk-armenia-azerbaijan-conflict/bodies-of-armenian-pilots-removed-from-helicopter-crash-site-idUKKCN0J60EY20141122 (date of retrieval 28-08-2018).

RFE/RL (Radio Free Europe/Radio Liberty) (2018a), "Armenian PM calls for 'More Strategic' relations with Russia," September 7, in https://www.rferl.org/a/armenian-pm-pashinian-strategic-relations-putin-russia-visit/29477245.html (date of retrieval 08-09-2018).

RFE/RL (2018b), "Kazakhs say relatives in China held at 'reeducation camps,'" September 21, in https://www.rferl.org/a/kazakhstan-china-detention/29502334.html (date of retrieval 21-09-2018).

RFE/RL (2016), "Armenia warns of 'full-scale war' amid fresh casualties in Karabakh fighting," April 4, in https://www.rferl.org/a/nagorno-karabakh-fighting-fresh-casualties-aremenia-azerbaijan/27653202.html (date of retrieval 06-09-2018).

RFE/RL (2014), "Gagauzia voters reject closer EU ties for Moldova," February 3, in https://www.rferl.org/a/moldova-gagauz-referendum-counting/25251251.html (date of retrieval 04-07-2018).

RIA Novosti (2014), "Medvedev raises doubts on legitimacy of new powers in Ukraine," February 24, in https://sputniknews.com/russia/20140224187851752-Medvedev-Raises-Doubts-on-Legitimacy-of-New-Powers-in-Ukraine/ (date of retrieval 01-08-2018).

Risse, Thomas (2002), "Constructivism and international institutions: Towards conversations across paradigms," in Ira Katznelson and Helen V. Milner (eds.), *Political science: State of the discipline*, Washington, DC: American Political Science Association, pp. 597–629.

Roach, Ashley, and Smith, Robert W. (2005), "Caspian seabed boundaries," in David A. Colson and Robert W. Smith (eds.), *International maritime noundaries, Volume V*, The Netherlands: Koninklijke Brill NV, pp. 3537–3549.

Roberts, Geoffrey (1995), "Soviet policy and the Baltic States, 1939–1940: A reappraisal," *Diplomacy & Statecraft*, Vol. (6)3: 672–700.

Roper, Steven D. (2001), "Regionalism in Moldova: The case of Transnistria and Gagauzia," *Regional & Federal Studies*, Vol. 11(3): 101–122.

Rossiĭskaia Gazeta (2014), "Churkin: Rossiya ne stremitsya vernut' Biktora YAnukovicha k vlasti" [Churkin: Russia does not want Viktor Yanukovych to return to the government], March 3, in http://www.rg.ru/2014/03/04/chyrkin-anons.html (date of retrieval 31-07-2108).

Roth, Andrew (2014), "In diplomatic defeat, Putin diverts pipeline to Turkey," *New York Times*, December 1, in https://www.nytimes.com/2014/12/02/world/europe/russian-gas-pipeline-turkey-south-stream.html (date of retrieval 10-07-2016).

Rothschild, Joseph (1974), *East Central Europe between the two World Wars*, Seattle: University of Washington Press.

RT (Russia Today) (2014), "Putin, Xi Jinping sign mega gas deal on second gas supply route," November 11, in https://www.rt.com/business/203679-china-russia-gas-deal/ (date of retrieval 17-09-2018).

Rukhadze, Vasili (2013), "New rhetoric, but old policy on Adjara autonomy," *Eurasia Daily Monitor*, Vol. 9: 215.

Rywkin, Michael (2010), "The geopolitics of the Caspian Sea basin," *American Foreign Policy Interests: The Journal of the National Committee on American Foreign Policy*, Vol. 32(2): 93–102.

Saakashvili, Mikheil (2005), "Speech delivered by President Saakashvili at Tbilisi Ivane Javakhishvili State University," *The President of Georgia*, February 16, in http://www.saakashviliarchive.info/en/PressOffice/News/SpeechesAndStatements?p=2773&i=1 (date of retrieval 13-08-1982).

Saideman, Stephen (2014), "In Crimea's sham referendum, all questions lead to 'yes,'" *The Globe and Mail*, March 10, in http://www.theglobeandmail.com/globe-debate/in-crimeas-shamreferendum-all-questions-lead-to-yes/article17396854/ (date of retrieval 01-08-2018).

Sakwa, Richard (2015), *Frontline Ukraine: Crisis in the borderlands*, London: I.B. Tauris.

Salem, Harriet, Walker, Shaun, and Harding, Luke (2014), "Ukraine's Crimean eye alliance with Russia," *The Guardian*, February 28, in http://www.theguardian.com/world/2014/feb/24/ukraine-crimea-russia-secession (date of retrieval 31-07-2018).

Sanchez, Alejandro W. (2009), "The 'frozen' southeast: How the Moldova-Transnistria question has become a European geo-security issue," *The Journal of Slavic Military Studies*, Vol. 22(2): 153–176.

Sankoyan, Markar (2016), "Lanthanousa isxys tou Azerbaijan: 'Ollandiki Astheneia' kai synepeies sto perifereiako yposystema" [The latent power of Azerbaijan: 'the Dutch Disease' and its repercussions on the regional subsystem], *Tetradia Eurasiatikwn Meletwn [Eurasian Studies Notebook]*, Vol. 1(2): 45.

Saparov, Arsene (2012), "Why autonomy? The making of the Nagorno-Karabakh autonomous region 1918–1925," *Europe-Asia Studies*, Vol. 64(2): 281–323.

Sasse, Gwendolyn (2009), "The European neighbourhood policy and conflict management: A comparison of Moldova and the Caucasus," *Ethnopolitics*, Vol. 8(3): 369–386.

Scandoil (2007), "Eni and Gazprom sign the agreement for the South Stream Project," November 23, in http://www.scandoil.com/moxie-bm2/news/eni-and-gazprom-sign-the-agreement-for-the-south-s.shtml (date of retrieval 10-09-2018).

Schmemann, Serge (1992), "Russia votes to void cession of Crimea to Ukraine," *New York Times*, May 22, in http://www.nytimes.com/1992/05/22/world/russia-votes-to-void-cession-of-crimea-to-ukraine.html (date of retrieval 31-07-2018).

SCO (Shanghai Cooperation Organization) (2107), "SCO secretary-general: the accession of India and Pakistan is evidence of SCO's openness," June 11, in http://eng.sectsco.org/news/20170611/295818.html (date of retrieval 22-06-2017).

SCO (2001), "The Shanghai convention on combating terrorism, separatism and extremism," June 15, in http://eng.sectsco.org/documents/20010615/202880.html (date of retrieval 22-06-2017).

Seaman, John (2010), *Energy security, transnational pipelines and China's role in Asia*, Paris: Ifri.

Shapovalova, Natalia (2014), "The politics of regionalism and decentralization," *FRIDE/Policy Brief*, No. 183, http://fride.org/download/PB_183_The_politics_of_regionalism_and_de centralisation_in_Ukraine.pdf (date of retrieval 01-08-2018).

Shaw, Malcolm N. (1997), "Peoples, territorialism and boundaries," *European Journal of International Law*, Vol. (8)3: 478–507.

Shlapentokh, Vladimir (2007), "China in the Russian mind today: Ambivalence and defeatism," *Europe-Asia Studies*, Vol. (59)1: 1–21.

Sidikov, Bahodir (2004), "New or traditional? 'Clans,' regional groupings, and state in post-Soviet Azerbaijan," *Berlin Osteuropa Info*, No. 21: 68–74.

Simon, Gerhard (1991), *Nationalism and policy toward the nationalities in the Soviet Union: From totalitarian dictatorship to post-Stalinist society*, Boulder: Westview Press.

Sindelar, Daisy (2014), "Was Yanukovych's ouster constitutional?" *Radio Free Europe/Radio Liberty*, February 23, in http://www.rferl.org/content/was-yanukovychs-ouster-constitutional/25274346.html (date of retrieval 31-07-2018).

Skocpol, Theda (1979), *States and social revolutions*. New York: Cambridge University Press.

Slider, Darrell (1985), "Crisis and response in Soviet nationality policy: The case of Abkhazia," *Central Asian Survey* Vol. 4(4): 51–68.

Sneider, Noah (2014), "Two choices in Crimea referendum, but neither is 'no,'" *New York Times*, March 7, in https://www.nytimes.com/2014/03/15/world/europe/crimea-vote-does-not-offer-choice-of-status-quo.html?_r=0 (date of retrieval 01-08-2018).

SNG (2018), "O Sodruzhestve Nezavisimykh Gosudarstv" [On the cooperation of Independent States], in http://www.cis.minsk.by/page.php?id=174 (date of retrieval 13-02-2018).

Snidal, Duncan (1991), "Relative gains and the pattern of international cooperation," *The American Political Science Review*, Vol. 85(3): 701–726.

Socor, Vladimir (2012), "Azerbaijan drives the planning on Trans-Anatolian Gas Pipeline Project," *Eurasia Daily Monitor*, Vol. 9(164).

Socor, Vladimir (1995), "Moldova's Gagauz republic organizes and becomes a precedent for Europe," *Prism*, Vol. 1(7).

Solchanyk, Roman (1994), "The politics of state building: Centre-periphery relations in post-Soviet Ukraine," *Europe-Asia Studies*, Vol. 46(1): 47–68.

Sotiriou, Stylianos A. (2017), "The irreversibility of history: The conflicts in South Ossetia and Abkhazia," *Problems of Post-Communism*, DOI:10.1080/10758216.2017.1406310.

Sotiriou, Stylianos A. (2016), "The irreversibility of history: The case of the Ukrainian crisis (2013–2015)," *Southeast European and Black Sea Studies*, Vol. 16(1): 51–70.

Sotiriou, Stylianos A. (2015a), *Russian energy strategy in the European Union, the Former Soviet Union region, and China*, Lanham, MD: Lexington Books.

Sotiriou, Stylianos A. (2015b), "The status of the Caspian Sea and its legal implications: A basic understanding," *Perspectives on Central Asia (PoCA)*, Issue 7: 14–18.

Sotiriou, Stylianos A. (2010), "I Rosiki epixeirimatiki oligarchia se mia dynamiki schesi exousias me to Kremlino" (in Greek) [The Russian oligarchs in a power struggle with the Kremlin], in Emmanuel Karagiannis (ed.), *I Rosia Simera: Politiki, Oikonomia kai Exoterikes sxeseis* [*Russia today: Politics, economics and foreign relations*], Athens: Ekdoseis Papazisi: 51–81.

Sotiriou, Stylianos A., and Karagiannis, Emmanuel (2013), "I energeiaki tautotita tis Kinas: mia eisagwgiki proseggisi" (in Greek) [China's energy identity: a basic understanding], in Sotiris Petropoulos and Asteris Huliaras (eds.), *I Kina kai oi alloi: oi sxeseis tis Kinas me tin Europi kai ton Kosmo* [*China and the others: China's relations with Europe and the World*], Athens: Ekdoseis Papazisi: 299–326.

Sputniknews (2015) "TurkStream falls under Russia's restrictive measures against Turkey," November 26, in http://sputniknews.com/world/20151126/1030796887/turkish-stream-russia.html (date of retrieval 10-07-2016).

SSR (1925), "Sotsialisticheskoi Sovetskoi Respubliki Abxazii" [Socialist Soviet Republic of Abkhazia], in http://abkhazia.narod.ru/constitution1.htm (date of retrieval 13-08-2018).

State Statistics of Ukraine (2004), "About number and composition population of Autonomous Republic of Crimea," in http://2001.ukrcensus.gov.ua/eng/results/general/nationality/Crimea/ (date of retrieval 31-07-2018).

State Statistics Service of Ukraine (2010), *Promislovist Ukrainyi y 2007–2010 pokaz*. Kyyiv: Derzhavna Slyzhba Statistiki Ukrainy [The Ukrainian Industry 2007–2010, Kiev: State Statistic Service of Ukraine].

Statista (2018), "Degree of urbanization in China from 2006 to 2016," in https://www.statista.com/statistics/270162/urbanization-in-china/ (date of retrieval 12-09-2018).

Stein, Arthur (1982), "Coordination and collaboration: Regimes in an anarchic world," *International Organization*, Vol. 36(2): 299–324.

Storey, Ian (2006), "China's 'Malacca dilemma,'" *China Brief*, Vol. 6(8).

Strassler, Robert B. (1996), *The landmark Thucydides: A comprehensive guide to the Peloponnesian War*, New York: Free Press.

Strategic Comments (2010), "Moscow plays both sides on Nagorno-Karabakh," Vol. 16(5): 1–3.

Stulberg, Adam N. (2007), *Well-oiled diplomacy: Strategic manipulation and Russia's energy statecraft in Eurasia*, Albany: State University of New York Press.

Suny, Ronald G. (1999/2000), "Provisional stabilities: The politics of identities in post-Soviet Eurasia," *International Security*, Vol. 24(3): 139–178.

Suny, Ronald G. (1994), *The Making of the Georgian nation*, Bloomington: Indiana University Press.

Suny, Ronald G. (1993), *The Revenge of the past: Nationalism, revolution, and the collapse of the Soviet Union*, California: Stanford University Press.

Sutter, Robert G. (2008), *Chinese foreign relations: Power and policy since the Cold War*, Lanham, MD: Rowman & Littlefield.

Sutter, Robert G. (2000), *Chinese policy priorities and their implications for the United States*, Lanham, MD: Rowman & Littlefield.

Sutyagin, Igor (2015), "Russian forces in Ukraine," *RUSI*, in https://www.rusi.org/publications/other/ref:O54FDBCF478D8B/ (date of retrieval 01-08-2018).

TCN (2014), "U Kharkovskikh separatistov izyali pistoleti i v yashchikov c 'kokteylyami Molotova'" [In Kharkiv separatists seized pistols and boxes with Molotov Cocktails], in https://ru.tsn.ua/ukrayina/u-harkovskih-separatistov-izyali-pistolety-i-6-yaschikov-s-kokteylyami-molotova-359433.html (date of retrieval 01-08-2018).

The Constitution of the Azerbaijan Republic (1995), in http://azerbaijan.az/portal/General/Constitution/doc/constitution_e.pdf (date of retrieval 11-09-2018).

The Guardian (2016), "The conflict erupts between Azerbaijani and Armenian forces," April 2, in https://www.theguardian.com/world/2016/apr/02/conflict-erupts-between-azerbaijani-and-armenian-forces (date of retrieval 06-09-2018).

The Molotov-Ribbentrop Pact (1939), in http://sourcebooks.fordham.edu/halsall/mod/1939pact.html (date of retrieval 26-07-2017).

The Straits Times (2018), "Project Kra Canal not priority project for Thai govt," February 13, in https://www.straitstimes.com/asia/se-asia/proposed-kra-canal-not-priority-project-for-thai-govt (date of retrieval 15-09-2018).

The Washington Times (2005), "China builds up strategic sea lanes," January 17, in http://www.washingtontimes.com/news/2005/jan/17/20050117-115550-1929r/ (date of retrieval 29-06-2017).

Thomas, Timothy L. (2009), "The bear went through the mountain: Russia appraises its five-day war in South Ossetia," *The Journal of Slavic Military Studies*, Vol. 22(1): 31–67.

Tilly, Charles (1992), *Coercion, capital, and European states, AD 990–1992*, Cambridge, MA: Blackwell.

Tkach, Vlada (1999), "Moldova and Transdniestria: Painful past, deadlocked present, uncertain future," *European Security*, Vol. 8(2): 130–159.

Toal, Gerard, and O'Loughlin, John (2013a), "Inside South Ossetia: A survey of attitudes in a de facto state," *Post-Soviet Affairs*, Vol. 29(2): 136–172.

Toal, Gerard, and O'Loughlin, John (2013b), "Land for peace in Nagorno Karabakh? Political geographies and public attitudes inside a contested de facto state," *Territory, Politics, Governance*, Vol. 1(2): 158–182.

Tokluoglu, Ceylan (2012), "Perceptions of state and leadership in post-Soviet Azerbaijan (1991–2009)," *Middle Eastern Studies*, Vol. 48(3): 319–343.

Tomkiv, Lydia (2015), "What is a fencer Su-24? What to know about the Russian plane shot down by Turkey," *International Business Times*, November 24, in http://www.ibtimes.com/what-fencer-su-24-what-know-about-russian-plane-shot-down-turkey-2197848 (date of retrieval 10-07-2016).

Torosyan, Tigran, and Vardanyan, Arax (2015), "The South Caucasus conflicts in the context of struggle for the Eurasian heartland," *Geopolitics*, Vol. 20(3): 559–582.

Tsentral'noi Izbiratel'noi Komissii [Central Election Committee] (2006), in http://ugo-osetia.ru/6.101/6.101-13.html (date of retrieval 13-08-2018).

Tsygankov, Andrei P. (2016), *Russia's foreign policy: Change and continuity in national identity, Fourth Edition*, Lanham, MD: Rowman & Littlefield.

Tsygankov, Andrei P. (2015), "Vladimir Putin's last stand: The sources of Russia's Ukraine policy," *Post-Soviet Affairs*, Vol. 31(4): 279–303.

Tucker Bernkopf, Nancy (2005), "Dangerous strait," in Nancy Bernkopf Tucker (eds.), *Dangerous strait: The U.S.-Taiwan-China Crisis*, New York: Columbia University Press, pp. 1–15.

Tudoroiu, Theodor (2016), "Unfreezing failed frozen conflicts: A post-Soviet case study," *Journal of Contemporary European Studies*, Vol. 24(3): 375–396.

Tudoroiu, Theodor (2011), "Structural factors vs. regime change: Moldova's difficult quest for democracy," *Democratization*, Vol. 18(1): 236–264.

Umbach, Frank (2010), "Global energy security and the implications for the EU," *Energy Policy*, Vol. 38: 1229–1240.

UN (United Nations) (2006), "Georgia-UNOMIG mandate," in https://peacekeeping.un.org/mission/past/unomig/mandate.html (date of retrieval 13-08-2018).

UN, A/55/309: letter dated 18 August 1998 from the permanent representative of Turkmenistan to the United Nations, addressed to the secretary-general. United Nations General Assembly, in http://www.un.org/en/ga/search/view_doc.asp?symbol=A/55/309 (date of retrieval 10-07-2016).

UN, A/53/453: letter dated 30 September 1998 from the permanent representatives of the Islamic Republic of Iran and Turkmenistan to the United Nations, addressed to the secretary-general. United Nations General Assembly, in http://www.un.org/en/ga/search/view_doc.asp?symbol=A/53/453 (date of retrieval 10-06-2016).

UN, A/52/983: letter dated 13 July 1998 from the permanent representatives of Kazakhstan and the Russian Federation to the United Nations, addressed to the secretary-general. United Nations General Assembly, in :http://www.un.org/en/ga/search/view_doc.asp?symbol=A/52/983 (date of retrieval 10-07-2016).

UN, A/52/424: letter dated 1 October 1997 from the permanent representative of Kazakhstan to the United Nations, addressed to the secretary-general. United Nations General Assembly, in http://www.un.org/ga/search/view_doc.asp?symbol=A/52/424 (date of retrieval 10-07-2018).

UN, A/52/324: letter dated 3 September 1997 from the chargé d'affaires a.i. of the permanent mission of the Islamic Republic of Iran to the United Nations, addressed to the secretary-general, United Nations General Assembly, in http://www.un.org/en/ga/search/view_doc.asp?symbol=A/52/324 (date of retrieval 10-07-2016).

UN, A/52/93: letter dated 14 March 1997 from the permanent representatives of Kazakhstan and Turkmenistan to the United Nations, addressed to the secretary-general. United Nations General Assembly, in http://www.un.org/ga/search/view_doc.asp?symbol=A/52/93 (date of retrieval 10-07-2018).

UNCLOS, United Nations Convention on the Law of the Sea of 10 December 1982, December 10, 1982 (United Nations, Oceans & Law of the Sea: Division for Ocean Affairs and the Law of the Sea Resolution 2749), in http://www.un.org/Depts/los/convention_agreements/texts/unclos/unclos_e.pdf (date of retrieval 10-07-2018).

UNCTAD, United Nations Conference on Trade and Development (2017), *2017 Handbook of Statistics*, New York: United Nations Publications.

UNHCR, United Nations High Commissioner for Refugees (2008), "Revised figures push number of Georgia displaced up to 192,000," September 12, in http://www.unhcr.org/news/latest/2008/9/48ca8d804/revised-figures-push-number-georgia-displaced-192000.html (date of retrieval 13-08-2018).

Upadhyay, Rakesh (2017), "The five biggest strategic petroleum reserves in the world," *Oilprice.com*, March 29, in https://oilprice.com/Energy/Energy-General/The-5-Biggest-Strategic-Petroleum-Reserves-In-The-World.html (date of retrieval 18-09-2018).

U.S. Department of State (2016), "Azerbaijan 2016 human rights report," https://www.state.gov/documents/organization/265608.pdf (date of retrieval 06-09-2018).

Van Parijs, Philippe (2011), *Linguistic justice for Europe and for the world*, Oxford: Oxford University Press.

Vienna Convention on Succession of States in respect of Treaties 1978. 1946, UNTS 3, entered into force 6 November 1996.

Vitkine, Benoit (2016), "Dans la guerre sans fin du Haut-Karabakh" [Inside the war without end in Nagorno-Karabakh], *Le Monde*, April 11, in https://www.lemonde.fr/europe/article/2016/04/11/au-haut-karabakh-l-etat-de-guerre-permanent_4899722_3214.html (date of retrieval 06-09-2018).

Volkov, Konstantin (2017), "Abkhaziia byrazila gotovnost' priznatm' nezavisimost' Katalonii" [Abkhazia ready to recognize the independence of Catalonia], *Rossiyskaia Gazeta*, September 27, in https://rg.ru/2017/09/27/abhaziia-vyrazila-gotovnost-priznat-nezavisimost-katalonii.html (date of retrieval 13-08-2013).

Vorob'ev, Vladislav (2018), "Dodon poobeshchal predotvratit' grazhdanskuyu voynu v Moldavii" [Dodon promised to prevent the civil war in Moldova], *Rossiyskaya Gazeta*, February 2, 2018, in https://rg.ru/2018/02/02/dodon-poobeshchal-predotvratit-grazhdanskuiu-vojnu-v-moldavii.html (date of retrieval 13-02-2018).

Voronkova, Anastasia (2013), "Nationalism and organized violence in Nagorno-Karabakh: A microspatial perspective," *Nationalism and Ethnic Politics*, Vol. 19(1): 102–118.

Vzglyad (2016), "Prem'er Armenii poprosil Medvedeva uckorum postavki voennoy produktsii iz Rossii," April 7, in https://vz.ru/news/2016/4/7/804171.html (date of retrieval 06-09-2018).

Wagstyl, Stefan (2008), "Contested caucasus," *Financial Times*, July 14, in https://www.ft.com/content/0287616e-5108-11dd-b751-000077b07658 (date of retrieval 13-08-2013).

Walker, Shaun (2014), "Ukraine's president flees Kiev as opposition takes control," *The Guardian*, February 23, in http://www.theguardian.com/world/2014/feb/22/ukraine-President-yanukovych-flees-kiev (date of retrieval 31-07-2018).

Walsh, Declan (2013), "Chinese company will run strategic Pakistani port," *New York Times*, January 31, in http://www.nytimes.com/2013/02/01/world/asia/chinese-firm-will-run-strategic-pakistani-port-at-gwadar.html?ref=global-home&_r=0 (date of retrieval 19-09-2018).

Waltz, Kenneth N. (1990), "Realist thought and neorealist theory," *Journal of International Affairs*, Vol. 44(1): 21–37.

Waltz, Kenneth N. (1986), "Anarchic orders and balances of power," in Robert O. Keohane (ed.), *Neorealism and its critics*, New York: Columbia University Press, pp. 98–130.

Weingast, Barry R. (2002), "Rational-choice institutionalism," in Ira Katznelson and Helen V. Milner (eds.), *Political science: State of the discipline*, Washington, DC: American Political Science Association, pp. 660–692.

Welt, Cory (2006), "Georgia's rose revolution: From regime weakness to regime collapse," paper presented at the Center on Democracy, Development, and the Rule of Law, California, April 28–29.

Wheatley, Jonathan (2009), "Managing ethnic diversity in Georgia: one step forward, two steps back," *Central Asian Survey*, Vol. 28(2): 119–134.

White, Stephen, Light, Margot, and Lowenhart, John (2001), "Belarus, Moldova and Ukraine: Looking east or looking west?" *Perspectives on European Politics and Society*, Vol. 2(2): 289–304.

Wilson, Andrew, and Birch, Sarah (1999), "Voting stability, political gridlock: Ukraine's 1998 parliamentary elections," *Europe-Asia Studies*, Vol. 51(6): 1039–1068.

Wilson, Andrew, and Popescu, Nicu (2009), "Russian and European neighbourhood policies compared," *Southeast European and Black Sea Studies*, Vol. 9(3): 317–331.

Wilson, Jeffrey D. (2017), *International Resource Politics in the Asia-Pacific: The political economy of conflict and cooperation*, Cheltenham, UK: Edward Elgar Publishing.

Wong, Edward (2013), "China allows media to report on air pollution crisis," *New York Times*, January 14, in http://www.nytimes.com/2013/01/15/world/asia/china-allows-media-to-report-alarming-air-pollution-crisis.html?ref=global-home&_r=0 (date of retrieval 14-01-2013).

World Bank (2018a), "DataBank: World development indicators," July 4, in http://databank.worldbank.org/data/source/world-development-indicators (date of retrieval 04-07-2018).

World Bank (2018b), "The World Bank in China," April 19, in http://www.worldbank.org/en/country/china/overview#1 (date of retrieval 12-09-2018).

World Bank (2018c), *Commodity markets outlook, oil exporters: Policies and challenges*, Washington D.C.: World Bank.

Xinhua News Agency (2013), "Beijing chokes on smog amid annual legislative sessions," January 23, in http://news.xinhuanet.com/english/china/2013-01/23/c_132123210.htm (date of retrieval 23-01-2013).

Xinhua News Agency (2011), "China Russia pledge closer energy cooperation," June 1, in http://news.xinhuanet.com/english2010/china/2011-06/01/c_13904057.htm (date of retrieval 01-09-2012).

Xinhua News Agency (2010), "42,000 tonnes of crude oil delivered to China from Russia after new pipeline's operation," January 2, in http://news.xinhuanet.com/english2010/china/2011-01/02/c_13674262.htm (date of retrieval 27-08-2012).

Xu, Bo, and Reisinger, William M. (2018), "Russia's energy diplomacy with China: Personalism and institutionalism in its policy-making process," *The Pacific Review*, DOI: 10.1080/09512748.2018.1428675.

Xu, Xiaojie (2007), *Chinese NOC's overseas strategies: Background, comparison and remarks*, Houston: The James A. Baker III Institute for Public Policy of Rice University.

Zabrodina, Ekaterina (2014), "Sezd v Kharkove: Na Ukraine sovershen gosperevorot" [Congress in Kharkiv: In Ukraine it was committed a coup], February 22, in http://www.rg.ru/2014/02/22/siezd-site.html (date of retrieval 31-07-2018).

Zhao, Suisheng (2008), "China's global search for energy security: Cooperation and competition in Asia-Pacific," *Journal of Contemporary China*, Vol. 17(55): 207–227.

Zia-Ebrahimi, Reza (2007), "Empire, nationalities, and the collapse of the Soviet Union," *The School of Russian and Asian Studies (SRAS)*, May 8, in http://www.sras.org/empire__nationalities__and_the_collapse_of_the_ussr (date of retrieval 28-07-2017).

Zimnitskaya, Hanna, and Von Geldern, James (2011), "Is the Caspian Sea a sea, and why does it matter?" *Journal of Eurasian Studies*, Vol. 2: 1–14.

Index

Abashidze, Aslan, 38n20, 106–107
Abkhazia, 38n22; administrative status of, 97–98, 113; Aydgylara in, 98, 99; critical juncture period (1980s to early 1990s) for, 97–98, 102–103, 112, 113; ethnic populations and divisions in, 102; Five-Day War (2008) and outcomes for, 95–96, 109–111, 112, 113; frozen conflict in, xvi, xx–xxi, 10–11; independence efforts in, 102–103, 106, 111, 112, 114n9; languages in, 98; political preferences in, 97, 103, 110, 111; Russia bilateral agreements with, 10–11; Russia relations with, 10–11, 102–103, 114n7, 136n31; Russia role in conflict in, 102–103; wars and violent conflict in, 95–96, 102–103, 106, 109–111, 112, 113, 114n10
accessibility, definition of, 39n41
Ademon Nykhaz, 97, 98, 99
Adjara, 38n20, 97, 106, 112, 133
AIOC. *See* Azerbaijan International Operating Company
Akhmetov, Rinat, 94n7
Aliyev, Heydar, 11–13, 38n28, 150
Aliyev, Ilham, 38n28, 116, 129, 136n30
alliances: energy, xix, 156, 157, 181, 183; human nature role in forming, 18, 22, 24, 29, 34, 91, 102, 113n4, 134n6, 178; international level, 24–25, 28; security

in formation of, 18, 182
"Ambiguous Warfare" doctrine, 94n6
anarchy/anarchic political environments: in Georgia, 10, 104; international level, 22, 24, 25, 33; national and international levels of, compared, 33; in post-Soviet era, xx, 80, 177–178; reactions to, 18
APF. *See* Azerbaijan Popular Front
April War. *See* Four-Day War
Armenia/Armenians: Azerbaijan violence against, 116, 121–123, 128, 136n31; ceasefire agreement (1994) with, 126, 127; corruption in, 136n27; defense budget of, 134n5, 136n31; Four-Day War (2016) for, xvi, 14, 115, 117–126, 127, 129–131, 133, 134; Free Democrats Party of, 131, 136n28; Iran gas swaps with, 158n11; military weaknesses in, 136n27; NK relations with, 11, 35n6, 115–121, 123–126, 136n31; Russia relations with, 128, 135n15, 136n23, 136n30; Sumgait riots and, 11, 119, 120
atomized socio-political reality: in Azerbaijan, 12–14, 127; in Georgia, 10, 103–104, 113, 113n4; in Moldova, 6–8, 65–66; national identities in, 7–8, 10, 12, 33, 38n22, 71–72, 80, 85, 89, 92, 93, 103–104, 113, 126, 127, 129, 136n27, 178; in Ukraine, 8–9, 71–72,

Central Asia Gas Pipeline (CAGP), xviii, 169, 174n24

China: BRI of, 17, 168; Central Asia energy relationship with, xviii–xix, xxi, xxiin6, 16–17, 31, 157, 168–169, 172, 180–181; coal production in, 160–161; economic power/status of, 34n4, 159–160, 171, 173n3; energy policies, environmental, 160–161; energy policies, foreign, xxi, 16–17, 157, 159, 166–167; energy policies, geopolitical dimension of, 165–171; energy policy-making institutions and process, 161–164, 173n10–174n12; energy relationships and human rights concerns, 166, 172; energy security for, 17, 162, 165, 166, 167, 169, 170, 171–172, 175n30; environmental/pollution concerns in, 160–161, 171, 173n7–173n9; ethnic populations and divisions in, xix, 181, 182; Kazakhstan energy relationship with, 148, 149, 168–169, 183n5; Kazakhstan natural gas exports to, 148, 149; "loan-for-oil" deals of, xviii, xxiin6, 166, 172; market reforms historically in, 159, 171; oil and gas market, xviii, xxiin6, 17, 163, 165–166, 168–170, 172, 183n5; population density and concentration in, 159, 173n1; Russia energy relationship with, 169–170, 172, 175n27, 180–181, 182; Russia relations historically with, xxiin8, 181–182; Russia relations in 2018 with, 182–183; SCO Energy Club and, xix; Special Economic Zones in, 173n2; "String of Pearls" energy agreements of, 166–167, 174n19; Turkmenistan energy relationship with, xviii, 151, 153, 169, 174n24, 183n5; USSR relations with, xxiin8, 181–182; Uzbekistan energy relationship with, xviii, xix, 166, 169; XUAR relations in, xviii–xix, 168–169, 181, 182, 183n5

China National Petroleum Corporation (CNPC), 163, 168–170

Chisinau, 4–5, 53, 54–55, 58, 59

CIS. *See* Commonwealth of Independent States

civil rights, 18

CNPC. *See* China National Petroleum Corporation

coal, 160–161

Collective Security Treaty Organization (CSTO), 68n10, 136n29

Commonwealth of Independent States (CIS): member states of, 68n10; Russian support of, 135n15; in Transdniestria war (1992), 53, 56, 69n15

Communist Party: in Abkhazia, 98; in Azerbaijan, 121–122; in Georgia, 9; in Moldova, 46, 47, 48, 49, 64, 68n2; non-Russians treatment under, 2–3

Copenhagen Summit, 161

corruption: in Armenia, 136n27; in Azerbaijan, 14, 126–127; in Georgia, 10, 104, 106; measurement methods for, 33; in Moldova, 66; in Transdniestria, 70n26; in Ukraine, 9

Crimea: annexation from Russia of, 84; Constitution of 1992, 93n1, 94n4; Constitutions of Ukraine and, joint analysis of, 74–77, 92, 94n4; crisis of 2013–2015 for, 83–87, 91; critical juncture period (1980s to early 1990s) for, 72–79; economic power/status of, 77; ethnic populations and divisions in, 8, 35n6, 73, 80, 84, 85, 86, 87; frozen conflicts in, xv–xvi, xx–xxi, 30, 71–93; political preferences poll (2008) in, 84–86; political preferences poll (2014) in, 86–87; Tatars in, 8, 35n6, 73, 80, 84, 85, 87; under USSR, importance of, 35n6

crisis of 2013–2015, 83, 142; for Crimea, 83–87, 91; for Donbass, 87–89, 91, 92; for Donetsk and Luhansk, 82, 83, 87, 88, 91–92; Minsk Agreements in settling, 88, 89–91, 92

critical juncture periods: for Abkhazia (1980s to early 1990s), 97–98, 102–103, 112, 113; for Crimea/Ukraine (1980s to early 1990s), 72–79; definition of, xxiin2; in EU-Russian energy relationship, 141–142; in NK (1980s to early 1990s), 117–126, 132–134; for South Ossetia (1980s to early 1990s), 97–101, 112, 113; for

language(s): in Abkhazia, 98; assimilation, 4–5; "Russification" with, 4, 45; South Ossetia barriers with, 97; Ukraine polarization and, 79. *See also* Russian language

Lenin, 3

Luhansk: crisis of 2013–2015 for, 82, 83, 87, 88, 91–92; in Minsk Agreements, 89, 90–91, 92

Mackinder, Sir Halford, 1–2, 34n2, 34n4

Mao Tse-tung, 159, 161, 182

MASSR. *See* Moldovan Autonomous Soviet Socialist Republic

Medvedev, Dmitry, 131, 180

"method of agreement," 72, 96, 117

methodology, 31–33, 34, 39n39, 39n41

military power/provisions: of Armenia, 136n27, 136n31; of Azerbaijan, 134n5, 136n31; in Caspian Sea region, 144, 158n6; of Transdniestria, 5

Mill, John S., 72, 96, 117

Minsk Agreements, 88–91, 92

"Mkhedrioni" (Horsemen), 9, 114n5

Moldova: atomized socio-political reality in, 6–8, 65–66; Berlin protocol (2016) between Transdniestria and, 64–65; Bessarabia relations historically with, 43–46; "big-four" enterprises in, 37n10; Communist Party in, 46, 47, 48, 49, 64, 68n2; Constitution, 57, 58; corruption in, 66; ethnic groups in, 5, 37n9; EUBAM in, 64, 69n25; history and evolution of, 35n6, 43–51; independence declarations for, 6, 57–59, 61–64; language policies in, 47–48, 49, 57, 62–63; national identities in, 7, 65, 67; Popular Front in, 46–49; population growth in, 45; quality of life in, 66, 67; Romania relations with, 35n6, 44–45, 48–49; Russian language in, 4–5, 45, 47–48, 57, 62–63; Russian nationalism and "Russification" in, 4–5, 7, 43–44, 45, 48, 68n3, 69n21; Russia relations with, 6–7, 43–46, 64; Transdniestria post-conflict relations with, 57–65; in USSR critical juncture period, 46–51; during World War II, 44–45; zero-sum politics

in, 46, 49, 50–51, 52, 54, 60. *See also* Gagauzia; Transdniestria

Moldovan Autonomous Soviet Socialist Republic (MASSR), 35n6, 44–45, 46, 57

Molotov-Ribbentrop pact, 35n6, 44–45, 50–51

Myanmar, 166, 167, 174n16

Nabucco Pipeline, 141–142

Nagorno-Karabakh (NK), 134n1; Armenia/Armenians relations with/in, 11, 35n6, 115–126, 136n31; atomized-turned-ethnicized national identities in, 126, 127, 129, 133, 136n27; "Black January" (1990) in, 11, 122–123; ceasefire agreement (1994) with, 126, 127; critical juncture period (1980s to early 1990s) in, 117–126, 132–134; economic power/status of, 135n7; fatalities in, 115; Four-Day War (2016) in, xvi, 14, 115, 117–126, 127, 129–131, 133, 134; frozen conflicts in, xvi, xx–xxi, 11–14, 115–134; human rights statement from, 132; independence efforts and support in, 120, 123–125, 126; political preferences in, 117, 124, 126, 131, 132, 133; Russian involvement in, 119–121, 123–126, 131, 134; territorial stance and conflict for, 117, 118, 121, 124, 125, 130, 131, 135n16; wars and violent conflict in, xvi, 11, 14, 115, 117–126, 127, 129–131, 133, 134, 134n6, 136n20–136n22; zero-sum politics in, 116, 135n18

Nagorno-Karabakh Autonomous Oblast (NKAO), 11, 115, 119, 120, 121, 125

national identities: atomized, 7–8, 10, 12, 33, 38n22, 71–72, 80, 85, 89, 92, 93, 103–104, 113, 126, 127, 129, 136n27, 178; atomized-turned-ethnicized, 103–104, 113, 126, 127, 129, 133, 136n27, 178; in Georgia, 96, 103–104, 113, 113n4; in Moldova, 7, 65, 67; in NK, 126, 127, 129, 133, 136n27; primordialism and, 37n13; socio-political development relation to, 6; in Ukraine, polarization with, 7–8, 80

Russia energy relationship with, xvii, xxiin3, 16; in SCO Energy Club, xxiin9; TurkStream negotiations with Russia and, xvii, xxiin3, 16, 142

Turkmenistan: Azerbaijan energy relationship with, 152; Caspian Sea legal regime for, 152–153, 156, 158n8–158n9; China energy relationship with, xviii, 151, 153, 169, 174n24, 183n5; natural gas exports from, 152–153; oil and gas market in, 143, 152–153, 158n8, 174n23

TurkStream, xvii, xxiin3, 16, 142

Ukraine: atomized socio-political reality in, 8–9, 71–72, 77, 80, 85, 89, 91–92, 93; Constitutions of Crimea and, joint analysis of, 74–77, 92, 94n4; corruption in, 9; critical juncture period (1980s to early 1990s) for, 72–79; on decentralization of power, 78, 89–90, 92–93; Dignity Revolution in, 9; Donbass impacted by independence of, 72, 77–78, 82; EaP Summit (2013) impact on, 71–72; economic power/status of, 72, 79–82, 92; ethnic divisions in, 8, 72–73, 80; EU influence in, 38n18; EU rapprochement negotiations with, xv; EU relations with, xv, 8, 38n18; GDP per capita, PPP in, 81–82; human rights declaration in, 72–73; independence, factors and outcomes of, 72, 77–79, 82; Minsk agreements with, 88–92; national identities and polarization in, 7–8, 80; Orange Revolution in, 8, 79, 93n3; polarization in, 7–8, 78–80; pre-crisis of 2013–2015 environment in, 79–82; quality of life in, 72, 79, 80–82, 92; Russia energy relationship with, xvii; Russian nationalism and "Russification" in, 5, 46, 78–79; Russia relations with, 8, 83–84, 87, 88; socio-political development in, 79–82; Transdniestria war (1992) and, 52–53, 55, 56; Turchynov administration in, 83–84; unemployment in, 72, 79–81; under Yanukovych, 71, 83, 93n3. *See also* Crimea; crisis of 2013–2015

United Nations Convention on the Law of the Sea (UNCLOS), 145–146, 148–149, 152, 156

United States (US), 34n4; China oil market control of, 165–166; energy security efforts of, 175n30; sanctions on Russian oil and gas, 183n1

USSR (Soviet Union), 37n12; anarchic political environments after dissolution of, xx, 80, 177–178; Caspian Sea region treaties under, xvii–xviii, 143, 144, 154, 158n6; China relations with, xxiin8, 181–182; Constitution of, 35n6, 118; Crimea importance in, 35n6; critical juncture period for, 46–51, 177–178; ethnic composition in, 3–4; frozen conflicts after dissolution of, xvi, xx–xxi, 29–30, 34, 177–179; "Heartland" of, 2; in Moldova history, 44–51; Molotov-Ribbentrop pact between Germany and, 35n6, 44–45, 50–51; nation-building in early, 3–4; Russian language nationalized in, 3, 4, 5–6

Uzbekistan, xviii, xix, xxiin7, 166, 169, 174n23

Vezirov, Abdulrahman, 121
vulnerability, definition of, 39n38

wars and violent conflict: in Abkhazia, 95–96, 102–103, 106, 109–111, 112, 113, 114n10; in Azerbaijan, xvi, 11, 14, 115, 117–126, 127, 129–131, 133, 134, 134n6, 136n20–136n22; China-USSR, 181–182; in Donbass, 94n6; in Georgia, 95–96, 106, 109–111, 112, 113; in NK, xvi, 11, 14, 115, 117–126, 127, 129–131, 133, 134, 134n6, 136n20–136n22; political leadership power agenda with, 134n6; in South Ossetia, 95–96, 98–101, 106–107, 109–111, 112, 113; in Transdniestria, 6, 51–57, 65, 68n6–68n8, 69n13, 69n15; World War II, 4, 44–45; in XUAR, 182. *See also* crisis of 2013–2015; Five-Day War (2008); Four-Day War (2016); frozen conflicts

Wen Jiabao, 162, 171

White Army, 2–3
win-win logic, 25, 27–28
World Island, 1, 2, 34n1
World War II, 4, 44–45

Xi Jinping, 169, 175n27
Xinjiang Uyghur Autonomous Region
   (XUAR), xviii–xix, 168–169, 181, 182,
   183n5

Yanukovych, Viktor, 71, 83, 93n3
Yeltsin, Boris, 53–57, 101, 123, 135n15
Yushchenko, Viktor, 8, 93n3

zero-sum politics: international system
   and, 24, 25, 28, 37n13; in Moldova, 46,
   49, 50–51, 52, 54, 60; in NK, 116,
   135n18

About the Author

Stylianos A. Sotiriou is lecturer of political science and international relations at the University of Macedonia. He holds a PhD in political science and international relations, with a specialization in energy security in Eurasia. He graduated from the Political Science Department of the Law School of Aristotle University, Thessaloniki, Greece, with a BSc in political science (2000–2004), and he received a master's degree (MSc) in political science from the Vrije Universiteit of Amsterdam, Amsterdam, the Netherlands (2005–2006). Dr. Sotiriou also holds a Rutgers scholarship and was granted a PhD in political science and international relations from the University of Macedonia, Thessaloniki, Greece (2009–2013). He has been a visiting professor at the International Hellenic University and as a visiting lecturer at the Turkish and Eurasian Studies Laboratory, University of Piraeus, Athens. He is the author of *Russian Energy Strategy in the European Union, the Former Soviet Union Region, and China* (Lexington Books, 2015), among other publications.

Made in the USA
Middletown, DE
26 August 2021

46995072R00144